HENRY ROLLINS

S0-ASN-127

THE FIRST FIVE

COLLECTED WORK 1983 – 1987

The First Five:
Collected work of Henry Rollins from 1983 – 1987

ISBN: 1–880985–51–9

Third Printing
This book is comprised of *High Adventure in the Great Outdoors, Pissing in the Gene Pool, Bang!, Art to Choke Hearts,* and *One From None*, which were originally published as five separate books.

Design: **ENDLESS** ∞
Cover drawing: Mark Mothersbaugh
Text Preparation: Alison Freer

2.13.61
P.O. BOX 1910 · LOS ANGELES · CALIFORNIA · 90078 · USA

JOE COLE 4.10.61 – 12.19.91

High Adventure In The Great Outdoors

South Bay... are there any real people here at all? Have you ever been to 7-11? Nothing but cellophane and youths humping the video games. 25 cent video youth, what culture! Those machines breed killers, I'm sure of it. Go, go video youth, go to the street, here's a quarter kill a queer, kill a nigger, kill a commie. Kill! Kill! Kill! I can see them now, storming into Westwood armed to the teeth with automatic weapons and quarters. Eddie Van Halen & Michael Jackson at the controls, distributing quarters and barking commands! This is a sick world we live in. Only Earth could come up with Philadelphia.

◆　◆　◆　◆　◆

My father took me to see *The Godfather* when it first came out. The theater was packed. The movie was underway and everyone very quiet. Behind us was a large black man. The man pulled out a bag of potato chips and opened them up. The bag made a bit of noise and my father said, "Hey shut up!" real loud. I sank into my seat and remained there for the rest of the film. I think it would have been real cool if: (a) the guy smiled and offered my dad some chips (that would have chilled his shit pretty good) or if (b) the guy slapped my dad upside his head.

My father took me to McDonald's one Saturday when I was young. It was springtime. We pulled into the parking lot and got out. There were two hippies parked next to us, a boy and a girl. On the side of their car they had some American flag stickers stuck on upside-down. My dad started yelling at them. He called them pinkos, fags, commies, and hippies. He told them to get haircuts and to take those stickers off their car. The girl got real upset and ripped her shirt open, her breasts fell out, right there in the McDonald's parking lot! I don't know why she ripped her shirt open to express her agitation, maybe that's how you did it back then. It might have been kind of neat if the girl kicked him in the nuts or something.

◆　◆　◆　◆　◆

I'm in my apartment
My left foot nailed to the floor
I just go in circles
A little blood seeps out
I'll be here tomorrow
If I can make it through today
A little blood seeps out
The days pass
Like passing your hands through broken glass
A little blood seeps out
I feel some pain here and there
I feel the days passing me
I choke on the exhaust
A little blood seeps out

◄● ◄● ◄● ◄● ◄●

I want to take a walk
A long walk
Into the desert
Into the heat
I see my name
Carved in the ruins
I see my number
Carved in the ruins
I can finally see myself
My reflection in sand
Reflected in light
Reflected in heat
I raise my hands to the sky
It is time to die
It's always time
There's always time to die
Didn't it always seem like time?
Didn't it?

The sun brings the blood to a boil
I drop to the ground

◦ ◦ ◦ ◦ ◦

Numbers are perfect, infallible and everlasting. You aren't. Numbers are always right in the end. You may see an incorrect figure but that's not the fault of the number, the fault lies in the person doing the calculating. How many times will your heart beat during your lifetime? Of course you don't know! But there's a number that will provide you with this small bit of information. Numbers are dependable! The sun may explode, you may lose your job, you may never be able to "get it up" again, but at the end of the day five is five. Get it? Good! Numbers do not cut in line at lunch time. Numbers do not write bad checks. Numbers sound cool, like when a fucking pig gets a call on his pig radio to go answer a 511. You can go to buy coffee at 7-11. Numbers make good names. Like at a party or soiree. I always wear a sticker that has a martini glass and the words: "Hi my name is:" printed on it, underneath the printing I write in "2-13-61." So I can say, "Hi, my name is 2-13-61, what's yours?" Then you can say to girls or guys, "Hey you're really the bees knees! What's your number?"

◦ ◦ ◦ ◦ ◦

He can take you to the desert. He can tell the time by just saying so. He can take you home if that's where you want to go. He told me the world was gonna get hit with a coat of black paint that was never gonna come off. He is insanity. Pure. I think he wants to burn the world down. I acknowledge my life through his deaths. With the perpetual delirium of an insane dream I think I know just what he means. I am afraid of the animals he understands. In a dream he touched me with a burning hand.

◦ ◦ ◦ ◦ ◦

You climb and climb
Hand over hand
You reach the top
You stand on the shaky ledge of your heart
You look at her eyes
You look into her eyes
You hold your breath and jump
You leap into her arms
Her arms fall to her sides
You fall past her window
You hit the ground
You are shattered
Like someone taking a bottle
And smashing it on the sidewalk
Sharp jagged broken pieces of yourself lie on the ground
You put the pieces back together again
They never go back quite the same
The outside is seamless, smooth
But inside
Broken glass mind
And a soul with little cracks in the sides
Loose splinters at the bottom stay to remind you
At times the soul glass splinters
Will give you a jab to remind you of your leap
After a time, when you start climbing again
You will forget about the soul glass splinters
She can break your fall
Or let you fall and break
And every time you jump
You just know she's going to catch you

❦   ❦   ❦   ❦   ❦

A man drove himself insane
He was driven
Insane

At least he was driven
I don't know about you
But it sure seems better
Than just sitting around talking about it

◄● ◄● ◄● ◄● ◄●

I want you to act like a human being
For you it is an act
Make the move
Make your flesh move
Get up
Tell me what you're looking at
Get up!
Make it move
Make your flesh move
Make it crawl
Oh please
Do something

◄● ◄● ◄● ◄● ◄●

Say if we were in a house that was burning down and there was
time for only one of us to escape. I would push you ahead of me
so you would be the one to reach safety. I would die happy
knowing that you were ok. If we were on a sinking ship and there
was only one life preserver, I would wrap it around you and tell
you to reach shore with all speed. I would die for you.

◄● ◄● ◄● ◄● ◄●

I sit in a different jailhouse. I wrap my fingers around my jail cell
eyes and beat my tin cup against my ribs. Someone left the gate
to the fields of humanity open. One night I crept in with a jail
house mind, with a thought, with a wish, and I slaughtered the
fields. I burned them to the ground.

◄● ◄● ◄● ◄● ◄●

Look at the people dancing in the fields. Human harvest. I watch all those in attendance through scarecrow eyes. The fields are on fire, and everybody's burning. Piles of lovers, stacked in twisted heaps, doused with gasoline and set to burn. Piles of dead bodies burning. I listen to the oily crackle of smoldering hair and flesh. I'm still alive. I'm too empty to burn. When I close my eyes I can still hear their screams. I remember their last dance, before I lit the fields aflame. It was beautiful.

◄ ◄ ◄ ◄ ◄

Tonight's summer night is a dead man wrapped in a wet blanket. I found him floating face up in my room. I'm lost in this swamp. Sinking in the quicksand of my loneliness. Sitting here, sweating, cursing and sinkin' all the while. My heart is making a dull, drumming sound and I'm thinking that my life is a waiting game and I'm sinkin' all the while.

◄ ◄ ◄ ◄ ◄

My mind and I had a meeting, and we came to the conclusion that you're going to let us down. We are here every minute of the day getting ready for the let down. So when you push me away, I'll just say ok, because we came to that conclusion a while ago. Like I said, we were ready for the let down. If you're ever walking down the way and you see me on the side of the road lying broken and scattered, you keep walking right on by.

◄ ◄ ◄ ◄ ◄

I don't think this road will ever end. Sometimes I get so tired that I think I'll fall off. I have looked high and low and I can't find anyone else here. The nights are so cold that I can't seem to ever warm up. I've been out here for awhile and I'll probably be out here forever. I can tell, this road hates me. This road does not want me here. I don't know where else to go. Sometimes I get so lonely that I think I'm going to break into pieces.

◄ ◄ ◄ ◄ ◄

There was a car crash, a powerful car crash. Heaps of twisted muscle machine. The engine died screaming, wrapped its teeth around a tree. In the bowels of the wreck was a girl. The most beautiful girl I had ever seen. The crash had been abrupt, crude. But even this could not mar her. Broken glass made a glittering necklace around her neck. Her head was crudely thrown back, splaying beautiful chestnut brown hair around her shoulders and face. Her eyes were wide open and staring out. It's hard for me to explain what her eyes were saying. They had a look of wise innocence, of jaded virginity. I'll never forget her eyes. Her face was composed, beautiful, saint-like. Her legs were rudely spread and broken as if the car had raped her before I had gotten there. One hand rested on her thigh as if to protect herself from attack and the other was thrown back over the headrest with submissive abandon. The night air was full of her perfume.

⬦ ⬦ ⬦ ⬦ ⬦

I see walking bombs on the street
Hearts not beating, but ticking
I am talking about detonation!
You're in McDonald's
And some guy's head explodes
Brains everywhere
I think there's some faulty circuitry here
You see some guy in a business suit
Walking home from work
Look at him closely
He's slumped over
There's a little smoke coming out of one ear
There's a buzzing, crackling sound coming from his head
Blown fuses
Poor machine!
But it's ok
The parts are interchangeable
We'll install a new one

⬦ ⬦ ⬦ ⬦ ⬦

I am made of leather
I am covered with run and hide
I come so cheap
So cheap
I come undone
I come from within
I got no heart so I can't die
I got no mind so I can't lie
Come on!
Untie me up

◂ ◂ ◂ ◂ ◂

The girl who moves with rustling music
Snakes
She has a head full of snakes!
When I see her
I feel like one of those snakes
Writhing
Squirming
Did you hear me?
Medusa
I burn for you
Sweat
Muscles pull
My heart
Writhing, squirming
Love me once
Then turn me to stone
Medusa
Snakes
Medusa
When will this end

◂ ◂ ◂ ◂ ◂

You want to take me down with you
I see your eyes
I know what's on your mind
I'm not like you
And you hate me for it
I'm not a drowning man
I got a mind of my own
And I'm going to keep it
I'm sorry I can't let you
Take me, define me, stop me
I know
You'll turn on me
Because I'm not like you

◆ ◆ ◆ ◆ ◆

In a state of delirium I dreamt that I came upon a female cockroach the size of a girl. She smiled at me and told me to come closer. She kissed me. The feeling of her belly scales against my flesh made me convulse and sweat. We made love. She wrapped her six legs around my back and pulled me close. Her antennas lashed my back. No girl ever made me feel like that before, ever. By morning I was covered with sweat, blood and a noisome yellow-green mucus. She had my children (twenty of them). They were semi-human in form, could reproduce in weeks not years and could lift up to six times their own weight. We are breeding. In the alleys in the sewers in the back rooms and brothels. Not a day goes by where my children don't grow in size and strength. We are everywhere. You try to kill us with motels and poison. This is snack-food for us. You will never rid the world of us. We will rid the world of you. You will witness the destruction of your species.

◆ ◆ ◆ ◆ ◆

I woke up this morning in the truck. I like sleeping in the truck. It's quiet and dark. Rain was falling on the roof. Sounded nice.

Outside I heard tires screeching followed by a loud crash. I looked out the window. Head on collision. The song "Dead Joe," by The Birthday Party immediately came to mind. There was a child lying sprawled on the sidewalk in the rain. The mother was in hysterics. The child kept screaming, "Mommy! Mommy!" I tried to imagine what the mother saw when she looked down at her child. Was the child's head bashed in? Where any bones exposed? Was the child's blood mixing with the falling rain and making rivulets of bloody water into the grass? Did their eyes meet? When the child would scream, the mother would jerk as if hit by lightning. Do the jerk mom, c'mon mom, do it in the rain. C'mon ma, jerk it. Use your hips mom. Jerk it.

◂ ◂ ◂ ◂ ◂

I put my cock in a noose
The bare bulb hanging from the ceiling
Is like some kind of cancerous growth
Just hanging around
Love and hate exist
On both sides of a one-sided coin
I enter the womb of a silent, sullen depression
I wait to be hatched out
I am always stillborn
Cold, blue
Bad as good as dead
As gone as never was in the first place
The last place is the same as the first place
Only now I'm more skilled in self-abuse
I take lessons from the quiet phone
The unknocked on door
The unopened mailbox
And the clock that won't shut off
Someday I'll substitute a bullet for two Tylenol

◂ ◂ ◂ ◂ ◂

She lit my soul and inhaled deeply
Flicking my ashes occasionally
Finally, she ground me out
After a time, she reached for another
Cracked
Crumbling
Ruptured soul
Shattered
I wrote out a road map to get back home
I threw it away
Here I am
In uncertain time
And a shaky place
And this is alright
Not somehow
But alright
This isn't the way it is
It's the way it is around these parts

◦ ◦ ◦ ◦ ◦

I am the end
The end of everything
Ashes, ashes
I am the end
I am the living end
I am
The end
I am the end of all
And it all falls
It all falls
It all falls down
I am what I am
I am the end

◦ ◦ ◦ ◦ ◦

I wish I kissed that girl in the summertime. I wished I touched that girl in the summertime. But I didn't. Her summer dresses were flower prints. I wanted to touch them with my hands. She cried in front of me, but never over me. After all confessions submitted, no crimes committed, my feelings were omitted with a drop of the eyes and the slam of the door. She left an empty house in my heart. The lights don't work anymore, the heater's broken. The roof leaks, the rent's overdue, the walls and doors are all smashed out. I'm trying to fix it up you know? But so far, construction's moving mighty slow.

◆ ◆ ◆ ◆ ◆

It's raining tonight. The rain and the smell of the streets remind me of Washington DC. Like walking home from Haagen-Dazs to my apartment. Those walks did me good. Cleared my head of a day's worth of shit at work. The rain makes me remember walking from Simon's house w/CFE to the Wisconsin Avenue 7-11 to get some ginger beer. And how on the same night I walked and wrote "Wound Up". That was about two weeks shy of a year ago. I would like to go to DC again for a visit. I like it there in the summer. The nights especially. I like Georgetown, not the places you would think, but my places like Montrose Park, Q Street, P Street, N Street, R Street, my 7-11's.

Always walking. Did you see what they did? To the pet shop, they turned my pet shop into an Italian restaurant. Steve sold Haagen-Dazs. They put video games in the Little Tavern and actually keep the place clean and don't let bums sleep on the floor by the cigarette machine. I can't even recognize the Calvert Deli anymore. Nicky's Pub uses frozen pizzas. They jack-hammered the Old Europe's parking lot. They put bullet-proof glass in Pearson's Liquor Store. Donald the dog died and sits in a heap of ashes in a brown plastic box in the hallway. The MacArthur Theater turned into the MacArthur 1-2-3. I'm twenty-three and I sound like I'm fifty-five.

◆ ◆ ◆ ◆ ◆

My ghetto gets getting and it pulls you in. See that mangy black dog looking at you through one good eye? You know that beast is from my ghetto because he's hungry, and low running. My ghetto gets getting and it invites you in. You walk into my ghetto and I hand you a sack of sad bad trash, slap you on the back and say, "Glad you could come on down!" My ghetto gets it right and sunshine ignores this heap of bad timing. My ghetto gets horny and it sucks you in. Do you see those boss hot rods slither by? You know those heaps are from my ghetto. Because they are wrecked and low riding. My ghetto gets desperate and it drags you in.

Dig my trash!

Hear my cry of love over the buzz of one thousand flies!

Stay with me!

For a moment or forever

Because I got nothing and I'll give it all to you

❧ ❧ ❧ ❧ ❧

Daddy, you're in your bed asleep

Your wife is lying next to you

She's yours

Your woman

I've come to your house

In your sleep you feel a sharp pain in your head

I have just slapped you

You're awake, your eyes widen in fear

It's dark, you don't recognize me

Our eyes meet, I'm looking in you, through you

My eyes are like two bullets ripping through your face

The tables have turned

It's good now, your wife has turned into a mass of putrid black tar and she's oozing off the bed. I have muscles, they are strong. I can utilize crushing power. You are older, weak, your bones are brittle. You are completely defenseless. I know this and fully take advantage of it. Your mouth is open. Your jaw is working. You're making faint rasping sounds, but no words come from your

mouth. Get up! Get up! I told you to get up and you do. Now, say my name. Tell me who I am. You say nothing. You're making choking sounds. What's my name? Who am I? Do you remember me? I am 2.13.61. My left fist comes straight at you. You see it in slow motion. Your face explodes like a pane of glass. Something broke. Your right cheek bone is crushed completely. You would fall to the ground if I wasn't holding your trachea. I'm not even sweating. This is easy, similar to beating a child. You remember now. You're seeing bright blue flashes and spots in your eyes. I am squeezing your trachea shut. The cartilage makes a rubbery snap-crack-pop as I crush it. Your feet are off the ground. They dangle as I shake you.
Hey dad
I learned
I learned respect
I learned discipline
I have strength
Your eyes are riveted to the ceiling

◆ ◆ ◆ ◆ ◆

Some of us live in the dark. We never see the light unless it comes through the window. Street light at night creeps through the venetian blinds and lies broken and scattered on the floor. Some of us wait in the dark. Quietly. Patiently. Sharpening our claws, waiting for you to slip just once. Our bodies are warm. Our muscles are tight. We press our eyes up to the keyhole and look around. We wait in the dark, grinding our teeth. Waiting. Waiting for you to slip just once.

◆ ◆ ◆ ◆ ◆

I live in disguise
I move from station to station
My dreams smash like glass acts in jagged formation
Like the fool that I am I swallow the slivers
And spit dead empty songs in the face of ms. givers
Memories get pulled like teeth from the shelf

I look in the mirror but can't see myself
The one that I can't see is the one that I am
The one that I can't be is the one in demand

❧   ❧   ❧   ❧   ❧

Alone
Don't you know
Alone
Like always
You're alone
In the end
Alone
No matter what you say
Alone
By yourself every day
You're alone
Give your grief to someone else
Alone
It's such a desperate grab
You're alone
Once you go, you know
You're alone

❧   ❧   ❧   ❧   ❧

In the dark unmoving still of the night
Two lovers
Their bodies twist and coil
Like loops on a hangman's noose
As the sun approaches
They shrink and separate
And speak in human tones
Death trip
In here
Right now

❧   ❧   ❧   ❧   ❧

My vision of you is marred by sight
The things I feel are nullified by sense
The things I want from you
The things I want to do to you
The things I want to do to myself
Here comes the dust

➤ ➤ ➤ ➤ ➤

I was in a men's room at one of those big gas-rest-food stops. At the urinal I saw six men pull down their zippers and pull out their cocks almost simultaneously. It was fantastic, like a firing squad, or like some kind of secret Masonic pud grab ritual. Men act differently in the men's room. They don't talk much, and if they do it's real loud as if to say, "Hey, I'm not afraid to talk in the men's room!" They act very manly in the men's room lest someone think they are gay. There are no weaklings in the men's room! We are in the men's room. We have our cocks in our hands. We are urinating our way. Right. A man who is henpecked and owned by his wife or girlfriend transforms into a virtual bedrock of masculinity upon entering the men's room. It's a temporary club, where men, united by a need to urinate, are men.

➤ ➤ ➤ ➤ ➤

The junkman sees everything
Picking up odds and ends
Never misses a thing
And do you know how?
Because he's seen his life
Written in the filth
Written on the shit that hangs on walls
The stuff that stares back and tells you what
He heard about himself at some fuckin' party
Now his life is background music
He found his life in a pile of trash

Over by Madam's Organ
He's been wearing it ever since
The junkman
Other's waste is his life

◂ ◂ ◂ ◂ ◂

The sound I feel the most is the still night air. Only broken by the
song of a bird somewhere. Have you ever been out there,
swallowed up in that inky night air? The smell of the trees and
lawns and streets. I feel the best when I'm there, alone. I am
always alone there. My mind's knots come untied. I can close my
eyes, let out a breath and my life as I know it becomes more
exacting. My eyes dull and my head hangs. Drunk on night air.

◂ ◂ ◂ ◂ ◂

I hate to want
You make me want
I hate to want
You make me want you
I hate to want
You make me want to hurt you
I hate to want
It hurts to want
I hate to want
I want to want

◂ ◂ ◂ ◂ ◂

I saw her
She was surrounded by light
I put my arms out
I wanted to touch her
I ran toward her
I put my arms out
I came to her

She pushed me away
I smashed her face in
I wanted her to want me
She didn't want me
She was porcelain under my fist
Porcelain cut my knuckles
I wanted her to want me

◆ ◆ ◆ ◆ ◆

The light reflects from her hair
She carries light in her heart
She radiates
If she touched me I would heal
She walks toward me
She walks right past me
She walks away

◆ ◆ ◆ ◆ ◆

I poured salt on a large slug. The slug writhed and squirmed. The slug tried to escape me and my burning salt. The slug made no sound. I'm sure if I was turned inside-out and dipped in salt, I would scream. I remember how the slug glistened and respirated until I put the salt on it. I remember how it tried to get away, secreting yellow-green mucus in great quantities that bubbled slightly. My fascination turned into revulsion as the slug writhed and tossed from side to side, secreting even more yellow-green mucus to try and beat the salt. It was a losing battle for the slug, because when the slug had succeeded in rubbing off some of the salt, I would simply turn the salt shaker over on the slug and the game would start again. Eventually I got bored and left the slug, still writhing, trying in vain to get free of the salt bath that would eventually suck the slug dry. Later I imagined that my whole body was a tongue, and I was dipped in salt.

◆ ◆ ◆ ◆ ◆

Home. The streets lie, the sidewalks lie. You can try to read it but you're gonna get it wrong. The summer evenings burn and melt and the nights glitter, but they lie. Underneath the streets there's a river that moves like a snake. It moves with smooth, undulating, crippling muscle power. It chokes and drowns and trips and strangles and lures and says, "Come here, stay with me," and it lies.

❧　❧　❧　❧　❧

I saw a man slither down four blocks of gutter with his face pressed against the ground. He called himself the snake man, said he could do just about anything. He didn't say a word about right or wrong or once or twice. He just talked about doing it. He bled dirt, he was down in the gutter, crawling low, he was invincible. I saw a man jam a needle into his arm. He looked my way and told me he was free. I saw a man who had cried so much that he had trenches bored into his face from the river of tears. He had his head in a vice and every once in a while he would give it a little twist. I saw a man who was so run down that he was pissing blue. He was pissing the blues, now that's what I call blue.

❧　❧　❧　❧　❧

What is it? Is it my hair? Am I ugly? I know, I'm boring, that's what it is. I'm a drag to be around. I don't understand, maybe I don't hammer down hard enough. I'm spineless, that's it. Please make me understand because all the shit hurts a lot. Frustration, all locked up. I'm stupid. For the rest of the day I'll try not to be so stupid. I'll try to keep the parts together. No! I don't ask for much. I should ask for a lot, then maybe I might get some. Everyone seems to have it together a lot more than I. I know I'm fucked up in the head, but Johnson, open the gate! Holy cats! I learn over and over. Slowly over time, the pain goes away. And I say, "I won't play that game again. Hey man! I don't play that game!" Well that's just another game to play. With all this playing going on, how does any work ever get done?

❧　❧　❧　❧　❧

Don't show me to the door
Just show me to the floor
And I'll crawl on home
Oh please miss, don't misunderstand me
I don't want to fuck with you
I just want to fuck you
So sing my song and beat my gong
I'm dead and gone but not dead yet!
I'm sorry for not being sorry that I'm not sorry
Don't show me to the door
Just show me to the floor
And I'll make like a snake and crawl for real
No useless limbs flailing around
I'm so low that I flirt with the dust
I flirt with the dirt so howza bouta date
Howza bouta night on me on you on the floor?
And we can crawl for real
Can you get lower than low-life?
Yes

◖ ◖ ◖ ◖ ◖

Something inside
Something from underneath
Flower
Dead
Girl
Street
Something is growing
Something is going on
Hit
Cry
Girl
Rain
Not again
Play it again

Fade
Eyes
Girl
House
Room
Grey
Dirt
Waste

❧   ❧   ❧   ❧   ❧

I remember I said to Ian, something along the lines of: "We had the best good times anyone ever had." He and I both agreed that while there are some really great days, some real good times, they really don't seem to roll like they used to. I know that sounds stupid, like let the good times roll, but they used to seem endless. You would look over the hood of your car into the street and it was good. Time goes by and I become less blind or I can look back and see more or something, do you know what I mean?

I get tired of the summer time. The people with their dates, getting drunk, laughing, having a good time, fucking with me. I'm so busy having the time of my life that sometimes I just want to curl up and die, but that's only sometimes. Like sometimes when you're at a party or you're hanging out and you're with all these people and you feel more alone than if you were lost in the desert. You feel lonely-blue-fit-to-die, and the more people around you, the more alone you seem to be. Well, what if you were on a stage with all these lights on you, with all these people looking at you, calling out your name? Might make you feel kind of funny. Not like funny ha ha funny, but funny like you come from a different planet. And you know that you could quit anytime you want. You might think, why can't I have one without the other, or neither, or both, but not feel it so hard, or something? Good times, good times.

❧   ❧   ❧   ❧   ❧

She was made of glass, she broke in my arms. The shards cut so clean, so deep, so good. My heart bled the only song it knew. It hurt to pull out the slivers but I knew that I couldn't bleed anymore, I had lost too much blood already. Now I remain, scarred and regaining strength.

◆   ◆   ◆   ◆   ◆

The ritual
The ritual, saying thank you
When I mean fuck you
The ritual has been beaten into my skull
The ritual
The ritual called my number
And they put me up here
And killed me with stones
I've got the ritual bored into my skin
I've got the ritual tattooed into my brain
The ritual
The ritual turned on me
Like a cornered animal
I was so close I could see its teeth
The ritual won't let me sleep
I lay awake in bed
With my brain screaming
The ritual won't let me say: I love you
The ritual won't let me
I bleed for the ritual
The ritual turns me on
The ritual turns on me
The ritual hangs above me
Like a dead man swingin'
The ritual
See the scars, remember the beatings?
Remember?
Remember the ritual?

The night gives birth to ugly depression children
Who tug at you and scream
Mommy-Daddy!
The stranger you recognize, self-infliction
Alone in your room with self abuse
A vice on your brain
Your hands know how to cut and fix and stick
Whatever-wherever
Hear it pounding in your ears
It's the ritual
Your fists-your tears-the blood
The strength to feel it over and over
It's the ritual

◄▷ ◄▷ ◄▷ ◄▷ ◄▷

Watching this dude shoot up: I like sticking needles in my arm.
Every time I do, I get high. I feel good. I say fuck you. When I
throw up I throw up on you. When I nod out, I nod out on you
and your fucked up world. The tracks on my arms are all the
times I won, all the times I said fuck you. I like sticking needles
in my arm! I do so much sticking that I don't even think of
sticking it in. You know, I don't get hard. I don't need no fucking
bitch to fuck with me. No girl can make me feel like this. I like
sticking needles in my arm!

◄▷ ◄▷ ◄▷ ◄▷ ◄▷

The sidewalk squirms
It wriggles underneath my feet
I look into the street, it's boiling
Moving like a black river
I step off the curb
I submerge into the asphalt
I have been christened
Blessed into the street

◄▷ ◄▷ ◄▷ ◄▷ ◄▷

Kicked down the stairs
Felt good to bleed
After awhile it hurt so bad I wanted to kill
I couldn't see
All the lights were off in the basement of love

◄ ◄ ◄ ◄ ◄

I was playing at this club in Birmingham, Alabama called "The Nick." I was sitting at the bar staring at the picture of Amanda Strickland. I had found the flyer at a restaurant a bit earlier that evening. The guy next to me said, "Yea they found her." "In how many pieces?" I asked. He said, "One. She was shot twice in the back of the head." The two abductors had her about six to eight hours, drove her to Atlanta, killed her and tossed the body. The body was found about two weeks later. The guy next me added, "She was bisexual. You know, kind of strange. A real nice girl."

◄ ◄ ◄ ◄ ◄

On the day of October 1, 1984, Katherine Arnold bought a shotgun at a K-Mart in Lincoln, Nebraska. Katherine, twenty-eight, mother of a son, took the shotgun into the parking lot of the K-Mart, sat down against a retaining wall and blew her brains out. On October 2, I came to Lincoln to play at the "Drumstick." The Drumstick is one hundred yards away from the K-Mart. I sat most of the day in the Drumstick writing. Now and again I would hear snatches of conversation about how "This lady blew her brains out." Later on that evening some people were telling me about it. This kid came up with a McDonald's cheeseburger wrapper all wrapped up. He opened it, inside was some of Katherine Arnold's brains. After the show I took a flashlight and went out to the K-Mart parking lot. I walked down the lot, parallel with the retaining wall. I saw chalk markings on the pavement. I guessed that was were the motor-cycle had been. I made a right and hopped over the wall, I shined the light against the wall. I found the spot. The wall was tinted brown from blood and gunpowder. The grassy area around the stain had been clipped. There was a sliver of brain still stuck on the wall, I peeled it off. There was a very strange smell in the air. I have never smelled anything like it before. I felt around in the surrounding grass area. I found some portions of brain tissue. I sat there alone with the remains of K. Arnold and that smell. It seemed to be in my pores, in my brain. I remember getting the feeling that this was a very special place, some kind of hallowed ground. I wanted to stay longer, I wanted to sit down exactly where she had. At this point I was overcome by a feeling of being watched, watched from the trees or from some place outside the distance of the flashlight's reach. It was time to leave. I picked up the pieces of brain tissue from the grass and went back to the club. Waiting outside to leave, I sat down and thought about the whole thing. After awhile, the blood would wash off the wall, the grass would grow back and it wouldn't look like anything out of the ordinary. Maybe some kids would come there in a car, park and drink some beers, legs dangling, feet hitting against the spot where Katherine Arnold's head rested. I wondered if the partyers would become aware of an odor. I wondered if they would just get up without a word and get the hell out of there. I found the article on Katherine Arnold in the local newspaper. I cut it out, and drove all night to Minneapolis.

◉ ◉ ◉ ◉ ◉

Katherine, who would ever think that your trail would end at K-Mart. Did anyone tell you? If you were alive right now, I mean if your brains hadn't been blown out of your skull with that shotgun you put to it, would you have believed that you would have done such a thing? Katherine, you didn't see what I saw. Oh girl, some kid had a hunk of your brains in a cheeseburger wrapper and was showing it to people. I went to the place where you shot yourself, You know the place I'm talking about, you were there about twenty-six hours before me. Katherine, I searched through the grass with my hands, I found pieces of your brain covered with dead grass and dirt. I peeled a piece of your head off the wall. You might be interested to know that your husband found you. Imagine what he saw, you with no head, brains all over the place. Katherine, I hope you aren't angry with me. I kept part of your blasted up brain. I wrapped it up in a piece of tin foil and put it in my back pack. I think about you from time to time. Hey, you made the local papers and everything. Who would have thought your trail would end at K-Mart?

◄ ◄ ◄ ◄ ◄

I just got off work. I work at an ice cream store. I scoop ice cream into cups, cones, pint containers, quart containers, coffins and body bags. I work behind a counter. I'm kind of like a bartender. I watch the pretty girls pass the window that looks out onto the sidewalk. I'm the guy in the ice cream store. I have been here eleven hours, my legs ache. I just got off work, it's 2:30 a.m. I'm hungry so I go to the only place that's open. 7-11. I get the same thing every night. I sit alone on the curb and eat. I have to walk to my apartment. My apartment is home. I don't want to go home. Home is dark, home is lonely. Home is cold storage. I'd rather go almost anywhere except home. I just got off work. I signed on for extra hours at the ice cream store so I could have somewhere to go. I go back into the 7-11 to get a coke for the walk to the apartment. It's a long walk. I don't want to go to the apartment. The apartment knows I'm coming. The apartment knows I have nowhere else to go. The apartment is smiling. It shuts off the heat and waits for me to fall in. I leave the 7-11 and walk down Wisconsin Avenue. I walk past the ice cream store and check the door to make sure it's locked. I just got off work. I hate my life. I hate myself. I feel ugly, unwanted, mad, mean, cold and condemned. I make the walk to the apartment. I pull out my folding shovel and dig down six feet to my front door.

◄ ◄ ◄ ◄ ◄

Fuck you Alan: I have been here all day. It's 6 p.m. I look forward to getting off work. It's cool not to work at night for once. I got nowhere to go but still...I'm waiting on Alan to come in and take over. It's 6:15, he's fifteen minutes late, fuck you Alan. Forty-five minutes later, Alan comes in, he's bleeding from his eye, his forehead is smashed up. Alan also works at this fancy shoe store up the street. At six o'clock the shoe store got robbed and the robber beat Alan's head in with the butt of a gun. Alan wants to know if I can pull his shift for him so he can go to the hospital. I ask him if he is sure he can't work. Alan stares at me in disbelief. Alan goes off to the hospital in a cab. The night shift is here. I might as well be here. I don't need the extra money and the store beats the apartment, but still...fuck you Alan.

❦   ❦   ❦   ❦   ❦

This guy had just got off work, he felt miserable. It was 3:23 a.m.. He went to the 7-11 and bought some microwave food. He sat outside the 7-11 and ate in silence. He felt low and lonesome, this was the usual. Just like the plastic bag taste of the microwave food, always right there. He thought of girls a lot. One in particular. She never thought of him unless she needed a ride or shoulder to cry on. After he would finish eating, he would walk to his apartment. He hated the apartment, it made him feel hateful to be all alone in there. It was hard to sleep in the apartment, always too damn hot, or too damn cold. Lots of couples on the street earlier that night. He would watch them pass by his work. They made him feel ugly, inhuman, like trash. He got up and started on his walk home. He had to cross a bridge to get to the apartment. The bridge was very high, it crossed over a large and powerful river. Almost every night he crossed that bridge he contemplated throwing himself off. That night he did. Stood on the edge and walked off, no shit.

❦   ❦   ❦   ❦   ❦

The crew. They live way back there. Some wash dishes, some work at record stores. They don't bum me out. They don't break my heart. They do something that falls somewhere in between. I feel strange around the crew sometimes, I feel cheap. Like some big shot who everyone hates. I never wanted to be big. No, I never cared. I wanted out. I looked at the back of a record jacket, I knew everyone in the picture. I listened to the words as the record played. I could almost see them coming out of his mouth. I remember when I was in Baltimore last. One of the crew came up and spoke to me. I had these girls crawling all over me at the time and I felt like an asshole as I tried to separate myself from them. It was hard for me to face him. I don't know, I felt like shit for reasons I can't explain. Every other sentence started with "Remember." I'm only twenty-three. I looked at the back of that record jacket and wrote all this. They ask me what I'm up to. I usually lie, I say nothing much so they won't ask anymore questions that make me feel like a person who won some kind of prize.

◆ ◆ ◆ ◆ ◆

I was at Dischord House. The Washington Post came by to take pictures of me for an interview I had done with the paper earlier. I took the photographer to Ian's room so no one would have to see him or listen to him. He insisted on going down to the living room and taking pictures of me with the rest of the guys "in the background." I felt like the big shot who uses people he knows merely for props. The photographer annoyed the Dischordions, no fault of his really, no fault of mine I don't think. It made me feel like I was rubbing some imaginary shit in their faces. It made me feel crummy.

◆ ◆ ◆ ◆ ◆

One day, I stopped hating
I ceased all meaningless activity
I completed the circle
I set my sights straight
Like an arrow I flew

I stopped acting
I got tired of playing with you
Violence and destruction
Became my reason for living
My out, my excuse
What is your excuse?
Destruction
Without hate, without fear, without judgment
I am no better than you
No one knows this better than I do
I just got tired of playing parlor games

◄ ◄ ◄ ◄ ◄

Look at your eyes.
Your eyes will lie to you
You have to take a walk in the desert
You have to understand the way things are
You have to take a walk through the desert
You have to understand
When you see yourself mirrored in the desert heat
Your eyes can never lie again

◄ ◄ ◄ ◄ ◄

Every second
I murder my life
I am alive
I am serving a death sentence
Born onto Death Row
Walking around
Dancing on my grave
By living, I am killing my life
Die, die, die
I breathe in
I breathe out
I am killing, digging a grave

Pounding coffin nails
I'm alive, I'm the killer
I'm the victim, I'm alive

◈ ◈ ◈ ◈ ◈

The world is lame
Painful, and hard to explain
In order to live inside your brain
You have to go insane
You have to die
Don't cry when you bid the world good-bye
You know you have to die to live in here
Circular vision games
Break down in calculated pain
Oh, you have to die to get by
To live in the world's eyes
You have to die
So you can look back
And see yourself wave goodbye

◈ ◈ ◈ ◈ ◈

I played this club in San Francisco. The night before, another band played. All night long the guitar player sat in a small room with the lights out. He spoke to no one. He played two sets, he stood in the shadows and played his guitar. Between sets he went back to the small room and sat in the dark. The next day they cleaned up the room, they found the ashtray full of camel non-filter butts. The ends were caked with heroin. What a life.

◈ ◈ ◈ ◈ ◈

He walked down the hallway, he stuck a key into room 21361. He sat down at a small table in the middle of the room. He wrote a short note on the back of an old paper bag. It said: "Could not hold on anymore." He pulled a .38 caliber pistol from his coat, put the barrel in his mouth and pulled the trigger. Click. No

bullet. He flipped the paper bag over and wrote "Memo: buy
bullets on way home from work."

⚫ ⚫ ⚫ ⚫ ⚫

Lying in the dark
Lying on my back
Rats crawling around
Breeding underneath my skin
Waiting on that last train
Heart slamming against its walls
Blood hurtling down my veins
Waiting on that pendulum blade
To cut its path across my flesh
Every day it swings a little closer
And sometimes I can feel the wind as it passes by

⚫ ⚫ ⚫ ⚫ ⚫

We are monsters
We create monsters
We mate and create
Monsters
Sluts and killers
Mean bloodspillers
Whores and fuckers
Fools and suckers
Monster fucker fathers
Monster slut mothers
Coors to you Redondo
Coors to you Hawthorne
Inglewood, this Bud's for you
Lawndale, welcome to Miller time
South Bay lovers
Hiding in trash heaps
Surfacing to dump trash
We are monsters

⚫ ⚫ ⚫ ⚫ ⚫

My eyes are two smashed out windows
Through my broken gaze I see
I stare at my hands and I wonder
What has happened to me
It's so cold when the wind comes whistling
Through my house
My mind is in the attic
Pushed aside piles of junk
Dark, cluttered, locked up
I can't get out
It's lonely
I'm alone in my house
My heart is in the basement
I don't dare go down the stairs
The door's been closed for so long
There's something down there
It's so quiet
No one comes to my house

◂● ◂● ◂● ◂● ◂●

I hear voices
When no one is around
I have seen the inside of my skull
I have crawled inside my skull
I am not alone
There are killers in there
I have met them
Sometimes they kick at the inside of my skull
It makes me twitch
There are killers living in my skull
Murderers in my skull
They make use of my body
They take my body and kill with it
I feel no pain
My body is the weapon of my mind.
I have pressed my hands against the inside of my skull

I have felt the insanity
I can mutilate
I can kill
I have before, it was just flesh in my hands
It was easy
I have murderers living in my skull
I have met them from time to time
They are my true friends
Don't disturb my insanity, don't you dare
There are killers in this house
They say you're ill, cure the illness
I listen to my skull
I have killed many inside my skull
I live with killers
It's time to come out

❦ ❦ ❦ ❦ ❦

I have dwelled in total absence of light. I have been inside my skull. I was not alone, someone touched me. He was cold. His touch was cold. It was dark, I couldn't see who it was. I remember his hands, they were cold. He said, "Come here, come here, come here. There is nothing to fear. In darkness, no fear."

❦ ❦ ❦ ❦ ❦

The insanity brings my soul to boil. The insanity brings my blood to tears. The insanity. The lines become so straight. I finally understand, my friend is here. I have finally met my friend. Now I understand everything that I need to understand. My friend is here. I'm not alone anymore. I'm free, my friend is here. Insanity.

The insanity is no twisted blade. It's like running your hands along a marble pillar. Cool, smooth and right. Calming, like a sanctuary for your wiggly brain. I don't need my soul tied in knots thank you. I remain in the field of the insanity, scouting around for the gate to infinity.

❦ ❦ ❦ ❦ ❦

The bad lands. Never to return. Forever living the end, leather skin, ashes underfoot. All saints fall but not now, that comes much, much later. Now here's a shovel, some nails, wood and a hammer. Go make history. Leave a trail. I don't care how you do it but do it. You know what I mean. I know you know. There's not the time to fool around. The clowns die. No more breathing. We're gonna make it oh so hot. Ashtray life, ashes, ashes oh so hot, incineration. We came to the end, we found nothing, nothing!!! And we cursed because we were hoping for so much less.

◖   ◖   ◖   ◖   ◖

I am a fool. Every night I want to die. I think how great it would be to be torn limb from limb by their greedy little hands, to be kicked into the grave by their dirty feet. Torn to bits. When they destroy me, they destroy themselves. I'm easier! So let it be! I like it, I love it! When you kill yourself, you're loving me. When you kill me, you'll die a thousand times. That's the only reason that I'm here, for your love. I revel in my stupidity. I wallow in my mortality. The cowards of the world come to me for pro tips! I'm the king of fools with nothing to prove, and everything to lose. Now if you think you lost it all, you're wrong. You can always lose a little more. So come on, get on up, rise up! Hey girls, hey! Come on down and lose. Right here, right here in the here and now. We're naked in the eyes of time so come on. Wrap your mind around mine. Look into my eyes and lie a thousand times and die a thousand more. If a coward dies a thousand times, then I have never lived. I'm too busy dying to even breathe.

◖   ◖   ◖   ◖   ◖

Open the door
Put me in an apartment
Make it cry
Make the walls convulse
Loop the extension cord around the light fixture

Do it for me
I can't do it myself
I'm helpless
I need you to help me
I'm calling out to you
I need help and assistance
Put the chair underneath the light
Help me die
I can't do it myself
Help me die
I want you to watch
Help me
Don't leave me
Tell me to get on the chair
Put the cord around my neck
Don't let me down
I'm counting on you
Tell me to get up on the chair
Good
Put the cord around my neck
I want you to watch
Push me off the chair
I'm hanging, I'm swinging
I'm doing my time
I'd whistle you a tune
But my tongue is turning black and swelling up
My head feels like it's going to explode
Are you watching, I can't see you
My eyes are riveted to the ceiling
My throat is thrust forward, exposed
My throat is shiny with oily sweat
Get a knife and cut my throat
Cut it
Disembowel me
Take the knife

And cut my stomach open
Gravity
Will cause my guts to fall all over the chair and floor
Now leave me
Leave me
Turn the light out
Remove yourself

◆ ◆ ◆ ◆ ◆

Cut and stick
Cure the illness
Close your eyes
Don't come back
Close the door
Give the knife to the girl in my dreams
Tell her about the long nights
Tell her about the self infliction
Tell her to cut me down
I'll fall right into her arms

◆ ◆ ◆ ◆ ◆

She goes to the 7-11. She buys a six pack of Miller (High Life), a box of tampons and a pack of cigarettes. She walks home to her dingy room she rents at the Edison Hotel. She sits and drinks and smokes and bleeds and watches the sun go down. It hurts to be alone when it's cold outside. It hurts to be alone when it's cold inside. It hurts to be alone when it hurts to be alone.

◆ ◆ ◆ ◆ ◆

Seen too much
Hit too hard
Too much damage
Just imagine someone walking
Around smoldering from an o.d. of life
A walking wreck

A pathetic shell
What I feel
Pain, depression
I'm tired
I don't want to react
I'm wrecked
Pull me off to the side for a breather
What do you mean there's no time?

◂ ◂ ◂ ◂ ◂

Sitting on the steps at 7-11 eating my burrito and big gulp thinking of where I'm going to sleep tonight. I just got off work and I'm still tense but cooling out on Wisconsin Ave. is making me unwind a little, occasional cat calls from cars no sweat. I got my car. I think I'll sleep in front of Ian's house because I got spooked real bad last night in that parking lot. Nice night breeze tonight, the air smells good. I like it out here.

Hanging out with Nathan in back of the 7-11 on Connecticut Ave. I got a burrito and a big gulp. Nathan, he likes that hippie girl with the big tits at work. We both work at the same place. Yea, just sitting there unwinding and enjoying the cool night air. It's not too late to us, 3:30 a.m., the night is still young. If you drank eight cokes and ate your fill of ice cream and nuts, you'd be wired too. I feel as if I have been working this job for a long time. I feel burned out and relieved that my shift is over.

◂ ◂ ◂ ◂ ◂

I've got an alienation
Sitting right here
My friend and me
I'm all the way alone
Hand in hand with me
In my alienation
In the desert of my alonity
I've got a black hole

So deep and dark
I live there
Inside my black hole soul
Where you can't go
Where you can't see
Where you can't hurt me
Anymore
I'm living in my alienation
I've got an alienation

◆　◆　◆　◆　◆

I was running on the strand down near the Hermosa Beach Pier.
It was a clear day. Everybody was outside. I saw all these people
in shorts and bikinis, having beers, playing volleyball on the
sand, running around, laughing, calling out to each other,
cooking hamburgers on hibachis, playing ZZ Top, fooling around
on skate boards. Beautiful girls, all tanned and slim, smiling and
talking with guys. People getting drunk, talking loud and laugh-
ing like a bunch of hyenas. Might have been nice to have been
part of it.

　　I saw this guy walking down the street with this girl. They
were both smiling, they were holding hands. You know she was
one of those blondes, and she had these nice clothes on, and they
were laughing and talking just walking down the street, prob-
ably going to eat dinner and then go to a movie or a play...I would
have traded places with the guy in a second.

　　I was in this apartment in the East Village. I saw this guy
shooting up heroin. He tied off his left arm with an extension
cord. He put the needle in his arm. The blood went up through
the needle and mixed with the heroin. He had hit the vein. He
shot the heroin and blood mixture into his arm. He released the
extension cord and pulled out the needle. He bent forward and
vomited all over his lap. He leaned back against the wall. A trail
of spittle came from his mouth onto his shirt. His arm was
bleeding, I noticed black and blue bruises from previous needle

punctures. He didn't bother to wipe up the blood, vomit or spittle, he seemed unconcerned. He seemed happy. Seemed kinda nice.

◂ ◂ ◂ ◂ ◂

I got a desert in mind and I go to get lost because I've been found too many times before. Sunrise burning brightly, burning eyes into the back of my head. Like I said, I've been found before when I'd thought I'd locked the door. I'll step behind the blinds of my mind and walk along that lonely desert road. Talking about my only trail, my only friend, like any desert scene. I have come to complete the circle. When I am done I will be one. In death I will be one. I am a snake that has been stepped on, lying scattered shattered and forgotten on the side of a trail. Squirming severed I feel no pain. Just the heat of the sun and the crawling famine that is my name.

◂ ◂ ◂ ◂ ◂

I am my end
I am the crawling famine
I am my end

◂ ◂ ◂ ◂ ◂

I've got a place
I've got a desert
I've got a good thing going
Don't climb down here
You put me on the outskirts of town
Now you want in?
You think you do
I'll turn your lights out
I'll take your virginity away again
I live in a hanging garden
Suspended from your world

In alienation: No Sears and Roebuck dreams
No credit is good
In alienation I am whole
Complete
The full circle realized
In alienation
In the alienation
In the peace of 21361 minds
It's only cold in your world
When I'm with you I'm cold
Alien
Your world is such a lonely place
When I am there
I am cold
You are a bad trip
That's why I quit you
That's why I spat you out
That's why I went up river
Into the desert
Into the jungle
Into the sun
I exist in alienation
I am not alone
I am joined by those who know that paradise
Lies

◀ ◀ ◀ ◀ ◀

I'm looking through the window at these guys sitting at a bar.
They stare into the darkness, they smoke, they drink, they try not
to exist. They drink and curse and burn and weep and drink and
hate it, and drink and grind their teeth, and drink and wring their
hands and drink and live a slow life-like death and drink and sink
into their stools.

◀ ◀ ◀ ◀ ◀

I am the incineration man. A disciple of the sun. I'm your man. I don't want to waste your time. I don't want to take you just anywhere. I want to take you nowhere. I've got a magic touch. Blow out the candles on your birthday cake, get in the car, we are gonna flame, brother.

◆　◆　◆　◆　◆

Take a walk but not alone
Take me with you
Please
Unravel, unfurl, come undone
Please
Open the curtains of your heart
Let me see inside your theater
I want a front row seat when the movie starts rolling
No
I want to touch you
But I can't
Not with these despicable hands
My hands are ugly
Often washed, but never clean
The filth is below the skin
I want to see you
I can't look at you for too long
You might notice me
This would be a disastrous thing
My eyes are ugly
I didn't keep them closed enough
I looked at things too closely
I don't touch, I defile
Please don't look at me
I don't look, I stare
I must go now
Watch me scurry away

◆　◆　◆　◆　◆

I'm walking on a tightrope
They say
If I keep straight I'll cope
I can't mess up
They touch me and I scream
They tell me to live
They tell me how
I can't go on like this
I want to live
I don't want it to be taken away
I know they have places for people like me
This can't be the only way
Just to exist on a tightrope
I'm not living
I'm already dead inside
No, not again
I can't go through it
I think tomorrow
Is going to be too much

◄ ◄ ◄ ◄ ◄

It is painfully simple to understand. You're gone and I miss you.
I think I have died a few times since you've been gone. I wish you
would come back to me. I lie awake at night and think about you.
I feel lonely. I feel weak. You're gone and I miss you. I feel like
I want to die. You've heard this before in a million songs I know.
But my room has turned into a penitentiary. It's cold and I got
rings under my eyes because I don't sleep good anymore. I know
I sound like a pathetic fool but I can't help how I feel right now.
See? I've been hurting myself again. The pain takes my mind off
the other pain. Girl, I miss you so bad. I don't know what to do
with myself. I don't know what to do. Please come back.

◄ ◄ ◄ ◄ ◄

It's December 24, 1984. Christmas Eve. I always spend these jolly times in places where the lonely and forgotten types seem to gravitate. Look at those broken faces in the diner window, melting into their coffee cups, cigarette smoke curling up around the sockets of their dead eyes. Merry Christmas dead man. It's the season to be with family and friends. I look at the people sitting in the bar, getting numb, toasting their loneliness to the winking Christmas lights strung up around the men's room. Back a few years ago I can remember sitting in my apartment alone on Christmas Eve watching the cars pass by my window. I was feeling mighty low, nowhere to go. I didn't know what I hated more, having nowhere to be or feeling that I had to be somewhere. Oh man, look at those people at the Georgetown Theater on Wisconsin Avenue! A guy pays his $3.50 and sits through four or five showings of a film so he can hear some voices other than the ones screaming in his head. I am wishing that the ice cream store that I work at was open so I could go and do a shift, turn on the radio and forget myself in the fluorescent light. Christmas Eve is here and the cold stove is burning.

◄ ◄ ◄ ◄ ◄

By December 27 the dead had started to fill the streets. I stepped around the corpses on my way back from 7-11. On the afternoon of the 28th the refuse truck came to pick them up. The bodies were so emaciated that the workmen could pick them up and pitch them into the truck without any trouble. When the truck bed was filled to the top, it would be driven to the outskirts of town. The bodies would be dumped into a large pit and incinerated. This was an efficient method of disposal. By January 2nd, a few more bodies had been dragged out of the houses and deposited in the streets. There they lay mixed in with Coors light cans and used condoms. They would soon be hauled away and incinerated. By January 3rd the streets were clear. All the Christmas trees had been reduced to ash.

◄ ◄ ◄ ◄ ◄

They go around and around
Their hearts beat
They live
They exist
But they don't know why
Everything they know
Is a matter of fact
Instinct
Drive
The need to sleep
But they don't know why
From start to finish
They don't know why
Instinct drives to survive
But they don't know why

❧ ❧ ❧ ❧ ❧

The man liked his uniform. He liked the way it looked in the mirror. He liked what it did to people. He got off on the fear and hatred and jealously in their eyes. He liked to touch his gun. His gun felt good, hard, cool and smooth. He didn't like girls. He only got hard when his uniform was on. That gun felt so good. He nearly shot a man once. Some fucking black piece of shit. He couldn't pull the trigger. His hand was shaking too much. He couldn't come for weeks afterward. He came home one evening and stood in front of the mirror. He couldn't get hard, he tried different poses with his sunglasses on and off, nothing. He closed his eyes and stroked his cock and remembered that night the summer before when he had that man face down on the sidewalk. He had the gun at the man's head. Make one move you piece of shit and I'll blow your fucking brains out. His hand hadn't shook, he was hard, it felt good, so good. Still no erection, in a flash he was down on his knees, the barrel sliding in and out of his mouth, so hard, so smooth. The gun came.

❧ ❧ ❧ ❧ ❧

I am sitting at the bar, I am happy. Drinks are 1/2 price, it's happy hour. I'm watching the game on TV. All my friends are here. Boy are we getting fucked up. I have enough courage to kind of flirt with the barmaid. She can't see how my stomach folds over my belt, that particular view is obstructed by the height of the bar. I call her Boo-Boo, she calls me Yogi. I think she likes me. She talks about this singer named Prince. Some nigger on MTV. I'll buy her some coke, she might fuck me then. I have a wife. Maybe by the time I get home the old bitch will be asleep and I won't have to look at her. I yell and laugh with my buddies as we watch the game, "Look at that nigger run, look at 'im!" I am jealous of the football players. I can't play so I just drink beer and watch. I am pathetic and stupid. I am drunk. I am fat and fucked up. I should be destroyed.

◆ ◆ ◆ ◆ ◆

To find the truth, you have to L.I.E. The big truth is the big lie. When you see the truth you'll know what I mean. The truth exists in a lie. The truth is a lie. L.I.E. – Living In Exile. To tell the truth, you must lie. The truth is told when you are alone. The truth is admitting to lies.

◆ ◆ ◆ ◆ ◆

The desert is on fire. The desert is burning for me. Spirits rising out of the ground. When I say that the desert is on fire, I mean to say that the desert is on fire! I mean to say that I am on fire. I'm standing up, walking around and burning down. I am incinerating. The desert is burning, the spirits are rising out of the ground. The snakes and the spiders and the vultures and all the other sisters and brothers are on fire, it's us. We are burning. At the end we are painless, charred, black and silent.

◆ ◆ ◆ ◆ ◆

When I was nineteen, I worked for awhile at a lab facility in Rockville, Maryland. The place had mice, rats and rabbits. I was a drone. Mondays I mopped the facility. Tuesday I loaded dirty cages into a huge washer. Wednesday, Thursday and Friday would pass in similar fashion. One day whilst transferring the three hundredth batch of mice into a clean cage, Mike, the head man, came into the room. He told me that there was an outbreak of a rodent disease called Ectromelia throughout the entire facility. All the animals in the facility were to be killed and incinerated.

Mike: Henry, do you want to do it? I mean would it make you squeamish?

Me: Hell no.

Mike: So you'll do it?

Me: Sure.

Fine. By order of the National Institute Of Health, fifteen to seventeen thousand little beasts were to be destroyed. Fine, clean their cages, mop their floors, sterilize their rooms. Now I kill them. Most of the staff were relocated to another facility. It was pretty much just me and the animals. I had a room all empty and waiting. I was to gas them. The procedure was simple enough. I would put twenty to thirty animals in a glad bag, squeeze the air out, stick in the gas tube, turn on the gas. Fine. I would go into the rooms and pull out the carts that held cages. I would wheel the cages into the death room. I had the bags and the gas tank of CO_2. I would kill, cage by cage. When the boxes would fill up with dead rats and mice I would take the boxes over to the big N.I.H. facility where I would incinerate them. From 7:30 in the morning, until 4:30 in the evening, I killed them. Each time I would gas, I watched the animals die. When the mice would be put into the bag, they would crawl around, sniff and try to figure out what they were doing there. Then when I would stick the tube in and turn the gas on, they would leap up the sides of the plastic bag as it ballooned full of the gas. They looked like they were jumping for joy or something. They would fall back down to the bottom, gasping, soaking in their own urine. They always died with their eyes open. I would look through the bag and look at their eyes, their bodies stacked in a heap. The bottom of the bag was always warm from their piss and shit. I would tie the bag off and throw it in a specially marked box. That sound, I'll never forget that sound, the gas hissing, and the scratch of the little claws scurrying up the inside of the bag. They always died the same, wide-eyed and with no idea why. I was Adolph Eichmann. I was ordered to terminate. I was not a murderer. I was just trying to get the job done with maximum efficiency. I would terminate and incinerate. I like the way that sounds. Yes, I brought them to the camp in carts that held up to two thousand at once, efficient. I gassed them in enclosures, that contained the bodies, their wastes and their disease. Efficient! The corpses were taken to the ovens and incinerated, leaving behind disease-free ashes, efficient. They called me a murderer. A saint maybe, a murderer, no. After all, it was I who cured the illness. It was I who stopped its spread. I destroyed the ill and the weak, those who were not fit for survival. Can't you see? I did a job that had to be done. I tried to give rise to a strong, perfect, disease-free race and you call me a criminal? I am a humanitarian in the strongest sense of the word.

Inside of a week and a half the facility was silent. All were incinerated, except for one load that I dumped in Burger King and 7-11 dumpsters. I quit the month after and started working in an ice cream store. A while ago, I was thinking that it would have been a lot more fun to distribute the boxes in more interesting locales. How about taking boxes of dead mice and rats to a nice residential neighborhood and putting a box on each doorstep? How about UPS'ing a whole bunch to your old high school or girlfriend's house. You could open up the boxes and bomb people on the sidewalk. How about taking a bag, putting it on someone's doorstep, lighting the bag on fire and ringing the doorbell. The guy comes out and stomps the fire out and ... gross, rodent flambe underfoot! You could freeze 'em and throw them at people in Westwood — fun!!! With an open mind, the possibilities are endless.

◄ ◄ ◄ ◄ ◄

Keep me preoccupied
Keep me busy, busy, busy
So I won't have to think
I don't want to think
Because it only brings me pain
I keep running away from my problems
Keep me busy
Give me a million things to do
So I can keep running away
From myself

◄ ◄ ◄ ◄ ◄

Black:
The color of silence
The color of the earth
Burnt to a crisp
The color of dead, charred bodies
Black:
The color of peace
The color of no pain
The color of nothing
Nothing!
The end of war
The end of hate
The end of noise
Black:
The color of infinity
The color of alienation's vacuum
The color of insanity's dream
The color of reality's nightmare
The color of the full circle realized
Ultimate
Final
Harmony

◄ ◄ ◄ ◄ ◄

Walking down Artesia Blvd. I walk past this souped-up Chevy. There's a man inside. He's lying in the back seat. He looks like a corpse, arms folded on his chest, baseball cap over his face. I breathe in his aftershave and keep walking.

◄ ◄ ◄ ◄ ◄

Phone calls, friends, Valentine's day cards, cats, parties and the countless games that make people hurt, cry, laugh, etc. These things are hands that stick out the window and catch you and break your fall after you have thrown yourself off the roof. The sound of their voices, the pain they inflict, the games they play, the noise. The noise, keeps you from going insane. They keep your mind off your mind. Down the road apiece in the house of the alive, there is darkness and silence. You can hear the water dripping off the roof of your skull. There's nothing there to stop you from hearing the silence. You wish for a phone call, a human touch, anything will do. But it's too late. You know too much. Your ears turn deaf to the noise. Jumping off the roof and the bottom is becoming clearer.

◄ ◄ ◄ ◄ ◄

They were cleaning up the place, it looked like a party that had gone too far. Looked like a garbage dump. Body bags for the whole ones, and glad bags for the parts. Custodians cleaning up, picking up limbs, guts, bodies. You could smell the semen, blood, and burned flesh. Everybody was dead. Luggage, body bags and custodians lumbering around, stepping over charred corpses.

◄ ◄ ◄ ◄ ◄

She has seen people shot down in the street, imprisoned in death camps. She has seen starvation and utter hopelessness of survival. Now she wants warmth, peace and quiet. She has lived in days of pain, darkness, cold and death. When she smiles, it's for real.

◄ ◄ ◄ ◄ ◄

I look across the way. I see that man in his room-cell. Blue light flickering through the window. All the lights are off. Just that blue light flickering, blinking, wrapping tight. O, he's got the blue light on. He's got that blue light on. He's turning cold blue. Lights off. He's cold when that blue light's on. He sits alone in the darkness, his face reflecting the cold blue light.

❦ ❦ ❦ ❦ ❦

Sleep tight. I hope that nothing comes and steals you away in the night. I have many frozen miles to travel before I see your eyes again. I'll reach you in your dreams, reach out and catch me, pull me down. I've lost my way.

❦ ❦ ❦ ❦ ❦

Saturday afternoon, ABC Wide World of Sports. Films of men in kayaks paddling down white water rapids, beautiful, sunny mountain footage. The announcer cuts in: "Some people will do anything to get to the great outdoors!" Scene cuts to black and white footage of the Belsen death camp in Germany. Men are pitching dead bodies into the back of a wide body truck. One of the men turns to the camera, waves and smiles.

❦ ❦ ❦ ❦ ❦

Walking among the handshakers. Watching them feed, breed, kill and shake hands. Watching them watch me. I want to be a pendulum blade, swingin' and a'killin' and a'slashin' down the way. Stamping them out like cigarettes.

❦ ❦ ❦ ❦ ❦

When we are lying next to each other, I look at her naked body. I try to imagine someone else entering her, kissing her. I try but I can't. I can, but I can't really.

❦ ❦ ❦ ❦ ❦

I have seen you throw people around and shit. The ones that enjoy their work are the ones that this little missive concerns. I saw this show in the summer of 1981. The bouncers had been a bit over the top that night. Well, here's the funny part. One of you boys was going to his car to drive home. One of the "bounced" walked up and sunk an ice pick into the bouncer's side, all the way, up to the handle. I of course thought this was cool. A few weeks after that, a highway patrol pig was blown off his bike by a shotgun blast. This brought a smile to my face again. I thought about you boys and how every once in a while you get what you need. It will happen again, yes it will, next time it could be you. We can only hope.

◂ ◂ ◂ ◂ ◂

There's a crazy man with vacuums in his eyes
He says he can hear the sun rise
He says it makes him a bit off balance
He says it makes his soul scream
Now all the cities burn down
In the slums and the gutters
Of his mind and dreams
All the cities burn down
Down through the times of his childhood memories
That strike and ignite with burning pain
Now burn down
The cities burn down
He closes his eyes
And the cities burn to the ground
The streets are full of ashes
He walks alone
His eyes pull in the wind
And the abandonment
Of every city that passed through him
And left him cold

He closes his eyes
And the cities burn down

❧ ❧ ❧ ❧ ❧

Life's abandonment is painless
Life's abandonment is silent
The abandonment grows inside
Like a freezing, killing, crawling cancer
Born, and left in the dust
The sun comes up
You're walking down the street
You realize that you've been left in the house all alone
It's cold inside
The doors are locked
You're never coming out
Who left you?
No one left you
You're looking at yourself
And there's nothing wrong
You're looking at yourself
And there's no one home inside
You say: Hey where have I gone?
You went nowhere
That's the abandonment
I open my eyes and I see it
I feel it
It consumes me
That's the abandonment
Turn me off
Or cut me
Take my mind off my mind

❧ ❧ ❧ ❧ ❧

I was standing on this bridge that crosses over four lanes of traffic. I was standing there, swearing, spitting on the traffic below, minding my own business, the usual. This kid comes up to me, he says, "Hey mister, have you seen a brown and white dog go by?" I said, "Forget the dog, kid, get up on the rail here." I · patted the marble guard rail with my hand. The kid got up on the guard rail and looked down at the whizzing traffic below. "Now jump." The kid jumped. Stupid kid.

◂ ◂ ◂ ◂ ◂

Come home
Close the door
Lock the door
Make sure you lock the door
Pull back the curtains
Look outside
The streets are full of killers
Snakes at your feet
Feel the dirt touch the disease
Cure the illness
Stop the hurt
Cure the illness
Stop the vision
Still the turbulence
Sit down on the couch
Take a load off
Take out the gun
Put the barrel in your mouth
Close your eyes
Think of the filth
Think of the alienation
Become the isolation
Embody the alone
Use it as a weapon

Alienate others
From yourself
From themselves
Use the weapon
Pull the trigger
Show them what you're made of
Stop flailing around
Pull the trigger
End the joke
Make it real
End it

◄ ◄ ◄ ◄ ◄

I'm in my shed
In the backyard
A little bit of sunlight
Your sunlight
Filters through the window
It gives itself silently
Walks right through the window
From your world
Into mine

◄ ◄ ◄ ◄ ◄

The world can be such a cold and lonely place. This is something that everybody knows. So cold and dark that sometimes I think I'm going to disappear and go spinning down the drain. Down to some cold sewer. Self-destruction becomes a straight line. Striking back at a world that doesn't even know your name. You can't hurt it, it can only hurt you back.

◄ ◄ ◄ ◄ ◄

When I'm down in the subway
Trying to find my way

Down in the refrigeration mind
Down in the basement of my alienation
I see her face
Coming through the walls
Shining
Down on me

◀◉ ◀◉ ◀◉ ◀◉ ◀◉

The baby was born, it was slapped. The baby started to scream. The greasy, bloody baby made a lunge, threw itself back onto the gurney where its mother lay. The baby tried to crawl back inside the mother. The child's oily fingers clawed, its head straining forward. The doctor grabbed it back into his hands. The baby screamed, "No!" The doctor was so shocked that he nearly dropped the child. The child was washed and put in the maternity ward with the rest of the infants. Later that day, a nurse found the child, cold, blue, dead. Its hands wrapped around its throat.

◀◉ ◀◉ ◀◉ ◀◉ ◀◉

When I die, bury me in the backyard of the Ginn's. It's really nice back there. The yard is covered with clover and pine needles. There's an old grey cat that hangs out, there's a nice offshore breeze. It's quiet, nobody's ever back there except for me. Wrap the body up in a sheet, dig a hole and throw the body in, cover the corpse with dirt, go back inside and watch Benny Hill.

◀◉ ◀◉ ◀◉ ◀◉ ◀◉

A bum stood at the Lucky Market right in front of Artesia & Blossom. He was begging for money. He looked pretty pathetic, dressed in rancid, oily clothes. He smelled like cigarettes and urine. "Can you spare a dime?" he would ask. People would shake their heads or walk around him. He was getting nowhere. Two hours went by, no money, not a cent. "Please, a dime!" cried the bum. A middle-aged man walked by him, heard his plea and laid upon him a mint new dime. "Thank you, sir! Thank you!" shouted the bum. Dime in hand, the bum limped over to a phone booth and called in the airstrike.

◄ ◄ ◄ ◄ ◄

I'll be back in a little while, I'm gonna go down to the store, then I'm gonna go shoot Mr. T. I'm gonna sell all that gold around his neck, gonna buy me some drugs, gonna buy me some guns, gonna buy me some bullets, gonna shoot every pig I see. Gonna watch the pigs get shot down to the ground. Pigs, dying, squealing, bleeding like stuck pigs. The only way they know.

◄ ◄ ◄ ◄ ◄

She's kind of druggie. On again off again. The times when she's on, she's on. She's bumming on having to come down. When she's off, she's talking about getting on. She's not an addict, it's an on again, off again kind of thing. You know, like those "heroin weekends" people go for, meth runs, etc. You know what I'm talking about. She pulls an apple cart, the driver has a stick with an apple on a string, he dangles it in front of her nose. She sees a syringe, the needle shines. She likes the word "spike." The needle is a lover, she likes the words "doing a dime." The needle is boss, the needle is her best friend. If she says, "Tie me off, lover" one more time I'll scream.

◄ ◄ ◄ ◄ ◄

Her eyes
Her touch
Her voice
Takes my breath away
She's nice enough
To give it back
Thanks friend
I needed that

◄ ◄ ◄ ◄ ◄

I'm swingin', a noose wrapped around my neck. The rope is tied
to the sky. I'm floating through the air, dead. People look up in
the air and see my dead, bloated body pass. Two lovers are lying
in the dirt, pushing each other around. They look up and my eyes
meet theirs, burning down the world. The two lovers start
making animal sounds. They sink their claws into each other's
flesh and fuck until they are loveless, breathless, sexless and
alive. They say, "Thanks dead man!" Oh, my death is a turn on!
I made the world cry, shudder and crack. I made the flowers
burst into flame, floating along, turning everything on. I am
black as any dead sun. Shining down a dead light to make it all
come alive and burst into flame. Handing down a dead light.
Like a message. Firing down a dead light.
O, they see me coming on a harvest wind
They see me burning hotly
They see me shining blackly
Their lungs fill with fire
They embrace every breath
Like a dead friend come back to life

      ◄   ◄   ◄   ◄   ◄

I am the bubonic plague
I turn you black
I make you drop and die
I fill you with pain
I make you convulse and scream
They burn your corpse
I am the rats
I am the grey wind
I am a sex machine
I fuck you slow
I fuck you all
I fuck you until you die
I've been gone for a long time
But it's time for me to come back
I see the pigs

I see the killers
I see the alienation
You feel superior to the vermin
You need to feel superior to the vermin
You call the pigs on the vermin
You call the exterminator on the vermin
I am a superhero
I am the divine punishment!
I'm going to destroy your life
I'm going to terminate your existence thoroughly
Unbiasedly, yes
I'm not racist
I'm not sexist
I have no political leanings
I'm not in this for the money
This is the best deal you ever had
I do not hate!

❧   ❧   ❧   ❧   ❧

They're at a bar, sitting at a table. The waitress comes over to take their order. She orders a dry martini, he orders a cup of coffee. Shortly after, the waitress comes back with the drinks. She says: "I'm confused, which is which?"
The lady says, "I'm the martini."
The gentleman says: "I'm the coffee."
The waitress puts the drinks down and leaves

She is the gin. Cold, intoxicating. Gives you a rush, makes you warm inside, makes you lose your head. Take too much, it makes you sick and shuts you down.

He is the coffee, hot, steaming, filtered. You have to add stuff to it to make it taste good. Grinds your stomach, makes you jittery, wired and tense. Bad trip, keeps you up, burns you out.

Coffee and gin don't mix, never do, everybody keeps trying and trying to make it taste good.

❧   ❧   ❧   ❧   ❧

Don't get all uptight. Relax, really, you could pull a muscle or something. You cut them, they bleed. You shoot them, you beat them, they die. It's simple. It's just flesh in your hands. It's just bodies lying at your feet. It's ok to want to "do it." It's not bad to "do it." It's ok to kill them. That's what they are there for. Now there's some things you really shouldn't do, like get all uptight and shit, really. Kill, relax and destroy. And don't sweat it!

◆　◆　◆　◆　◆

In the Ginn's backyard
Shirts hang from branches of a tree
They look like ghosts
Billowing souls at attention
Pettibon's pot plant grows in a clay pot
He doesn't smoke pot
He thinks it's funny
Ms. Ginn sits in a lawn chair
Reading a book about Adolph Hitler
I sit in the shed
Listening to the MC5

◆　◆　◆　◆　◆

You know what they say:
A man's got to do what
A brainless idiot's got to do

◆　◆　◆　◆　◆

Got a shield of armor
Wrapped around my soul so tight
Sometimes even I can't get in or out
Held prisoner to myself by myself

◆　◆　◆　◆　◆

He bought the stuff from a guy in a beat-up pinto. He went home. He fixed. He tied off. Sunk the nail into his arm. The sun came streaming in through the window. God was born.

◆ ◆ ◆ ◆ ◆

Madonna. She makes me want to drink beer. She makes me want to drive fast and go bowling. She makes me want to shop at Sears. She makes me want to kick vegetarians. When I hear her sing, I know she's singing to me. She wants to get nasty with me. When I see her face, her eyes, her lips, talking to me, telling me to come on, I get to feeling mean. I get to feeling like I wanna do a whole lot of pushups, or go to a hardware store. Then I have to cool down. I gotta cool down, man. It's either gonna be a cold shower or a Bruce Springsteen record.

◆ ◆ ◆ ◆ ◆

Saw you walking down the trail
Singing a dead black bird song
Getting small in the eyes
Needle hanging out of your arm
Talking about the divine punishment
And screaming at the gods
And how you gotta get out of here
And how it's such a shame to have to go so soon

◆ ◆ ◆ ◆ ◆

Standing on the roof
Just after the rain fell
Ozone
Sirens
Staring out
Feel like jumping off?
All the time, yes
Moist breeze

2:47 a.m.
Maybe the sun won't come up today
Maybe if that happens
All the bus drivers would be more polite
The cab drivers wouldn't be insane
And this nice stillness would last awhile
But the sun is on its way
And I'm not going to let it burn me up today
If I could fly off this roof right now
I would
But if I fall down again
I don't think I'll be able to handle it
So I'll just stay alive
Amongst the animals of summer

◆ ◆ ◆ ◆ ◆

I was at this guy's house. I met this girl who was hanging out
there. She was real pretty, she had brown eyes and dark hair. She
was soft-spoken and real nice. I know that everyone has their
own life and they can do what they want and you shouldn't think
anything of it or anything. But man, I couldn't help but flinch a
little when I saw all those needle marks in her arm, they looked
so sore. Hateful little holes. I wanted to say something, but I
didn't.

◆ ◆ ◆ ◆ ◆

I have colors on my back
I am marked
Branded
Chosen
The air tears at me
Sometimes I feel
Like the gas chambers and the ovens
Of the world

Are inside me
Ready to choke and incinerate
Everything that wounds my eyes
And sometimes I think
That everything and everyone wounds my eyes
And the pain brings a lucidity
That brings sense to the idea of
Healing the wounds
And bringing the streets to a boil

⋆   ⋆   ⋆   ⋆   ⋆

When I look into her eyes
I see a fire burning
Not the fire of desire
Not the fire of love
The fire of dead bodies
Piled in mounds
The fire of plague and pestilence
She is napalm
Burned to death by napalm
Have you seen them running
Screaming
Flesh burning, curling back
My love for her is a crawling famine
Clawing at her soul
I crave her destruction
She lights up the jungle
She burns with napalm

⋆   ⋆   ⋆   ⋆   ⋆

I'm coming out of 7-11
A car pulls up
The door opens
A man yells:

Ok, fuck, you go get the beer. I don't care!
A pretty girl gets out
She passes me, and smiles
Her perfume mixes with the smell
Of the alcohol already consumed
The man in the front seat winks at me
And waits for the bud and the broad

◄ ◄ ◄ ◄ ◄

Don't think
Drink
Yes
Drink your fill
Drive
Kill
Yes
It's ok, really
It's ok to mow down innocent people?
Yes
Why?
Because no one is innocent
Or some shit
It's a good rap when you get drunk
When you get behind the wheel
When you get pulled over
For wiping out some people
Who got in your way

◄ ◄ ◄ ◄ ◄

I don't want to get out of bed today. I pull the covers over my head. I start to gnaw at the flesh on my chest. I rip pieces of my skin away from my body. I swallow hunks of my flesh. I chew a large hole in my chest. There. Fine. I crawl into the hole. I reach my hand out the bleeding flesh hole and pull the covers over the corpse's face. There. Fine. Dark, warm, quiet. I take out the gun.

I put the barrel in my mouth. I pull the trigger. My brains splatter all over my rib cage. I died inside myself. Goodbye. There. Fine.

❧   ❧   ❧   ❧   ❧

Man and woman
Forever ruptured
Forever severed
Clutching
Clawing each other's flesh
Fucking in shallow graves
Rolling in blood soaked dirt
He looks into her eyes
He reaches inside her
Deep inside her
He rips her uterus out
And shakes it in her face
He screams:
Whose idea was this?

❧   ❧   ❧   ❧   ❧

I drilled a hole into the back of my head. It was easy. I took a Black and Decker power drill and put it to my head. The drill bit chewed through my scalp, no problem, a little bit of smoke came up when the bit hit my skull. I gave it a good push and it crunched through to my brain. I stuffed a bit of paper towel in the hole, now, when the pressure gets to be too much I pull out the cork and let my brain drain out some. A little bit of sticky juice comes out. The pressure's off. If you want to get rid of problems, get rid of them.

❧   ❧   ❧   ❧   ❧

I saw this movie on TV today. This Polish spy was impersonating Adolph Hitler. He was on a flight with a bunch of other Poles dressed in Nazi uniforms. The only Germans on the plane were the two pilots. To get rid of them, a soldier came to the cockpit and told the pilots that Hitler wanted to speak to them personally to compliment them on their skill. The two pilots ran down the aisle to meet the man. The Hitler impersonator opened up the side door and said "Jump." They both saluted and jumped out, they did not question their leader. What control, what charisma. Sometimes I wish I could take everyone in the world to a cliff and tell them to jump.

◆   ◆   ◆   ◆   ◆

Be my oasis, make me want to stay by letting me go away when I need to go. Be my forest, make me want to stay by understanding my need to walk alone in the desert. Be my sunshine, make me want to be around you by knowing how good it is to run in moon lit fields.

◆   ◆   ◆   ◆   ◆

This morning they found you, in an alley, dead, face down, all shot up. Your bullet-ridden black-and-white still running. The lady on the 11:00 news said that your fellow officers are still looking for the reason why someone killed you. I did it because you're a fucking pig and I'm a pig killer.

◆   ◆   ◆   ◆   ◆

My love runs deeper than the wounds I inflict upon myself, deeper than the sweat that pours from my body. My love runs deeper than the tears that roll down my face. My hate runs deeper than the wounds I inflict upon myself, deeper than the sweat that pours from my body. My hate runs deeper than the tears that roll down my face.

◆   ◆   ◆   ◆   ◆

Cockroaches are your gods. You are weak. You should pray to them. They are a more perfect life form than you. You are fucked up with your idiotic idiosyncrasies. You have analysts, tranquilizers, you need vacations, you start wars, you commit suicide, you steal, you lie, you cheat. You are weak. You cannot survive, you are too busy hauling around that big brain of yours. You have to build jails to keep your own kind from killing you. You kill everything. You live in fear. You could never live with the simplicity and beauty of the roach. You have abortions. You engage in meaningless activity. You are weak, cockroaches are your gods. You're not even fit to kiss the smooth belly scales of the mother roach. You are repulsed by them, you fear them. There are more of them than there are of you. You get squeamish at just the sight, they make you sick. You are weak. Cockroaches are your gods. Give up your plate of food to them. Whether you do or not, they will survive you and your stupidity. You try to kill them with gas and poison just like you do to your own kind. The roach comes back, stronger, faster, immune. You watch television, you lock your doors to protect yourself from your species. You put needles in your arms, you sell your bodies, you find new and inventive ways to mutilate yourselves and others. You are weak. Cockroaches are your gods.

◖ ◖ ◖ ◖ ◖

I got a brain but I don't know it
I got feelings but I don't show it
All my friends are going nowhere
They are nobodies
How come I'm always with them at the bar?
I drink to sink
Partying takes away the pain
I don't want to think
If I'm wrecked then I don't have to explain
All my buddies give me the push
I fly the flag for Anheuser-Busch
When I'm wasted
I know that I've escaped the grind of 9 to 5

But sometimes
I think that I'm running from something
I heard on the radio
That everybody's working for the weekend
When does the weekend start?
What comes at the end of the week?
The end?
Picture a tired dog chasing its tail

◄ ◄ ◄ ◄ ◄

Attention! Attention! Husbands and wives with young, or those expecting young ones! In the near future you will be relocated! You will be stationed at breeding centers. The males will be slaughtered painlessly. The females will be kept in large pens, one male to stud pens of thirty breeders! You breeders will have a meaningful and productive life. You will have a child every eleven months until you are no longer adequate for breeding status. Then you will be put to sleep painlessly. In plain words: You will no longer be allowed to have children unless they are kept and maintained in designated breeding centers. If any infants or young are found outside the breeding confines, they will be immediately destroyed, along with the parents of course. Thank you for your cooperation.

◄ ◄ ◄ ◄ ◄

They are rolling out the carpet for you to get sick on. They are getting your head size for a custom fitted lampshade. They are lighting twenty-three candles tonight. Twenty-three little flames for you to blow out. Twenty-three years in one breath. I'm in the background backyard digging a hole, waiting for the party to be over. Make a wish.

◄ ◄ ◄ ◄ ◄

Family Man, with your glances my way
Taking no chances on the new day

Family Man, with your life all planned
Your sand castle built
Smiling through your guilt
Here I come
Here I come Family Man
I come to infect
I come to rape your woman
I come to take your children into the street
I come for you Family Man
Family Man, with your Christmas lights already up
You're such a man when you're putting up your Christmas lights
First on the block
I want to crucify you on your front door
With nails from your well stocked garage
Family Man
Saint Dad
Father on fire
I've come to incinerate
I've come home

◆ ◆ ◆ ◆ ◆

The manifestation manifests itself in every way imaginable. We
are folded, spindled and mutilated. We are not blinded! Disillu-
sionment smashes its fist through the pavement and grabs us by
the ankles, trips us up, trips us out. Our eyes fill with dirt, we try
to scream but our mouths become filled with the dirt. We spit
and curse but we eventually chomp the bit and pull forward and
lurch to the next screeching halt. The brakes (our eyes) keep us
in our seats. We go along with it, due to a safe facade of
ignorance. But we're always looking through the keyhole, prob-
ably the closest we shall come to reckoning. We are born,
immediately infected, and plagued for the rest of our lives. Our
private eternity, our own forever. All of our thoughts are purely
impure. We try to understand the pain of others but we can only
understand it our way. We sit in your apartment. We are leeches,

sucking each other dry. We are each other's heroin, always trying to fix our relationship which is full of holes and sinking fast. Wanting to kick so bad. We are monkeys on a monkey's back. I'm a junkie—you're my monkey. The sun falls like a dying creature through the burning air. The air that stings our eyes, as the gasping final rays pass us. We take off our clothes, we find our bodies clawed, defiled, scarred, distorted, misshapen. Monkey on a monkey's back. Holding on to each other's tail, we run in circles just as fast as we can. Have you ever pressed your hands against the wall and thought, "Damn, I'm gonna die in this place." We are stuck here. Moored, entrenched by mortality. The stifling straight jacket of humanity does its job. We are passed around, hand-to-hand and led to the whipping post where our lovers are waiting. They hand us whips and we beat ourselves into sleep. We beat ourselves to death. They lay us down, lay us low, whip in one hand, a bloody monkey's tail in the other.

❦   ❦   ❦   ❦   ❦

We don't give birth. We abort, abort, abort. Jump ship. Drowning rats will cling with a tenacity seldom seen. I think they want to live more than you do, so why don't you step aside.

❦   ❦   ❦   ❦   ❦

In the deep well of the night, the silence surrounds you and seals off your pores. A silence so silent and powerful that you might think you are going insane. You hear a song that you've never heard before, and you think that you are going insane.

❦   ❦   ❦   ❦   ❦

The baby was born. A girl. She had her father's nose and cheekbones, her mother's high forehead and eyes. She had her father's knife scars and her mother's track marks.

❦   ❦   ❦   ❦   ❦

Lord, give me a gun
I'll give you acts of salvation and mercy
Give me a mobile artillery unit
I'll give you some constructive criticism
Give me napalm
I'll turn the other cheek
Give me a dime
I'll call in the air strike
Give me a chance
And I'll stop hunger
I'll stop disease
I'll stop world suffering
Give me a button
I'll give you peace

◂ ◂ ◂ ◂ ◂

I have found a way to beat myself
I win by losing, something like that
I'm told that I'm stupid
So ok, I'll be stupid
If I can't register the pain
Then it's not there
I'm not so stupid after all
I'll show them

◂ ◂ ◂ ◂ ◂

How lame it is for me to sit in some cushy living room watching Apocalypse Now, on videocassette no less. You think you have pain? That guy went up the river to kill a guy. I'm sitting in a suburban living room on a plush carpet with Search and Destroy tattooed on my back and I'm watching the real thing, it makes touring seem rather easy in comparison. I love that movie. I feel small when I see it because I want to do stuff that's as ultimate. Music is a far cry from missions into classified Cambodia. The guy sat in his room in Saigon and was going crazy waiting for a chance to get back to the jungle, and all I do is pull up to a club, set up and play for an hour or so, and leave. This is not living and dying, or anything close. I'm sitting in a living room in suburban Seattle with a full stomach, a cup of coffee in my hand, a pillow for my head, shit! That is the case. This nullifies any of my little hardships, I don't know the meaning of grueling. Pain, pain? Fuck my pain! The muscle aches, the neck aches, so what. I don't know the meaning of pain. "Doesn't your tour schedule tire you out?" I'm still alive, we can't be pressed that hard. You can't call in an air strike at the Perkins Palace. There's no backstage in the jungle, no sound-check, no set list, no men's room. What kind of an asshole am I anyway? Sitting on this rug, safe, about to take a hot shower, knowing that when the movie is over, I can flip a switch and watch MTV.

◆ ◆ ◆ ◆ ◆

He came home after work, like he did Monday through Friday. He felt good, he parked the car in the garage and came in through the kitchen door. His wife was in the kitchen, cooking dinner. She smiles, "Hi honey." She went to the refrigerator and got him a Coors Light. He looked out the window, the front lawn was good, trimmed, green. His wife talked about all kinds of things he didn't care about. That's good, women are supposed to talk about PTA meetings and casseroles. Good. She was ok. The house smelled clean, un-lived in. A real castle. He went into the bathroom to use the toilet. He thought about those magazines he saw at the newsstand. Young girls engaging in oral copulation with young males. That's what he wanted! Yes. He wanted to tell his wife, "Madge, suck me!" But he thought of her aprons and her casseroles and knew that he couldn't do it. What if he could! She might do it, then at the end (when he came), she would probably bolt downstairs and wash her mouth out with sink cleanser. He started to get an erection. He thought about masturbating, he hadn't done that since he was in college. He started to cry. Tears splashed onto his bare legs. The stench of his own waste filled his nostrils. He felt clean, un-lived in, held prisoner by the life he created for himself. His life was driveways, casseroles, television, miles of front lawns, kids and then death. Dinner would be ready soon.

◆　◆　◆　◆　◆

The whites stood, shackled and bound. They lined the streets of Hollywood. Some were being loaded into buses, others were being auctioned off right there at Hollywood and Vine. A father stood trembling and crying silently as he watched his daughter being haggled over by black men. She stood on a Knudson's orange crate naked. Men were laughing, grabbing her breasts and fingering her and sampling the goods in general. A man with a large erection was the highest bidder. He grabbed her roughly and led her away. The two got on an R.T.D. bus and were gone.

◆　◆　◆　◆　◆

My muscles straining. My soul almost ripping itself away from the bone. Pulling together the black circle. Trying to join the ends, thus eliminating them and eliminating myself. I understand now. I understand what it takes for me to be. These feelings, jolts of lightning in my nerves, they define me. I have come to the idea of rising below and letting the circle run its course. I will no longer fight the wheel inside me. Now I understand the strength of succumbing to the storm, joining the maelstrom, finding power in its turmoil. Pulling together end to end like a snake consuming its tail. Coiling tighter and tighter until consumption defines its implosion. End to end.

◆　◆　◆　◆　◆

I would crawl on my face and stomach
Down her street at night
To bask in the glow of the street lamp
Outside her house

I would
I would slither up the brick stairs of her front porch
And rest my chin at the top step
Gazing up into her room
TV flickering against the wall
Shadows
Shapes walking past the window
Ok
I'm talking snakewise
Summer like
Charmed?
Yes
I am that
There I am, on her street, on her porch
Some dude comes out and steps on me
Splat
What a drag

❧   ❧   ❧   ❧   ❧

Kill the father
Fuck the mother
Eat the kids
Burn the house down
Take over

❧   ❧   ❧   ❧   ❧

7-11 Prospect & Artesia
Inside:
Thirteen year olds
Smoking cigarettes
Reading rock magazines
They all have high water pants
The guy behind the counter looks like Clark Kent
Outside:
A guy gets out of the car

Says to the girl inside
What kind do you want?
I'm thinking of that police car on Prospect
Unmanned, parked, lights flashing
Someone should torch it
I can't
All I've got is a Snickers Bar

❧ ❧ ❧ ❧ ❧

The sun is dying
Lying on its side
One eye open
Every day the sun dies
It commits suicide
Drowns itself in the sea
Every morning the sun rises
It tears across the sky
Just to show 'em
I aspire to that
To give totally
And die every night
And then be given the chance
To die again
Sinking
Burning
Dying
And rising again
Just to show 'em

❧ ❧ ❧ ❧ ❧

The sun died
I killed it
Ripped it out of the sky
Choked the life out of it
Turned the world

Cold
Black
Dead
And in need
Take candy from babies
Step on ants
If you're in line at the supermarket
Kick the people in front of you
Kick your way to the front
Lie to people
Smile at them
And then bash their skulls apart with a crowbar
Probably too much sun

◄ ◄ ◄ ◄ ◄

Sitting alone in my cell. Around 8:30 the depression comes rolling in. Wraps itself around me like a big snake, suffocating me. Tonight when it got me, I turned out the light and I sat quietly in the darkness waiting for it to subside. Sitting alone, sitting still. Listening to the radio. Thinking, wondering what my father looks like now. Haven't seen him in about five years. I would hear people say, "I haven't seen my old man for five years." Now I'm one of them. Big snake made of lead, coiling around me, holding me down. Damn! I hate when this happens. I don't know what to do. It gets me. Turns me cold, leaden, makes me write, makes me sing. Do da, do da.

◄ ◄ ◄ ◄ ◄

Slicing up a cadaver
No pain
I tell you
The shit just doesn't hurt
Kicking a corpse
Sinking your jackboot into my side
The ribs crack

You can't hurt me
I don't feel it
You can razor me up
Dismember me
Disembowel me
I'll still offer you my hand
I hold no malice towards you
Because violence toward my flesh
Isn't the kind of thing
That hurts me these days

◆ ◆ ◆ ◆ ◆

Dangling corpse in cold storage. Big steel hook through the corpse's throat. Bare light sends out harsh, crude rays. They deflect off bluish, dead, corpse flesh. Ain't nuthin'! Just cows. I eat 'em, smiling men at McDonald's cook 'em. I want more meaning to my food, more soul. Some bovine, grass eating animal just don't cut the mustard with me. Like I said, I need, I want, I gotta have, more. I want to eat your children. Just the daughters. I don't want to eat no boys man. What the fuck do you think I am? I saw that little girl outside the laundromat on Artesia Blvd. I wanted one of those slim, tanned, hairless little legs, medium well, with some Grey Poupon. Soul food. I dig soul food. I'm not a vegetarian. I am carnivorous, an' I wanna eat your fucking kid. But only if it's female! Like I said, I'm no weirdo man. Eat the little girls, kill the little boys. The streets are open air markets. Playgrounds are restaurants, parks with built in hibachis are convenient and very thoughtful. Thank you.

◆ ◆ ◆ ◆ ◆

The sun will rise
The sun will burn the tears from your eyes
The sun will rise
The sun will burn designs in you
Some of us find strength

In our weakness
And are driven insane by the eyes of the sun
The eyes of the sun blind me in my darkness
There is strength in my blindness
There is light
Blinding
Scorching
Light

◄ ◄ ◄ ◄ ◄

Jack
I could never walk through her door
I would have to turn into a snake
And slither underneath
But I would crawl on the floor for her
I would slither across the floor to the bed
I would coil myself neatly
Next to one of her lover's shoes and wait
When he would put his foot down
I would strike and bite
Then try to turn back into my normal shape
But I could never do that
I was never one of her lovers
I was a snake
A creature crawling on the floor for her
I was never one of her lovers

◄ ◄ ◄ ◄ ◄

In discipline:
The blood roars
The brain turns to marble
The muscles turn to steel
When wrapped in the scalding arms of the discipline
I can't rip my eyes away from the sun

I feel no pain
If you know what I mean
Then you know what I mean

                  ❦   ❦   ❦   ❦   ❦

I'm starting to think that I'm not a human being. I don't feel like one. I think I was one when I was about seventeen. Now I think I'm something else. I don't belong here. Maybe I'm a snake, a copper snake, dusty, addicted, crawling slowly. I do not suffer. Only wounded suffer. I'm not wounded. I am inflicted. I inflict myself upon myself. I re-arrange, breakdown, deplete myself of myself, causing hunger, causing pain. People hate people who are free. People who are waiting for their "reward" will wait forever, content to hate, fear and condemn. I am up to other things in the mean time. Freaky misfits, disciples of the sun, you are the ones who understand the rhythm of disease. The cold, isolating, beautiful fire of the distorted soul. The flowers bloom for you! The birds in the sky sing for you! The sun shines for you! The copper snake crawls for you.

                  ❦   ❦   ❦   ❦   ❦

She touches me
The jungle lights up with incinerating fire
Looks like a flaming serpent
I look into her eyes
I see a movie flickering
Car crashes
People kicking corpses
Men ripping their tracheas out and shaking them at the sky
I think to myself:
I don't want to survive this one
I want to burn up in the wreckage
Cooking flesh in the jungle

                  ❦   ❦   ❦   ❦   ❦

I've seen too many drunks tonight
They stumble around the living room
Reeking of beer & cigarettes
Talking bullshit
Talking in my face
To me
Making me smell their good time
Wasting my good time
And making time drag
What a drag

◀ ◀ ◀ ◀ ◀

Get on the cinder trail
See the Indian man
Turn around
Feel the sun
Feel the forked tongue burn in your mouth
Turn around
See me awakening from a night's sleep
On an Indian Burial mound
In an Indian Burial ground
Soaking up death
Turn around
What do you see?
The sky is full of fire
The rain will burn you down
You spat when you saw me
When you saw your face mirrored in mine
Turn around, it's just a circle
It only takes a second
To open your eyes
To realize your circle
Turn around

◀ ◀ ◀ ◀ ◀

Dead
Oven
Come into the oven
Crawl into the oven
I'll wait
The vultures are clawing the roof
In the oven it gets so hot
And I burn
White
Hot
I've been burning forever
Burning over and over
Burning
White
Hot
I crawled in here to die
I crawled out of one hole
And into this
And I can hear the vultures clawing at the roof
And I burn
White hot

◆ ◆ ◆ ◆ ◆

Sometimes when the cold wind blows my way, I don't even need a coat because I just can't even feel it. I don't even know. It probably blows through me. It's like freezing a corpse, it doesn't even know that its ass is freezing off. Goddamn, sometimes it gets so cold in here when I feel it. When I don't feel it I hurt worse, and that shit hurts.

◆ ◆ ◆ ◆ ◆

I see sunshine
I see clear sky
I see palm trees
I see the ocean

I feel the ocean breeze
I see 7-11
I see Burger King
I feel the famine
I see the disease
I say:
Double double cheese cheese burger burger please
I see the body bags piled up in the streets
I see the trucks come
To haul the dead bodies away
To their incineration
Surf's up

❧ ❧ ❧ ❧ ❧

Crucify the rats!
Deify the roaches!
Canonize disease!
Don't forget the flies
Baptize the flies
Or they will eat your eyes
Ride in Daddy's station wagon
Inflict the divine punishment
Hail!
The divine punishment
Crawl
Yea
Don't forget the flies
Hail!
Saint Plague

❧ ❧ ❧ ❧ ❧

Burning light
Shining bright
Annihilating the darkness in my brain
You see me

Staring through to my soul
And you might think that I am insane
And you might be right

❖ ❖ ❖ ❖ ❖

I have learned a lot in the last few weeks. I have learned to question smiling faces. I don't trust smiling faces anymore. When someone smiles and reaches out to shake my hand, I try and guess what they want from me and when they will try to sink the knife in. It's so easy to get pulled in on a confidence scam. You feel shocked and amazed that a person you were helping was just getting over on you. He's shaking your hand and pulling you into your grave. When someone gives something away, they want something in return, some how, some way. This is a game that gets played on many levels. Don't take candy from strangers unless you're willing to take a ride in the car.

❖ ❖ ❖ ❖ ❖

I try to smile when people talk to me but I can feel the refrigeration man behind my flesh. I can't let them know the face I see. I chase myself. I always catch up. I never deny. I try to avoid myself. I am destroying myself to give birth to my soul. The other night I felt violent pain in my stomach. Something was inside me. My stomach contracted and I thought I was going to vomit. I felt something crawling up my throat. I opened my mouth. A large, greasy, rat squirmed out and fell on the floor. It quivered for a moment and crawled away. I gave birth. The man behind my face tells me to smile, tells me to speak. When I'm alone, the roaches come out of my pores, I give birth to rats. I catch up with my self. I pull away from the face that smiles and acts and talks. I am destroying myself.

❖ ❖ ❖ ❖ ❖

I am dying of hate. Suffocating. Fist over fist pounding down on my head. I am dying of hate. I got my hands wrapped around my throat and I'm squeezing myself shut. I'm trying to close my wounds. I am dying of hate. I feel ugly. I don't want to see light again. I don't want to hear those sounds again. I am dying of hate. A circle in a square. The lines are straight but the edges are smooth and there are no answers here.

❧ ❧ ❧ ❧ ❧

I took LSD, I came on at a Burger King. I was sitting in this girl's car about to eat this Double Whopper and it hit me. All of a sudden I thought that this warm thing I was cupping in my hands was an infant's head. At first I thought I couldn't do that, I couldn't eat an infant's brains, no way. But I did. Every bite I took, I could see every part of the head that I was eating. Meat juice dripped down my chin. There I was eating this kid's head, kind of like an all meat grapefruit. I ate every bite. Life is a loosening process. Things you thought you would never do before get done when you get rid of those inhibitions that hang you up. So take my advice and loosen up a little.

❧ ❧ ❧ ❧ ❧

White boy. Dog eye. White boy. Glowing, walking down the street, hands in pockets, skin glowing. Insane. Smiling, going down to the public pool to swim in the piss water. Going down to get beat up. Dog brain. White boy sending out vibes: take my money, scare me so my knees knock together. Bash my mouth into the water fountain. I know I don't deserve to live. White boy sweating off Ivory soap in the summer heat. White boy with bus token safety-pinned onto t-shirt. White, scared and trapped. Sealed inside a bottle of August heat.

❧ ❧ ❧ ❧ ❧

I am followed. Everywhere I go. I am followed by cancer man. He touches me and I bruise. I feel weak when he is near. From night to night, from club to club he follows me. He breathes on me. He makes me lonely, he makes me want for human kindness. He starves my soul. He steals my sanity. I hate cancer man for the emptiness he fills me with. He's next to me at night and he makes me feel the bottom of my heart over and over again. He's in the audience every night, sucking me dry, making me want for a human touch and making sure it never comes. He's close now, very close, so close. I am cancer man. Turning myself charred and lifeless. I am cancer man. I hate cancer man.

◄● ◄● ◄● ◄● ◄●

They smile
They will hurt you
Turn inside
Your only friend is inside
They will cut your heart
They will maim your soul
I need someone so bad
I think I'm going to break into little pieces
You cannot touch
You cannot be touched
You are dirty and insane
You come from a different planet
No one will ever understand
Ever
Turn inside
Remember
What always happens

◄● ◄● ◄● ◄● ◄●

A bare bulb burns in an apartment in my brain. In the middle of the apartment is a small table and a wooden chair. There is a cot in the corner. Pacing the floor of the apartment is a man who has never slept, ever. He stares out the window constantly. He is scarred and insane from his thoughts. Everything he thinks is true. That's why he lives alone. He writes words on the walls to remind and console himself:

Alienation
Hard road
Incinerate
Never
Heart ache
Soul
Forever

◆   ◆   ◆   ◆   ◆

We need to spend more time in the darkness. Yes we do. You and me, girl. Darkness smoothes things over. The soul is let free to be embraced. Come to me in darkness. You will see me. You will understand me. You will touch my desperation. In darkness we are secrets. In darkness we are every thing, we are safe, sealed off from the filthy light that defiles us and leaves us lifeless and cold. Touch me in darkness. Call my name and I will come to you. In darkness you will see that we are everything.

◆   ◆   ◆   ◆   ◆

My dearest, to live out there, you must have eyes that act as prisms, to dismantle and refract anything that comes before them. You must have skin as hard and as seamless as glass. More like elastic marble. Yes. A hard exterior is a must. Their talk, their eyes, their true motives, are like sand filled wind wearing you down. Taking away your edge, making you malleable, so slowly and evenly that you won't realize it until it's too late. It's only because you brought my blood to a boil, only because you looked into my heart and touched my soul. Only because you gave yourself to me completely that I tell you this. Get a lock for your door. They're everywhere. Remain intact. I will be with you again.

◆   ◆   ◆   ◆   ◆

I am the dismembered man walking dislocated and stiff, white skin glowing. Sending off bluish light. Looking and feeling unnatural everywhere I go. See me at the beach walking around like an asshole on holiday, talking loud and covering up my tracks with oaths and beer. At the end of the day I am red and swollen and all tired out from fighting with the flies.

❧   ❧   ❧   ❧   ❧

When she comes:
She pulls you close
She breathes in short bursts
Her eyes close
Her head tilts back
Her mouth opens slightly
Her thighs turn to steel and then melt
She is perfect
And you feel like you are everything

❧   ❧   ❧   ❧   ❧

Whenever I am in my home town, I am reminded of my father. I might have breathed the same air he had just a day before. I can feel him. I can feel his breathing. I can feel his heart beat. I think of the discipline. The instruction. The things he said. The fear and anguish and hatred. I walk on the same streets as he does. His foot prints glow in the dark. He got me good and it makes me want to kill.

❧   ❧   ❧   ❧   ❧

There are nights where I cannot sleep
They happen all the time
In these periods, I don't want to exist
Wouldn't it be nice to be no one right now?
When I'm lying there, I always think of two things
Sex and suicide
Wouldn't it be nice to be no one right now?
Sometimes I lie there and hope that I'll die right then
I don't want to exist

No big deal
No big sob story
I don't make a fucking sound
I just don't want it any more and nothing can pull me back
Wouldn't it be nice to be no one right now?
I wait for sleep to take me
To stop me from thinking
To rid me of me
Wouldn't it be nice to be no one right now?

◦ ◦ ◦ ◦ ◦

I want to be here for you
I want to be real for you
Am I real?
I don't know
Help me
Help me know that I am real
I don't know what I am
Am I alive?
Am I here?
Tell me
Show me
Touch me
Make me exist

◦ ◦ ◦ ◦ ◦

Follow the snake
He leaves a trail that glows in the sand
When you learn to crawl
The trail is so easy to understand
For a love that will never leave you
And for a soul that never dies
You don't have to live forever
To finally realize
The music of the sky

The scream of the sun
And the crawl of the snake
Limbless, perfect and absolute
Crawl

◄ ◄ ◄ ◄ ◄

Swirling above his body now
I find a world away from his pain
I'm living and dying in another brain
In the mind of a snake
I am cold and dusty but alive
And that's good enough in this reptile house
If I'm alive I will survive
And I will crawl this trail until my belly bleeds
And then I'll crawl it some more

◄ ◄ ◄ ◄ ◄

I have watched your people for a very long time. I have been taking very thorough notes and I've been making vocal entries into my tape recorder. I have been chronicling every vice, every fear, every weakness. Every one. I have weapons. I will use these against you. I will reflect you at yourself. You teach me so much about yourself. Your aversion to the truth and your fear of rejection and failure make you easy. I watch you from above. I will strike when you are at your lowest, weakest level. See you around.

◄ ◄ ◄ ◄ ◄

This is the house where you spent all those years
This is the house where you learned so much
This is the house that was home
The place that defines home
With all the warmth and comfort
That goes along with the thought of home
This is the place that you thought would last forever

This is the place you thought you would never leave
Or want to
This is the place
That you will someday want to burn to the ground

◄ ◄ ◄ ◄ ◄

I work at a diner
I don't hate this job
I don't hate anything
I don't know my name
I'm faceless
I look at them
They look at me
I heard about myself in a Bruce Springsteen song
I am no one
I am faceless
I don't know what to do
I come here and then I go home
I feel so blank today
Am I here?
Do I exist?
Help me
I am turning to wood

◄ ◄ ◄ ◄ ◄

I'm in favor of the right to bear arms. Guns. Fine. I'd like to take
it a bit further. Everyone should have the right to bear nuclear
arms. A revolver under every pillow, a silo in every back yard. If
it was up to me, I'd like to change things around a bit. I'd have
every Caucasian male castrated. The police would be taken to
black and Mexican districts and beaten three times a day.
Finally, they would have to crawl on their hands and knees
through Watts. You would not be allowed to drive your car
unless you were intoxicated. Signs would read: "If you don't
drink, don't drive." Drug abuse would be mandatory in all states.

Live sex in every classroom. All students would be de-virginized by the age of eleven, by any sex partner they choose. There would be only one version of the National Anthem. Hendrix's version from Woodstock. All ministers would be required to drop large quantities of LSD three to five times a week. They say they see God. I want to make damn sure. All cigarettes would be sprayed with angel dust. Nothing like a little dust to get things going. All TV religious figures would be required to enter mud-wrestling matches with MTV personalities. Anyone caught stepping on or harming cockroaches in any way whatsoever would be shot. Any children that look good enough to be eaten will be. The public parks in all states will provide bar-b-que pits in all outdoor areas for this purpose. Porno stars would be sent to the U.N. Madonna would buy me a pad in Malibu and seek me desperately. The time is now. Turn on. Take over. Let's get cancerous.

◄ ◄ ◄ ◄ ◄

This is a bad, dangerous and filthy place. Don't try to sway me with fashion magazines and commercials depicting people smiling about soft drinks or some shit, and then try to tell me that there's no place for me. You're wrong, pigs. You live in a place where you're allowed to buy guns and liquor. Imagine that, they let any idiot have access to this stuff. So that means you can get fucked up and wreck your car, kill some people. You are allowed to do this! Imagine how stupid that is to someone like me! To let you idiot pigs have total access to things that you can't handle is totally beyond me. You are idiots! And you're allowed to have guns! I cannot tolerate such stupidity without some kind of retort. The next drunk who gets in my face will be beaten. Not by me, by people who work for me. I will rip a pay phone from its cord in return for such aggravation. If you are allowed to drink and drive, allowed to have guns, then I am allowed to kick your kids, put bricks through your windows and take what's yours. You can't handle your freedom, you have proven this time and time again. I am beyond, worlds beyond your reproach. Idiots, little copulating homicidal children playing with big toys. I wait for you to slip. I will destroy you. I'm going to destroy you. You inhuman pigs, don't you ever, ever look down on me.

◈   ◈   ◈   ◈   ◈

I hear children yelling outside. Sounds like they are being skinned alive. They're only playing. I think about a scene that goes down in broad daylight. Phelan Avenue. Children in the back alley behind the apartment complex. Miniature ghetto back there. Children screaming like they are being skinned alive. They are. I am skinning them alive. I am high. Not on drugs or anything like that. I am high on the smell of garbage and blood. A young girl is across my knee. I'm peeling the flesh off her shoulders and I'm cutting away the skin that connects the flesh to the muscle. Her ribs are exposed and rubbing against my bare leg. Feels warm and greasy. There's a strong smell in the air. The smell of dying people in the air is a funny one. It smells like a closed room. Like lies. Like the end. I want to string the little bodies from the telephone lines on Phelan Avenue. It would look like some kind of celebration or prayer ritual. When I walk over to this girl's house sometimes, I see these little kids running around screaming like they are being skinned alive but they're only playing. I watch them and I think of their bodies, drenched in gasoline and torched. They catch on fire and keep screaming and playing, rolling over and over, spinning and burning. They deserve gasoline. You can get it on the corner. They should put signs up saying that the gasoline can also be used to torch children. I would like to burn the whole area down. Fire would look nice against the palm trees and the blue sky. It would be nice to see that happen. Helicopters over the beaches dropping napalm on the people on the sand. The screams would sound like sea birds. Dying like insects. Public executions again. At the Redondo Beach pier a crowd of angry white people surround this black dude who robbed a white boy down by the showers.

People are sitting on their rooftops yelling and drinking Coors. Some surfers are beating the black boy to death with sticks. One boy has a crowbar. He is scared to hit the black boy at first, but everyone roots him on and he goes to it with youthful energy. He will get laid for this. The locals will know him as "that totally crazed dude with the crowbar," and he will be famous on 21st street. I say exterminate them all.

◖ ◖ ◖ ◖ ◖

I will never feel a pang of remorse for the idiots who bought the dream and dug their own graves. I will never lose a moment's sleep over a tale of the downward spiraling man, trapped in his job, toeing the line, running in circles. Monsters living in a monster's world. They deserve knives, divorce, guns, liquor. They perpetuate their own pain and heartfelt desperation just as much as I do. I don't look for a hand-out. I don't beg for a way out. I know where the out door is. I walked through it a long time ago. The ones who spend their lives looking for virtue and a shining path to the dream they saw in a magazine and just die like common animals are not heroes, they are suckers. I cannot, will not feel for a sucker. I sit and watch the desperate parade run at full speed. I watch their houses burn. I hear their stories and I feel nothing. When their life suddenly turns and looks them in the face with rancid, burning eyes, they run to their keepers waving their arms. The keepers don't care. They just pat them on the back and put them on the 7:00 news. I cannot care about this trip. But I'll tell you what, you come on my property and I'll shoot you.

◖ ◖ ◖ ◖ ◖

My father died this winter. He just died. I am glad that he died in the winter. Just the idea of it, his body, sealed off in the season of cold. Doesn't it seem more clean to you? Less decay? I like that. I can almost imagine his face in death. The eyes, staring, tilted slightly upward. The mouth gaping open. Looking like almost every picture I have ever seen of a victim of the Nazi death camps. Yes, he died in the winter time. Sealed off in cold. That is my memory of his death. Cold, frozen, stagnant. Totally unaffected by the heat and damp of the summer. A heat that makes my thoughts fester and boil in decay and rot. No, memories of him live in the freezer of my soul. The warmth of compassion and tender feeling will never reach there. These feelings do not exist anyway. I did not attend the funeral. I missed the two events that I would have liked to be present at. I missed his last breath. I would have wanted to have had my eyes so close to his that his last breath would have blown right upon me. I would have breathed in every single solitary particle of his last breath as I stared into his eyes. I would have savored this breath of air for as long as I could before expelling it into a jar for later use. I also missed the autopsy. I would have loved to have seen his guts, his brains, his body. Mutilated in cold, precise surgical fashion.

...In my dream I hover above and study his gutted, sliced features. He looks pathetic. His cock, shriveled up grey/blue. He looks like dog meat. He looks helpless and stupid. I hate stupidity. I descend from my perch above and kick his brittle ribs with my steel cap jack boots. The coroner waves me off and asks me to hold off until he has conducted his investigation. Respecting a job that has to be done, I sit in a folding chair and read a magazine. I cannot concentrate on the magazine because the cutting up and squeezing of my father's corpse is captivating. I ask to help. I am refused, of course, as it is normal policy for the next-of-kin to have no part in the autopsy....

I would have asked the coroner for my father's cold, dead heart. Having received the heart I would have taken it home and cooked it in a hearty bullion. I would have invited very special guests over. We could chat about small, non-important matters, sip mineral water or white wine, and sup upon my father's heart.

To me that would be a very spiritual and intimate send-off. This would take a lot of intestinal fortitude on my part because I am a vegetarian. However, the opportunity to dine on my father's heart is one that is irresistible to me.

❦   ❦   ❦   ❦   ❦

I am waiting
I am waiting to be melted
I am waiting for the corn to ripen
I am waiting to be touched
I am waiting to have my name called
I don't know what my name is
But when she calls it, I'll know
I am waiting to be asked
I am waiting for the sun to explode
I am waiting for the flowers to rip open
I am waiting to be touched
I am waiting
Beyond silence
Beyond patience
Beyond time

❦   ❦   ❦   ❦   ❦

I am walking down a street. I cross the street. A car nearly runs me over as it plows through the stop sign. No respect. A pig works security at a show in his off duty hours and threatens and harasses the owner of the club that he is working for. No respect. A car waves me over, the driver asks, "Aren't you Henry Rollins?" I say yes, he asks "Playing tomorrow night?" I say yes. He flips me off and drives away. No respect. People will suck your blood until you dry up and blow away. No respect there.

This is for the girl's dad: Hey, Dad, you made a fine daughter, you and your wife should be proud. She is so fine. Dad. She is blonde, eighteen years old, slim, great tits. Checked out those melons lately, Dad? Lord have mercy! They look so ripe and fine, like peaches on a pretty peach tree. Dad, your girl sucks cock real good. How do I know this? Because she was in a back room of a club, sucking on my cock. You should have seen us. I had my back against the wall and that your daughter was on her knees sucking my cock. I stared down and watched her pretty little head go up and down, up and down, I looked at her knees, grinding into that greasy, filthy, rancid floor and I thought of you. Finally, I came. I came right into her mouth Dad. She was into it. Every drop. She stroked my cock to squeeze out every last drop of my cum, which she swallowed. That must have been a real drag for her boyfriend, who was waiting outside in the hallway. Oh well, what he doesn't know won't hurt him, but I hope it does anyway. Dad, during all that bliss, I forgot your daughter's name, but it's cool pops, because I don't give a fuck. No respect.

◆ ◆ ◆ ◆ ◆

It's 4:23 a.m. I cannot sleep. I feel so distraught and I cannot sleep. I roll to my left side and then to my right. No luck. I'm sinking so deep into myself that I cannot get out. I imagine myself in a jungle, wandering around, looking for a break in the trees. There is none yet. I sat on the front porch for a while, now I'm back inside the house.

What about those long nights spent alone, unable to sleep? Sitting very still, very quietly with your head in your hands. Not a soul around to watch you burn. That's some real bad blues. Alone, torn up and empty. With your head in your hands, you feel like dying.

The alienation inside me is growing all the time. I just can't identify. It hurts. Who will be the next "one of them?" I am helpless. I am alone. It hurts to feel this. It hurts even more to know that I am right. I feel on the outside of everything except myself and it's in myself where I choke and drown. I cannot sleep tonight. If my shoes didn't hurt so much I'd go for a long walk, but I can't. The sound of their voices is maddening. The more they talk to me, the more they push me away from them and into myself.

I am the vacuum man
Breathing in pain
Eyes sucking inward
Pores closing off
Skull clenching in on my brain
Turning inward
Bleeding
Internal bleeding
Rupturing
Living inside the vacuum
Silent
Vacant
Bottomless
Consuming
Turning inward
Behind the glass curtain
Going blind and eventually caving in

It reaches the point where the faces and the sounds bring pain to me. I will never break through. When I move forward I get knocked back immeasurable distances, and with this flight comes clear realization of the jungle that I live in. A move forward is idiocy. Pure idiocy. There must be a part of me that hates me, to make me go out and cut myself like that. There's music in my head. Music that won't let me be. The music is at a horrendous din. Deafening. Why do they turn on you like that? Why do they let you down and push you out and shut you in? Why do they make you hurt until the point of numbness and collapse? Why do they do it? How do they do it? How do I do it to myself? Why do I do it to myself? Please, help me break it down. Touch me, no don't. I'm sorry, touch me, please, I need, I need, I need, I ...

◄● ◄● ◄● ◄● ◄●

I am confused. People really make me spin out. Last night I was playing, and there were people coming up and touching me and grabbing me the whole night. This is not unusual, it happens all the time. Last night it hit me that I do not understand the difference between this kind of adulation and the affection of a girl I want to be with, who wants to be with me. If you have a few hundred people call your name and poke at you all the time, you might not value it, or maybe not consider it real anymore. If someone tied me up and started whipping me, there would come a point where I wouldn't feel it anymore. That's what I'm wondering about right now. I'm trying to understand myself. Sometimes I get to feeling so dry and hollow, like a stuffed animal. Things can get devoid of meaning, feelings can become numbed. I understand that it is I who must keep myself looking straight, but where the hell is the reference point? I can't find my feet. When I am with a girl, I'll look into her eyes until I start to shake. I need to see something that will make me understand. At that point, I want to be understood, totally, by her. The rest of the world does not exist, never did. I don't see it. I don't know if I ever will. I don't know what I'm looking for and it makes me feel dead inside. I sit in a corner after playing. I will go through fits of depression and satisfaction all in a breath. I do not understand what I need to understand and it makes me hurt inside. An understanding of pain is nothing, anyone can stick their hand on a hot plate and go screaming around the house. An understanding of pain is what I want. That's why I look so deep, so hard into their eyes. I look right through. Unfortunately, all I see is myself on the other end, staring right back at me. I feel locked inside for good. Never to breathe, never to understand, never to see outside. All I understand is that everything is starting to run together, their faces, their talk, their touch. Sometimes it feels like being run through a machine. It becomes meaningless. Maybe it will come to the point where I will open my eyes and see one of them. I will look into her eyes hard and see and feel nothing.

PISSING IN THE
GENE POOL

I saw it on TV. An L-1011. Full color footage. It looked like a ruptured toy. The men were out with their garbage bags, picking up limbs. There was luggage, clothes, bodies and big hunks of metal all over the place. I'll never forget the sight of that enormous plane ripped apart and gutted like a big foot had kicked it around. I wonder what that must have been like. Picking up heads, arms, fingers and assorted guts and loading them into Glad bags. I wonder if those guys go through the pockets of the dead, maybe get a little beer money. Why not? What the fuck is a stiff going to do with money? There must have been flies all over the place, being summer and all. Ask any fly and he'll tell you, there's nothing better than fresh guts on a summer day! The telecast turned to the chief coroner. He said that identification of the corpses would take a long time. He said that most of the bodies were covered with jet fuel, a lot were burned beyond recognition. He asked that the relatives bring any photographs, dental records, and doctor's info (operation scars) that they had to help speed up the process. In a few days Time and Newsweek will have good color pictures of the twisted metal and destroyed bodies. I dig those pictures, a few months ago they had some great color shots of dead bodies stacked high at the Belsen concentration camp. But anyway, when those mags come out with those airplane pictures, I'm gonna buy 'em, yes sir. And I'm gonna say, "Boy! Am I glad I wasn't on that plane! Look at all those people. They're dead, naked, and burned up!"

▸ ▸ ▸ ▸ ▸ ▸

To me, she's not even human, she's some kind of a germ. A concoction. She is neurotic, nasty and abusive. Pathetic is a word that springs to mind. When she is loud and drunk, it's torture being around her. She treats marijuana like some life preserving drug. She is most lively when she has a chance to get fucked up. Whenever she's spazzing out and drooling over pot, I think to myself, "coke whore" but I change to word "coke" to pot. She doesn't bathe much and sometimes the stench can be quite noxious. I don't like being associated with her because I see how nasty she is with people who I work with. When she comes into a room, I either leave or try to get out of earshot of her. I hope she goes on her painful little way and leaves my sight. Not a bone in me hates that girl. She has managed to turn off everyone around her. She sure did it to me. I never set out to feel like that, no way. Now it's at the point where it's totally irreversible.

▶   ▶   ▶   ▶   ▶   ▶

I overheard some people talking. This girl was complaining about having to shell out money every time she her period came around. She said that Midol and tampons should be given away in welfare boxes. I had never thought of that before. She had a point there. What if a guy had to put out a dime every time he took a piss. It would be nothing at first, but after a while those dimes would start to pile up and you might try and hold out to make that dime go a bit farther. Imagine saying, "Fuck, I spent a buck on urine today!" What if you were into beer? What if you are out of $$$? What if you had to write a check? A credit card? What if you had to say, "Brother, can you spare a dime? I gotta piss." You would be in bladder hell pal. Think about that!

▶   ▶   ▶   ▶   ▶   ▶

Living amongst straight people is like walking on a tightrope of dominoes set end to end. That's their lives. Straight, narrow, unbending, locked nose to asshole in a line. I don't walk on a line of dominoes. One step out of place and they're knocked out of place. Can't do it. Their fear and numbness to their own pain chokes me. I stay away from straight people. They make me feel uneasy. When they're "nice," it makes me think of the word "cordial" and it makes me think that this is what they have been taught rather than what they feel —like getting a handout. They call me filthy, crazy and crude. Of course this has no effect on me. Their lies and self torture raise a stench that they will never live down.

‣ ‣ ‣ ‣ ‣ ‣

I understand
I understand you
I understand me
I understand them
I can't shut it off
Sometimes I wish I didn't understand
The shit hurts
I know what I'm talking about
You know what I'm talking about
They know what I'm talking about
We all understand
Understand?

‣ ‣ ‣ ‣ ‣ ‣

You know there's nothing at the bottom. I've been there so many times. Empty handed, empty hearted just empty, brittle, hollow. Like a shell. At the bottom. So many times. When I'm there I know where I am. Nowhere. I open my eyes and there's nowhere everywhere so many times.

‣ ‣ ‣ ‣ ‣ ‣

It's cold here, cold and raining. It's August but it feels like October. Even the air smells like autumn. Autumn time makes me think of working at the ice cream store in Washington, DC. I lived in this really dingy apartment in the fall of 1980 and I used to avoid it as much as possible. I would do this by hanging out on the street and working extra shifts at the ice cream store. I would spend a lot of time alone. While my car still worked, I would go for drives at night with all the windows open, just to have the cold air wash over me. I would drive through different neighborhoods in NW just to clear my head. I later stopped driving as much because I started to enjoy walking more.

I would go for long walks by myself. That made me feel old, getting enjoyment from going for walks by myself. I'll never forget how the autumn air smelled that year. I spent a lot of time out and around because I only used the apartment as a last resort. At the time it seemed that everything frustrated me. I would work behind the counter at the ice cream store and the customers would just wear me down. I would take orders all day long. I felt like an old shirt going through the laundry over and over. By the end of the shift I was burned out on people, their talk and their bullshit. The walks did me good. It was so great to be outside when the air was clear and cool. Everything looked good.

Sometimes I would get invited to a party or to go out to dinner by one of them and I would decline. Part of me wanted to go but those kind of outings always made me feel even more alienated than usual. Hearing them talk made me feel lonely and hateful at the same time. Lonely because I didn't fit in, never did. When I was reminded, it hurt. And hateful because it re-affirmed what I already knew, that I was alone and on the outside.

I spent a lot of time feeling alienated and lonely. But with all of that also came a real solid feeling of independence. I came to enjoy eating alone and spending my off time for the most part, alone. I was walking down the streets here today, cloudy sky, on and off drizzle and it all came back to me in waves, perfectly structured memories. That was the autumn I remember most clearly. I was no longer in school and it was a strange feeling for it to be autumn and for me not to be sitting behind a desk. I was more aware of each day and each night and all the time in between. Sometimes I miss that way of life. I enjoyed the nights at the ice cream store. A place to be doing something that wasn't the apartment. I would walk home slowly, enjoying the street lamps, smelling the cold air. The apartment was like a prison cell. I felt like kicking myself every time I slept late. It was a long walk to Georgetown but I knew the sooner I got out of that apartment, the better. Damn, I was lonely that autumn. I wished for a girl I could hang out with. I never really did anything to meet girls, too shy, too fucked up. Autumn makes me think of women.

At the ice cream store I would get one or two days off a week. But as I took on more responsibility at the store, the days off decreased to almost none. That autumn I almost always got Friday nights off. Friday is my favorite day of the week. Friday night was either spent walking around until I got tired or spent at Mike's or Chris' house. We would sit around, drink cokes and play a lot of records. That became one of my favorite memories.

I'll never forget how the depression and loneliness felt good and bad at the same time. Still does. The sidewalks, the trees, the storefronts, they became my friends. Every time I would pass a house that had a wood burning fire, I would try to imagine what the people inside were doing. Sometimes I felt so outside of everything that I wanted to die. I felt terrible, but then out of nowhere would come an overwhelming wave of relief and calm. It was my life! My depression! Good for me! The air and the leaves and the street lights would smile at me and I would feel okay. I realized that autumn that yes, I was alone in this world, totally alone. Alone and on the outside, but at the same time I wasn't alone. I had myself. I was always alone as a child growing up but this was the first time that I ever clicked on what it meant to be alone. I felt invincible. I felt as if I could withstand the longest winter ever.

I feel uneasy when my mind gets crowded with memories that I can't shake. I write them out of my system and hope it works. I run breathlessly from one word to the next. Sometimes I think I'm dissecting my brain into little pieces. When I'm forced into a frame of mind and time by outside elements such as season or geographical location, it drives me nuts. I feel I have to write a telephone directory size book to get it out of me.

Nothing gets me like autumn, though, nothing. I can see myself walking down "P" Street right now, I can feel it. I can smell the fireplaces on "O" Street right now. I can see the street lamps glow on "R" Street. But at the same time, I can feel the consuming emptiness that paralyzed me and made me sullen and cold. I can remember sitting in that dark apartment that reeked of paint and insecticide wanting out so bad but not having the slightest fucking idea where to go. Every time the air turns cold, I am transported back to all those places. I have visions of the florescent glow of the ice cream store when it's observed from the People's Drug Store across the street. The place looks busy and cheerful. A lit glass cube in a dark, cold wall. It makes me feel like I'm watching the world from the outside. Walking the streets on the outskirts of earth. Alone and on the outside.

► ► ► ► ► ►

In the sea of amputated limbs: Bobbing heads, starved faces screaming upward. Creation gives birth to scar tissue. In the middle of my nowhere comes a reference point. Twisting like a crippled man driven insane. I'm all the way in this, lost beyond lost. The reference point, the disease, it drives me insane. The light is unstoppable. Once created, it will never be destroyed. The disease is total, the disease is addictive. The reference point sickens and infest me. The reference point, blinded on its own radiance sees no end. Blindness beyond total blindness. No end in sight.

► ► ► ► ► ►

I need to burn. Yes, I must burn. Tonight I take heavy tools to my mind. Touch me. Make me burn. Tonight, my heart. Burning, rising. Torch me. Reduce me. Tonight I melt iron with my soul.

Tonight I lay torched in my cell. Destroy me. My heart, tonight, my heart. Turn me to ash. Tonight I melt iron with my soul. Touch me. Annihilate. Annihilate. Annihilate.

► ► ► ► ► ►

It's all happening right now. All at once. Take your feelings. Every heartbeat. Wrap them around you. Build a fire. Burn yourself to the ground while you still can because it will be a long time before you see me again. Maybe never, maybe forever. Take hold. Touch the flame. Burn yourself to the ground while you still can because sure as my eyes crawl out from my head, it will be a long time before you see me again. Maybe never, maybe forever.

► ► ► ► ► ►

Living inside of a light bulb: Ideas, thoughts, thunder and lightning all the time. A real brainstorm. Hot and cold. The edges are so smooth you could slip and fall on your own soul. Like walking on a greased frying pan on a high flame. You don't walk or run, you jump and dance like someone stuck a red hot poker up your ass. Not brilliance. Heat, pain irritation, dark teeth grinding frustration maybe, but not brilliance. No. The flight of the imagination soars high above its execution in reality. That's the beauty. The struggle to take the imagination out of imagination. To try and walk through walls...brilliant people sit very still with contented smiles on their faces, their end calculated down to their last breathing moment. They know damn well that you can't walk through walls. That's brilliant. This brilliant guy once asked me, "How did you get all those bumps on your head?" — From trying to walk through a wall.

► ► ► ► ► ►

I see a man leaving his house to go to his place of work. He is the color of flesh, blood and bone. His breath is visible as it rolls from his nostrils. As he gets closer to his job, he starts to change color, like a chameleon. With every step the man becomes a darker shade of grey. The man crosses the threshold of the work place. He leaves behind heavy shoe prints of dark, dead blood.

The day drags very slowly. The sun starts to set. The air grows colder and colder. Finally it's dark outside. The door of the man's work place opens and the man comes flying out as if he were being bounced out of a bar. He lands with a heavy thud in the gutter. After a moment he slowly rises to his feet. The man is now dark grey. His flesh looks like lead. Even though the air outside is very cold, his breath is not visible as it passes through his nostrils. He is now as cold and dead as any corpse. The man is hard, sullen, and burned out. A bullet shot at this man would steer clear, knowing that nothing would happen to its target. The man turns and looks up the long, uphill avenue. He starts to walk up the avenue with slow deliberate steps. He is going to her house. He has no intentions of calling on her. He'll just walk by and look at the house. Maybe she might pass by the window. He makes this walk all the time. He always walks extra slow when passing underneath her window. The sight of the television's grey shadows sends the black plague to his glacial brain.

He's close to her home now. He watches the people on the street as they pass him, he feels like a different breed altogether. He turns onto the street where she lives. A pulsing, red glow is visible through his coat. The smell of molten lead is very strong. His boots are melting the brick sidewalk underneath his feet, leaving behind glassy footprints. He stands in front of her porch stairs and looks up. He might as well be looking at the top of Mount Everest. A small whine comes from his throat. He stands still for a moment or two, watching the television's images bounce silently off the walls. She's in there alright. At that instant he asks himself the same tired question for the millionth time. Why? Why torture himself this way? Does he need this? —Yes.

Yes! Because the feeling of desire, the feeling of wanting to be close to someone fills a need. Like a grave digger shoveling dirt back into the hole. But this? This futile exercise? Yes. Yes! The pain and the want are almost too much to bear but this is the most alive he's felt all week. He wants what he cannot have. This is a steadying consolation in the frozen wasteland of his futility. The chase can never end, the dream can never be destroyed. He probably couldn't climb those stairs if she opened the door and stood with her arms open wide. Damn! So cold outside. Heart burning like a coal. Time to leave. Damn! What if her face suddenly appeared in the window? What if she motioned for him to come to her. Would he go? Yes! No! Who knows? Would any words come out of him? Time to go. What would it be like to not feel like solid lead? Time to go! Time. To. Go. He lurches down the sidewalk towards his home. The smell of lead and automotive exhaust exudes from his body as he walks into the night.

He is Leadman. His flesh is cold, impenetrable lead. His heart is red hot, burning. Cold on the outside, burning on the inside. So hot on the inside, so hot.

▶   ▶   ▶   ▶   ▶   ▶

For a while there I was going out with this girl. A nice girl. She went to a girl's school out in the suburbs. She was beautiful, long brown hair, very tall, very nice. Something about that school uniform drove me crazy. The skirt. It looked so impenetrable. What was underneath it? Whatever it was, it had to be good. We would fuck. It was great. The sight of her skirt falling down and the knowledge that I would soon be falling in, filled me with great joy. Sometimes we would fuck after school. She would be on her way to a Bible class and we would go for it in my bedroom. I'll never forget that as long as I live. Broad daylight, the venetian blinds, and that uniform on the floor. I always insisted on taking that skirt off her, that cock-proof skirt. I felt like a magician. (..."And with a flick of my wrist, Voila! The skirt is in my hand..."

A round of applause erupts as the magician tosses the skirt over his shoulder.) I felt like a safe cracker.

The after school thing didn't last too long. When she would sit in her Bible study class with cum running down her leg, she said it made her feel guilty. And besides, she was afraid her mother would see the stains if she wasn't careful.

Her mother was crazy. Really crazy. We would go to her house and mom would look at us and say, "You're both going to burn in Hell! I know what you're doing! You can't fool me! Oh my God, my daughter! Damn the both of you!" That sent her into fits, she would cry and hide herself. After one of those ordeals, the skirt would stay on for days. Her mother was crazy alright. Crazy and correct. She never admitted it to her mother, ever. I would go to her place for dinner sometimes. Her mother would cook up a storm. I think we really blew it bad a few times, taking the car to go to the corner market for mustard and coming back forty-five minutes later, all sweaty.

The final blow came down. I'll never forget that night. We were at her house, downstairs in the den. Mom was safely upstairs watching television. The den was a good spot to fool around in because no matter how softly old Mom tiptoes down the stairs, we could always hear her and pretend to be talking about history or some such shit. But this time her mother got downstairs without us hearing her. My girl was on the couch and I was on the floor on my knees with my head planted between her legs. Her thighs were wrapped around my ears so I could not hear or see. She was enjoying herself to the point to where she wasn't listening or caring. All of a sudden, her legs spread wide. My head was pushed back. Hearing and sight restored, I instinctively turned around. There was Mom. I don't think she believed that scene because she just stood there with her mouth open. It was clearly time to go. Mom was foaming, calling us perverts and telling her that she was going to be thrown out. I thought both of them were going to have heart attacks and die right there on the rug. I had no ride home. Her mom drove me. I sat in the back, the two of them sat in front, no one said a word for the duration of the drive. I can only guess what was said after I was dropped off.

▸ ▸ ▸ ▸ ▸ ▸

I am ready to implode. Excuse me, cave in is more like it. I feel so empty inside. I wonder if I coughed, would dust come out of my mouth? After I play, I sit still and I swear I can feel the earth turning in my brain. My eyes feel dead. I feel like my soul is sucked dry. I sometimes expect to see myself in a mirror as just a skeleton. No meat, no blood, nothing. This is how I feel. I could say that my soul is thirsty, like a dusty snake crawling to an oasis. I could have said that a while ago but now I can't because my soul is beyond dehydration. It no longer thirsts. I see myself as an extinguished cigarette butt falling into a black hole, burned out and falling down into endless silent darkness.

▸ ▸ ▸ ▸ ▸ ▸

Every time they call my name I can feel a few more grains of myself fall away. The alienation. The isolation. The desolation is painless. It's a vacant parking lot in the middle of the desert. The trip hammers me flat. Where I once felt like a radiant, charged filament bouncing around, I now feel like a field of dead grass. I blame no one, not even myself. I am a dead planet. Moving slow, emitting very little heat. Relaxing in the ghetto of myself. I know how I got there but I have no idea how to get out.

▸ ▸ ▸ ▸ ▸ ▸

Annihilate! Alienate!
Come on, say it with me!
Shhh, not too loud, someone may hear you. We couldn't have that now, could we?

Annihilate, alienate!
I stood alone on the side of a mountain and I said those words. My vision flattened. The city below fell to rubble. Spirits of the dead rose from the collapsed remains. They rose pure and shining, cleansed by annihilation and alienation.
Annihilate! Alienate!
I flew with desperate wings. I wished for the birth of new animals so I could end this panicked flight. I wished for a discarded world to build my home. I touched down in the city. I cringed from the petty evil and the fraudulent fire. I wrapped alienation and annihilation around me and went forth. My world is clean.

▶   ▶   ▶   ▶   ▶   ▶

I snuck out the back door while the house burned down. I don't know how many bodies lie in the smoking remains. They had names. They had hearts. I don't care. I can still remember walking down that fiery hallway to the door. The exit was all too clear. It was a burning house but it could have been a sinking ship. They were burning people but they could have been drowning rats. I think I overheard some of the burning bodies say, "Come back, come back." But I wasn't really listening. The roar of the flames and the crackle of the burning flesh was deafening. I stood outside and watched the nameless fire destroy their world, their nameless existence. I will always burn alone.

▶   ▶   ▶   ▶   ▶   ▶

If you're going to do, do it alone. Try it. Cry alone. Drink alone, suffer alone. Not much fun is it? Home at night alone, you hear a sucking sound. You look up, the windows and doors of your house disappear. Yes. Locked in the room of yourself.

Turn down the lights. Glowing claws will grab the hands of your clock and stop them dead. This night has no end. The sun lies in an alley stabbed and dying. It's never coming up again.

Alone. A mirror. Get some bailing wire. Tie the mirror to your face so whenever you open your eyes you will be forced to see the person you are locked in with. Force yourself to realize its prison.

No one to hear you, no one to hand you a Budweiser. No place to wreck your car. No one to show your scars to. Do it. If you're going to do it, do it alone. Do it right. You'll see that you don't need them to exist.

► ► ► ► ► ►

I watched a man burn to death in a public park. He lit himself on fire and did the fire dance. (Soul inflamed! Dance! Faster, faster! Soul burning, dance on the water that fills the open graves! All lovers turn mekanikal in the dark!) He burned like a tree, waving his arms like a bird in flight. Like the last warning. Like the first smile on a dead man's face. He burned self-contained and all the way. I watched him burn to death. He danced to the end. I will be dancing at the end.

► ► ► ► ► ►

The three ass kickers talked through mekanikal leather hinged mouths. They talked about their kills and the right way to do it. They laughed about the obvious wrong ways. Each spoke easily. Their stories often told, flapped like old flags in the wind. Their stories, often told, increased with grandeur and might with every telling. Each ass-kicker upped the ante with every word, with every blow. Fascinating. So many ways to smash a man into little bits. The process was always different. But the result was always the same. Some dude all busted apart on a filthy floor. Another gust of wind. Another story. Another notch. Another step towards infinite darkness.

► ► ► ► ► ►

I'm sitting in an airplane. This airplane looks like a pregnant rat, skin pulled tight, belly distended, crammed full of little rat babes. The passengers in this plane are just like me, hoping that this stupid looking thing won't crash. If you toss a pregnant rat off of a rooftop it will smash like a ripe melon upon impact. The mother will be twisted and shattered, the bloody unborn will be scattered and broken. That's what's going to happen when this heap drops from the sky like a stone vulture. Shattered mother in a heap, stomach torn open and babes in suits and dresses and unscratched Samsonite luggage. Nice thing about Samsonite luggage, those suckers are really built to take it! Crash with 'em, hose the guts and fuel off 'em, use 'em again!

▶ ▶ ▶ ▶ ▶ ▶

I often think of getting out. Killing myself. No big deal, no public scene. Just doing it. I think about blowing my brains out with a pistol. The other day I was going through a textbook of dead bodies. I turned to the section that dealt with suicide. There were dead bodies swinging in prison cells, dead bodies with multiple, deep slash wounds on the inner arms. Dead bodies with throats cut, one lady nearly cut her damn head off. Finally the book came to the pictures of the ones who killed themselves with guns. One picture really caught my attention. A man had put the barrel of a rifle into his mouth and pulled the trigger. The man's mouth was twisted into an arrogant sneer. His nose was turned slightly upward due to the upward trajectory of the bullet. The rest of the man's head was gone. The face folded backward over the remainder of the skull. I said, "Someone had to clean all that up."

That would be a drag for someone that I like to walk in on my corpse. What if I blew my brains all over the wall? That's not fair. I would go to a place where I didn't know anyone. I would leave an envelope of money and a note apologizing for the mess and thanking them for cleaning my brains up. Maybe I would go over to a person's house that I hated and do it there, let him worry about the mess. That's a great idea. Blow your head off in somebody's bedroom. It will be a long time before he'll be able to get it up in that room again.

Sometimes I just want to get out. Nothing that I can explain very clearly. I've been like this as long as I can remember. Sometimes I feel like I want to get out. I get a lump in my throat and my stomach starts feeling cold. I sink inside myself and start to solidify. I try to cry to get things moving, nothing comes. Sometimes I want to get out. I feel as if I never knew anything but that cold paralysis. I don't want to be a picture in a text book that someone will use for a term paper. I just want to get out. Sometimes I just want to get out. Sometimes it gets so cold in here I want to build a roaring fire using my body for kindling. Another man torches himself in his cell. It happens all the time and I know why. Existence can be such a freeze out. You could wait forever for a warming touch, you could freeze solid waiting. Better to burn than to freeze. Incinerate. Turn to ash. If you dream in your sleep tonight and your dreams are of the sun, touch me. I feel so cold tonight.

▶ ▶ ▶ ▶ ▶ ▶

And now you're so far away and I don't know where I stand with you. I miss you. The wind blows cold around me and I think of you. Oh man, the sun always seems to come up too fast to get enough thinking done. I want to throw myself off a cliff and fall into the endless night. Sometimes I think I get so close to the edge of the big night that I can almost make myself believe that the sun will never come up again.

I put myself in the night room. Filled the place with pictures of death. Built a cold fire inside the night room. I let it burn. I sit alone and tend the fire that burns cold and solid blue.

▶ ▶ ▶ ▶ ▶ ▶

Pictures of car crashes take my mind off women. If the dead want to dance, LET THEM DANCE! Yes, by all means let them dance. Maybe they'll come back. Come back? No, no, no, you can't come back. Cross your heart and hope to die you can't come back. I came here. I tried to get back. Every time I looked behind me I could see the dense forest closing in. Cool darkness.

The night room is a holding tank, temporary solitary confinement. I can't come back. I sleep in the dark, under a rock in the forest of the night room. I have dreams of dark cold river water. I have river water in my veins. It makes me understand.

➤ ➤ ➤ ➤ ➤ ➤

I want to be on a river ride
They talk, they tell me that I'm nothing
If I'm nothing, then how come they talk so much about me?
You would think they would have more worthy topics to dissect
You would think
Well fuck that, Junior
I don't want to be on a river ride
I want to be the river
They will throw their stones into me
They will try to float their petty, leaky rafts on me
Their stones will sink and disappear
Their rafts will be sucked below
This river runs deep
This river has one fierce current and can not go home

➤ ➤ ➤ ➤ ➤ ➤

I walked along at a fast clip, my head expounding thunder. A mission.

I had just gotten finished hearing the talk. Have mercy, that's all they do. I almost made the mistake of adding to the stink. I opted for total insanity. I was walking, screaming, cursing and laughing to myself. They want to destroy me. The weather has gotten so cold and I know why.

Freedom.

▸ ▸ ▸ ▸ ▸ ▸

I don't feel human. I don't know what I am. I see myself limbless and skewered, cooking over hot coals. People come up and cut off slices of me and eat them. These are people who would vomit at the thought of eating human flesh, yet they gouge away and watch me burn. They say and do things to me that they would never do to themselves. I'm not human anymore. Their eyes, their talk, their cruel actions have robbed me of all human feeling. I feel so outside. I don't have a clue of how to return to human form. I am not human. I have no feelings for myself, for them, none. I'm not human anymore.

▸ ▸ ▸ ▸ ▸ ▸

The fires of hate burn me like a wooden witch. The flames consume me and turn me into useless dead ash. Sweat turns to gasoline, feeds the fire, ensures total incineration. Burning up in a stupid fire. Senseless heat, burns so fast, so easy. Too easy, almost irresistible. Sometimes I feel like a match. I want nothing more than to get struck so I can burn like a motherfucker.

▸ ▸ ▸ ▸ ▸ ▸

Soldier from Space. Soldier of a different kind. Soldier of a different mind, from the dark and into light, then back again. I find myself back again in darkness. Standing alone in the light of darkness. Dancing in a ring of fire and hoping I'll get burned to death.

Soldier of a different mind. The sands shift tonight. I am wrapped in a blanket of wind. I can see for miles and I thank my good judgment that I chose to go blind. From the dark and into light and back again. Into darkness where in my blindness I can see myself.

➤ ➤ ➤ ➤ ➤ ➤

I am paranoid of my brain. It thinks all the time, even when I'm asleep. My thoughts assail me. Murderous lechers they are. Thought is the assassin of thought. Like a man stabbing himself to death with one hand while the other hand tries to stop the blade. Like an explosion that destroys the detonator. I am paranoid of my brain. It makes me unsettled and ill at ease. Makes me chase my tail, freezes my eyes and shuts me down. Watches me. Eats my head. It destroys me.

➤ ➤ ➤ ➤ ➤ ➤

As your nerves bend and twist to accommodate yet inexperienced force, new thought and mutant hallucination come into light. I heard about this nervous breakdown that's been going around. Read a letter about how you broke down in the middle of nowhere, which is everywhere when you're broken down. Open your eyes. Your tears cut a trail. Your scars build a ladder that takes you to a place that you could not have gotten to any other way. Take a look around, remember every second, every breath, every choked scream. Scar tissue is stronger than regular tissue. Realize the strength. Move on.

➤ ➤ ➤ ➤ ➤ ➤

I just got back from the trip. The mission. It's impossible to come all the way back. I just don't seem to ever get there. Now I'm sitting alone in my cell, thinking about the whole thing. All my memories come to me in nightmarish form. Rearing their ugly heads, forcing me to remember the whole thing. You can't come back. Smoke slowly rises from the burnt villages I left back there. You can't come back, not all the way. Never.

▸ ▸ ▸ ▸ ▸ ▸

People say that I am a bastard. People say that I am a god. That's what they say. I know what I am. I'm a spirit. I live in a desert outside of life. Outside of time. Every day I rise phosphorescent and burning. I know this because I remember the day that I cleansed my eyes and rid my life of their putrefying, lying existence. The wind blew cold around my feet like a snake without a home. I realized that I live outside of their petty, hostile vision. Outside of their numbness to discipline and beauty and outside of their welcome shore. On that day I saw so far, so deeply that my vision went around and then came around and burned eyes into my back. I know what I am.

▸ ▸ ▸ ▸ ▸ ▸

Can there be a ghetto in the desert? I walk down Artesia Boulevard at night. It's a small neon desert. Narrow like a bowling alley. Doesn't give you much room to walk anywhere but down and through. We gotcha. This place has got all the inhabitants beat. The loneliness and liquor soaked desperation forces all into their heavy cold cinder brains. Locks them into unfurnished apartments of sullen sorrow. The neon desert eats itself and deposits a ghetto like a roach giving birth to a small ghetto in the neon desert. The infection is spreading and everybody is getting sick and slowing down.

▸ ▸ ▸ ▸ ▸ ▸

How are you today? Are you climbing that ladder? They told you all about that ladder. Climb that ladder and find that salvation. Sure is a hard climb I bet. Arms getting tired? Sure is a long ladder. Faith, is that the word they used? Hope? I've been watching you from a long ways off. You're not climbing on any ladder. You're running on a tread wheel.

▶   ▶   ▶   ▶   ▶   ▶

This summer has left me on an island all by myself. My mind goes its own way, usually to the streets of my home town. Walking alone on MacArthur Boulevard at night. Muggy, unmoving air. Watching the moths play around the street lamps. I walk through the night, ill at ease and alone. The sun will never rise on this street. MacArthur Boulevard is always dark and quiet. The street lamps are small yellow planets that keep me from falling into the distance. I feel the isolation. I sink inside myself so deep that I turn into the most pathetic, lonely, ugly animal there ever was. Summer becomes a jail, a ship run aground, a ladder to nowhere. Summer brings back the thoughts of the girl and her house. I would feel so small that I would sink into the cracks in the brick sidewalk. The summer animal, I can never outrun or hide from it. The journey in my mind continues along and I find myself standing in front of a house with a roofed front porch on Beecher Street. I see myself and others I recognize sitting on the porch, they are unmoving. They are statues. Suddenly I grow heavy, as if filled with water or sand. I grow tired, lazy and thoughtless. Stagnant and breathless. I know what I am, but I don't know what I'm supposed to do. When in doubt, I move. So I leave and walk somewhere else, trying to walk out of the mouth or asshole of the summer beast that has consumed me. The sunsets are the worst. They sink slowly and mournfully, burning and waving good-bye. I want to reach out and grab the sun and throw it back up high in the sky so I can have more time to figure out this dilemma. I know that it's too late to turn to other shores. I wouldn't even if I could. The summer bores me out, turns me into a hollow carcass. Fueled by insomnia and a thirst for everything. I turn into boneless limbo man caught in the middle. My skin turns to leather, I turn inside in. I seal off. Every pore, every orifice. Underneath this leather exterior I scream, twist, convulse and burn silently. I wonder to myself wouldn't I be better off far from everything that bears the least resemblance to this? You can change the scenery that surrounds you. You can run from the fists that pound you, but you cannot escape your feelings. I've crawled every sewer from here to there and I've never done it. And I burn silently.

► ► ► ► ► ►

I never want to sleep again! I never want to see the light of day, or see another human face ever again. I feel like I've been beheaded and cleaned like a trout for the skillet. I have no friends here. I've been in one place for nine days now and I can hardly remember how to breathe. Everyone wants to bind and gag me. My arrows fall short of the sun, my words and gestures make me feel like a mute amputee. Everything is bad and out to take a bite. The phone rings, it's for me every time. Now I hear it when it doesn't ring. I call someone that I want to talk to, the voice I hear sounds very different. I try to speak but I'm losing my grasp of this language. Flesh falls away as I stand with the phone in my hand. The friend loses all blood, bone and muscle. I am left with a porcelain shell of the person in my heart. The next beat smashes the shell into a million pieces, my heart caves in a little causing a slight pain, a slight freezing. The distance grows. My iceberg island sails steadily away from the mainland. Every time I turn around the mainland becomes more distant, more blurred. The things that used to matter, the people, they all start to melt and quickly vaporize, leaving nothing, not a trace of why or when or who.

I envy the lonesome coyote. Walking alone under clear night sky, moon reflecting off its coat. The beast howls, full of pain and desire. My howl would be thin and hollow. I want, but

I don't know what. I sometimes wish I could crawl into a painting and live. Maybe a mountainous backdrop. A road to a place where I could see things that didn't make my eyes hurt, maybe I would feel something. Desire! What is life without insane desire? It's slow death, like breathing mercury-filled air. Knives and unseen eyes line the paths of my existence. I never want to sleep again, or maybe I want to sleep forever. Hurry! Fetch my revolver. I want to get on with my life.

➤   ➤   ➤   ➤   ➤   ➤

I had a dream the other night. I lay on the floor and closed my eyes and the creatures came to life: A snake is crawling along a desert trail that parallels a straight, black paved road. The sun is going down but it's still quite bright outside. Over the horizon walking down the road in the opposite direction is a woman. The two get closer and almost pass each other but each stop just in time. They both step into the area that runs between the trail and the road. The wind gusts suddenly and the snake is instantly transformed into a man. He has dark hair. He is marked with scars and symbols, patterns of his tribe. The two walk towards each other and embrace. Another gust of wind comes and blows all vestiges of clothing off them both. The sun holds still for a moment and starts to slowly rise and as it rises it turns a deep crimson and gives off a low metallic whine. The couple are fully embraced and perfectly still. Their bodies fit together as if they were two parts of a jigsaw puzzle. Another gust of wind comes and blows the flesh and organs off the man and woman so all that's left are two skeletons locked in embrace. Their jaws open and they start to grind into each other, bone on bone, tooth on tooth. The sun is emitting a pitch that is making the ground rumble. The skeletal bodies grind together as if one was trying to destroy the other. Another gust of wind comes and forces the two to totally intertwine with each other until only one is visible, this lasts the duration of the blink of an eye before the image implodes and turns to a pile of sand. The pile of sand conflagrates with white/blue flame and nothing is left. The sun has now changed shape and has transformed itself into a double helix, bright red and twisting, it sinks into the distance, the rumbling quiets as the light fades.

▸ ▸ ▸ ▸ ▸ ▸

Denver, CO 1985 (Transcribed from tape by Rx): Now here's the thing... you all know what I'm talking about. And that's the nice thing about alienation: everyone has been there, everyone has felt pushed to the edge of their existence to where they're standing on the edge, on their toes, and it's crumbling and you're thinking, *They can't push me anymore!* and then all of a sudden you open your eyes, and everything in the world is shoveling dirt into your face. You try and talk, but all of a sudden your language doesn't work anymore, and you think, *Maybe I got the wrong planet!* You check your zip code, all of a sudden the earth doesn't work anymore. And the shit hurts, as you well know.

And you want for a different thing. A delivery to a different place. Maybe you could crawl into another world. Here's this thing I wrote about it:

Imagine a man standing on this island looking at the mainland as if you were looking at Cuba, standing on the coast of Florida.

I spent an entire summer apart from existence. My life. I denied myself life in hopes that the fast might sharpen my vision. I needed desperately to understand. The summer beat the air like a blacksmith. Beat it into the shape of a woman. She rose off the pavement and flashed her fangs. Cruel summer.

Through the keyhole of soul I caught a glimpse of myself, locked in the white-hot straitjacket of infinite isolation. I stood alone on a desert island. I looked out over the water. I saw islands of starvation. They reached out with scaly hands to grab me. I retreated into the jungle. Took a few times of searching for light before I saw any at all.

I crossed to the other side. I waded across a shallow, rancid inlet to the Island of Hope. I walked for miles on the Island of Hope. My legs grew tired, and then I realized that I could have walked forever on the Island of Hope. Suffocated and drained with every step, with every starving mile.

I called in the air strike. I incinerated the Island of Hope.

When you get pushed all the way out, for some stupid reason, you think to yourself that you need them, and you try and do it again with these people who don't understand you.

I went to the city to let the rats run over my face, to feel the depletion. I lay like a tomb in the bottom of the Cavern of Love, feeling like a dead soldier, crawling towards the womb of Death. Reborn as dirt, coming down like fire. Rain, as pure as cinder, walking on twilight through frozen roads to the Womb of Death.

I wiped my hands and spat and grinned and dreamed of annihilation, the beauty of pain, and the sound they'll never hear. I took a train to forever, and I found myself in a land of madness. I was washed and drenched by a torrential rain that threatened to drown my soul. I nearly gave up to the flood. I wished for the iron will of the rat, so I could survive. My will turned weak and cancerous. I blacked out and found myself washed ashore on the Island. I had reached the Womb of Death.

You get pushed all the way out there, and at your lowest low, suddenly you start to feel not so low anymore. Maybe the low is the high, and maybe at the bottom of all that darkness you see this big sun punching through. Nothing's going to stop it, and you start thinking that maybe this Alienation is not so bad. At least the air is clean.

I woke up one morning and found myself on the most lonesome trail. I came around from coming around and found myself in reality's jail. I've got a place. I've got a place I can go.

I've got an Alienation. Don't come down here. You put me on the outskirts of town and now you want in? No. Doesn't work like that. In the Alienation, no credit is good. No Sears and Roebuck dreams.

In the Alienation, I am whole. I am complete. I am the full circle realized. Your world is cold. Alien. That's why, when I'm with you, I'm cold. Your world is a bad trip. That's why I quit you. That's why I spat you out. That's why I went up the river, into the desert, into the jungle, into the Sun. I exist in Alienation, but I'm not alone. I'm with all of those who realize that Paradise lies.

▶   ▶   ▶   ▶   ▶   ▶

I like my headaches, they're pure. The ones I've been getting lately are the ones I like best. The pain jumps all over my head. Sometimes they come out of nowhere. The pain rushes through my head like splinters of lightning. The pain is sharp and pure. I see cold blue shards in my brain. They make my head expand, contract and distort into vile shapes. The pain sometimes makes me squint. Like a bullet entering my brain and then altering its normal path and wriggling about like a snake plugged into a light socket. Sometimes I think that something wants in and sometimes I think that something is trying to rip its way out of my head. Like a rising sun. Ulcerating. Burning. Destroying my brain cells. Spinning and aborting constantly. Maybe I harbor a colony of fugitive rats in my head, turning my brain into a ghetto and a rancid nest for dreams and hallucinations. They eat away at the center of my brain. Fortifying themselves, strengthening themselves so they can employ and embody plague and infestation. The pain strengthens and educates me. Forces me to understand, acknowledge, assimilate and enjoy pain and pain's by-products: Vision and brutal, absolute forward movement.

▶   ▶   ▶   ▶   ▶   ▶

I'm a multicolored man scar tissue. I'm a self-inflicted kind of guy and I'm self-inflicting down the road. DRAW THE LINE! I'll fall short. I guess I forgot to mention the overflowing cowardice, stupidity and sheer unadulterated pettiness. But I'm a stranger in your face and my mood swings like a guillotine and my hands aren't connected to my head bone and I got crazy muscles and wavy eyes and I got an urge with no name I don't know what to do with it muscles, cock, brain, knife —whatever. I just want to do it.

▶ ▶ ▶ ▶ ▶ ▶

Me and Ian went for a drive in his car. We went over Key Bridge where I used to walk home from work. We drove down "M" Street. We drove down "R" Street, past the place where that black dude slammed my head against the wall of the alley and took my tape player, past the place where that dog looked me in the eye a split second before he got hit by a car, covering my shoes with blood. Past the block where a hippie girl put flowers in my hair while her male companions turned over cars. Past Montrose Park. Past Jackson School where I went for first, second and third grade and got beat and harassed because I was white in 1969. Got held responsible for the death of Martin Luther King. I could still remember hearing them chant: "Fight, fight nigger and a white, beat him nigger, beat him 'cuz the white can't fight!" I could still remember how my stomach would twist and my head would grow light. Down 30th Street, over to "Q" Street, past my old bus stop, past that apartment where that young white boy was raped and made to play games with that black dude. Back on Wisconsin Avenue, past 7-11, past the library, past the Safeway.

We keep driving, we stop at Ian's parent's house. We park the car, we walk to Wisconsin Avenue. Ian goes into the bank, I take a walk down to the building that once held the pet shop I worked at for years. The building is an Italian restaurant now. I walk behind the building to see the back steps, the steps that I walked up and down for years hauling out garbage The steps that I sat on and ate my lunch. The steps that I stood on and destroyed litters of sick animals. Cats, rabbits, you name it. People would come in with their sick animals to have them put to sleep. Of course, we had no facilities for such things. Didn't matter to my boss. He took the money and I took the animals on the back stairs and killed them. Some, I broke their necks with a sharp twist. Others I took and bashed their heads against the wooden rail. The move was smooth and swift. I used to go home with my shoes covered with blood. The back steps. One time I went out to dump the trash and I saw a guy getting head from a stripper from the bar next door. I walk back up the alley and re-emerge on Wisconsin Avenue. I look around me, almost every building in the area has been torn down. I walk past the Italian restaurant and look inside. A family of well-dressed people sit at a table, they look up and see me, their eyes swell up. I pull away from the glass and walk back up Wisconsin Avenue towards the bank. I'm thinking about that family eating their food, their feet tapping on the floor. The floor that acted as a roof for more rats than you will ever know. We had rats all over that place, rat shit everywhere. Piles of it stacked high and rotting into every two-by-four in the joint. A miniature ghetto of sorts. Upstairs from where the family eats is a room where my boss used to fuck his boyfriends. One day he told me how hard it was to get the vaseline out of the sheets.

Keep eating, lady, the rats squirm, crawl and shit below you. Neurotic fags fuck and moan above you. You're surrounded entrenched in shit, sweat and vaseline, eat up, sleep tight. It gets so twisted, so distorted, that I lock myself out of my own house. I look at myself looking at myself, inverse to inverse, turning inside out and the other way around.

I'm going to wait until the ghosts come out again. I'll see my boss walk through the rear wall, naked, heaving, smelling of shit, complaining of the sheets and how bad he hates "the niggers in this city." That was one of his obsessions. He had a huge dog that he trained to hate blacks too. He would say, "Tannis, don't you want to eat a nigger?"

There's ozone in the air now. I'm sitting in a room with an open window. The ozone air comes flowing in gently. So gently, I might just drift off with it. I get lonely when the ozone comes out. The smell of it makes me remember lonely times, always. Grey, cool and empty, leading to a cave in. I've been to that window ledge before. I never jump, I never have the guts. I just sit in a chair and contemplate my body falling through the ozone. Thinking of girls, thinking of how it never works. Never. And then you die or just go to sleep...

▶ ▶ ▶ ▶ ▶ ▶

I go out on the street. I hear the cars and the people but that's not what I want. I want to hear jungle music. It's all lies out there. I think I understand the difference between dirt and filth. The dirt is clean and the filth is filthy and it's everywhere. It rips at my eyes. I can keep a better grip than a lot of people I know. And when I make an effort, I can maintain out there. But sometimes I get pushed and my brain goes into automatic pilot and I feel like kicking and walking a straight line right into their diamond minds. But you know you can't do that. You will never touch their minds. That would be like punching at thin air. If you're going to get all the way into it, you might as well take that straight line right into their flesh. You know what I'm talking about. With a smile on your face speak the international language: Dirt and filth.

▶ ▶ ▶ ▶ ▶ ▶

When I'm alone feeling lonely, feeling it all the way down to the marrow, I call out from a million miles away. It's like I'm in a cave. It can get just as dark as you want it to. Any time, any place.

The light gets so hard to find. You can get so gone that you wouldn't know a helping hand from one that wants to push your head under for good. I'm calling out. But I think the line's been disconnected. The screams go into the night. The whole place gets cold and hard. The edges get sharp and the whole thing shoots you down to the ground.

▸   ▸   ▸   ▸   ▸   ▸

The noise comes in, crowds me out of my brain. At first, the sound of children laughing mixes with the sound of rain. The sound of the children fades out and is replaced by the sound of gunfire. The gunfire remains at a steady pitch as the rain fades. Now I hear the sound of people talking, laughing, screaming, crying. Reminds me of when I was in the hospital. All night long they would scream for their medicine, they wanted to get better. The old woman in the room next to mine sounded like she was being cooked alive in her bed. The whole place was screaming. Made me think that I might lose my mind in there. In there, out there, I don't know the difference anymore. The sound, I can't shut off the sounds of their voices. When I'm all alone in my room I can still hear their voices screaming in my ears. I know that I am to blame for letting them in. I want to get better myself. I'm not running from anything. I'm just trying to free myself from their sounds. If I don't I'll become accustomed to them and that will be the end of me. The sound of rain, pelting down on boxes holding the dead. The rain mixing with dead children. What I see, what I hear. The whole place is an insane asylum. A screaming shit house. Gunfire off in the distance. The bodies are falling, crying, trying to get better, doing anything to get well. And you know how bad the emptiness feels when you're full of it. They fill you with emptiness, and then they come to get their pay. They want their pay, but they don't want what's coming to them.

It never fails. My weaknesses are always strong enough to knock me to the ground. My weaknesses are the greatest weapons I have when I turn on myself. It won't always be like this. I'm getting better every day. Maybe someday I won't want, I won't be such a sucker. It's all one big insane asylum, a screaming shit house.

The sound of children splattering, sounding like gunfire. For every voice, a bullet. For every scream, every prayer, every day, annihilation inside my room.

▸ ▸ ▸ ▸ ▸ ▸

Got the Southbay blues like a motherfucker right now. Walking down Artesia Blvd. White trash gas station junior college McDonalds Burger King meat stock minds on the street. A Budweiser flood would get sucked up within three blocks. Marlboro woman at the bus-stop clings to her Zody's bag and stares at me, hoping I won't try to steal the goodies: A loaf of Wonder bread, a carton of Marlboros and a TV Guide.

▸ ▸ ▸ ▸ ▸ ▸

I thought about you for so long, so many nights. All their broken ends strung together so many nights in the desert lost. So many nights, seeing your face mirrored in the moon. Ghost white. So many nights in that cold desert I wanted to feel you next to me. I thought of your touch, your breathing, how I wanted you buried alive in the night with me. Plague comes to me, pulls me inside the womb of my mind. I call out to you from the desert. Pull me out. I want to come out. I am lost. I don't know who I am. I want to climb your ladder and crawl inside your heart.

▸ ▸ ▸ ▸ ▸ ▸

S&D Vacation Package Pt.1: Organize leisure air tours during war time. Vacationers who could afford it would be flown over battle sites and would have the opportunity to drop napalm and bombs on the villagers below. I can see them now. Wagner's March of the Valkeries blasting through the quad system. Fat white tourists dressed in polyester pant suits and those silly Hawaiian shirts sit in their seats, each with his own personal trigger. "Can we do it now?" they ask. A smiling stewardess gives them a knowing wink and says, "Soon, very soon." "But I want to drop fire now! I want to kill now! I want to incinerate now! Now!" says a fat balding man. "Calm down honey," his wife says, "You heard the stewardess. We'll be in bombing range soon. See honey, the music's starting and everything." Soon they are dropping fire on the cities below. The conversation in the plane resembles one that can be heard in a boxing arena on a good night. The vacationers come home with pictures and souvenirs. Some pose with charred dismembered bodies. They smile and give the thumbs up to the camera. Some are wearing strings of ears around their necks. The women all want their pictures taken with the captain. Each will come back with their own story about the number of gooks they killed, each will exaggerate like crazy. Each will have their story about the one that got away. "One of those little bastards was hiding in a rice paddy. I was so plastered on those goddam huge drinks they were serving that I missed him. Madge blew the little sonofabitch right out of the water. What a woman."

► ► ► ► ► ►

I used to think that red, blue, green, and yellow were my friends. For a while there I thought that lines could go in circles if I wanted them to. I know better now. Black and white and the straight line are my friends. Inside my room I am free. Colors burst forth anytime they want to. The lines go wherever they please. Outside of my room I am not free and that's where the black and white are by my side and that straight line is my chosen direction. I know what it does to you. I know how it makes you feel. There is another side to this blade and I know that one too and I am tired of playing games with you. Thank you for all the gifts. I'll return them one of these days.

▶ ▶ ▶ ▶ ▶ ▶

Frozen night. Endless light. Aborting mother waving her arms. Make a flag out of human parts. Hack and sew. Make it so big that it blots out the sun. Eclipse. Another abortion. Take all the hacked off arms and stack them as high as you can. Climb to the top and know that you are that much closer to heaven. I am miles away from alienation. She is a frozen stone I can no longer even imagine. I am nothing, from nothing to nothing. Standing on a cliff screaming down into the black air. Heavy night. Sleepless, serpent night. I am nothing. From nothing to nothing.

▶ ▶ ▶ ▶ ▶ ▶

It hurts to let go. Sometimes it seems the harder you try to hold onto something or someone the more it wants to get away. You feel like some kind of criminal for having felt, for having wanted. For having wanted to be wanted. It confuses you, because you think that your feelings were wrong and it makes you feel so small because it's so hard to keep it inside when you let it out and it doesn't come back. You're left so alone that you can't explain. Damn, there's nothing like that is there? I've been there and you have too. You're nodding you head.

▶ ▶ ▶ ▶ ▶ ▶

I can't do it anymore
I can't act
It hurts to do it and I don't mind the pain

But this is a pain that I cannot take
And this is a pain that I won't take
To them it's life
To me it's a filthy lie
An act, a tight rope of fear and treachery
I can't hold my breath any more
Truth is everything to me now
More than your eyes
More than your smile
More than anything you could ever hold in your heart for me
I will walk hand in hand with truth and hate lies
And if I'm hated for that hate
that only means my love is true and absolute
Worlds beyond their shallow world of lies
I will travel miles up river
Far past their choking, stricken fields
Until time cuts me loose from this trip

► ► ► ► ► ►

Cold outside, cold inside, the smell of grease and disinfectant. The guys behind the counter look like they hate everybody that comes in. It's one of those jobs that you get, and all the while you're telling yourself that it's just temporary until the right thing comes along. It's one of those jobs that when you look up, you would swear that the clock hasn't moved a second since you looked at it an hour ago. The kind of job that you realize that you've been at for over a year now. Sure, you hate it, but it doesn't feel as bad as it used to. The brain numbs itself to everything except hate and the ability to take orders. But then again, who the fuck am I to say anything at all? For all I know, these guys might think that waiting on a bunch of meth dealers and whores is quite a great thing to be doing. Nobody understands anybody's anything.

► ► ► ► ► ►

The bus stop at Artesia and Hawthorne: The sun is almost gone from the sky. A woman sits alone and waits for the 116 to Hollywood. The woman doesn't move. The woman makes no sound. She sits like a black rock. I know that ride. I've taken that bus several times. It goes on Artesia for a while and then goes onto Crenshaw Blvd, which snakes its way through a fairly terrifying ghetto. I think about her ride. I think about the thing I saw on the news the other night. There was this gang fight on Crenshaw. Gang violence is common in this neck of the woods. The thing that grabbed the attention of the press was that while the bullets were flying, a nine month old child got its head blown apart by a stray bullet. This is the youngest person to be killed in the history of gang war in LA. I remember watching the reporter giving her "on the scene report." I recognized the block that she was reporting from. One time, I was riding the bus from Hollywood to the South Bay. The bus had just passed that block. We hit a red light and the door opened. About ten black dudes got on. They were all laughing and talking about the other dudes they had just fucked up. "You kicked that nigger upside his head! I think he's dead!" I looked out the window, there was this guy on the ground. He lay still, a pool of blood was around his head. I put my head down and hoped that they wouldn't kill me too. Most of the dudes got off at the next stop to go get him some more.

Another time, this big old fat black lady got on. She was all fucked up on angel dust. She was running up and down the aisle, screaming and telling everybody about how she went shopping that day. Finally she got off, everybody waved. The guy in front of me was this ugly old drunk guy. He tried to pick up every girl in the bus. He had this captain hat on, maybe he thought that made him look a bit more suave. He hit on every girl without any luck. Finally, this fat nurse got on. She sat down next to him and of course he went right to it. Several stops later, they got off the bus together.

The car I'm riding in speeds by and I look at the woman through the rear windshield and I think about her ride. I remember how the headmaster at my high school used to call the public buses "slave ships." He was making reference to the large number of maids that would get off the bus near the school grounds. One of the bus drivers called it the "Coal Train" Some people go home, others go home to it.

▶ ▶ ▶ ▶ ▶ ▶

It hurts when you see a friend burn himself down to the ground
One more until the last time
There you go...
Turning blue in the shower
Makes me wish you had the power to say no
Say no for me just once
There you go...
Falling back in rehab again
Forgetting the names of all your friends
Say no one time for me
There you go...
Telling me about a taste
That you got the time to waste
Say no one time for me
Just a little
Just one more time...
It never seems to be enough
Life got so much colder
Right after it got tough

▶ ▶ ▶ ▶ ▶ ▶

I was in this junk yard, staring at these jagged mountains of metal rubber and glass. One pile really caught my eye. Twisted metal and rubber, the pieces looked like human limbs all twisted. Like there had been an orgy of five hundred people and someone poured gasoline on the pile and torched it. I couldn't take my eyes off the heap. I started to imagine that it was a pile of bodies in a death camp. Made me think, *Gutted, dead, mutilated and totally erotic*. Now my mind goes out to the junkyard. I sit and long for a twisted heap. Two wrecks twist and grind in the dirt, alone under the moon. I want to feel the twisting grind. Call my name. Make me feel. Call my name. I want to contract the first disease. Tonight. In the junk yard, that's where I am. Screaming your name. Hot, twisted lover, come to me.

► ► ► ► ► ►

...But they came in and they put assassins in my brain. The assassins are killing and burning the villages to the ground. The sparkling water now is red from blood. How did they know that I was weak? How could they see my beautiful village? I thought I had it so well hidden. Now the assassins are after me. They're trying to destroy me. I won't let them take me alive. I won't give the bastards the satisfaction.

► ► ► ► ► ►

Darkside pulling at me. It's getting so hard to stay here. This place is not for me. I don't think it was meant to be. Everyday is becoming a struggle to maintain. I want to go away over there. I'll take my chances. There's no chance here. This place is not for me. I can see it, I can feel it, and the whole trip is making me crazy. The incineration of thought. The destruction of mind. Life after the great fire. Life after the crash. Life pulled from the ashes. Life during life. There must be no interruptions. Anything that in any way attempts to destroy the signal must be exposed and annihilated. The things that are most dangerous and threatening are the things that seem to be tolerated the most. This madness must end, a more pure and true madness must be sought.

▶ ▶ ▶ ▶ ▶ ▶

Why do people allow themselves to be compromised? Why will they give themselves away again and again? Why are those who stand up for themselves shunned, scorned and hated? Fear. Fear of being alone. Fear of being. Years and years of learning and the opportunity to teach themselves was never allowed. They can read and write but they can't walk through their front door. They fear and hate themselves. They are strangers to themselves. They see their feelings and desires, what they truly feel inside, as the enemy.

▶ ▶ ▶ ▶ ▶ ▶

Pushed aside. Pushed down a flight of stares. Pushed under the water, pushed to the end of the earth. "They got pushed out to the desert, man. They were crazy and desperate, like out of their minds, eating bugs and shit." Push... pushing... pushed. When that turn around comes around, and you know that's coming around sometime. When it comes down it would be such a lie if you said that you had no idea why.

▶ ▶ ▶ ▶ ▶ ▶

Obscene vision
Life is spelled wrong, doesn't sound right
Doesn't smell right, doesn't look right
Can't hear any screams
Can't smell fear or burning bodies
Can't see any pain or frustration
Nope, it's just not right

▶ ▶ ▶ ▶ ▶ ▶

Our Lady of Disintegration. I watch her as she passes by. Her head is disintegrating. She is catching fire as if to say, "You knew this couldn't last." As she self destructs she takes a part of you with her. She destroys part of you when she goes down, when she goes away, when she disintegrates and submerges into the street. She's gone. Somehow, you feel lucky.

► ► ► ► ► ►

Sometimes I just have to sit down and tell myself to hold on. Sometimes it gets very hard to hold on. It's happening right now. Honesty is a weapon I use upon myself like a gun or a knife. More like a razor that leaves little scars. Honesty is the isolation machine.

► ► ► ► ► ►

Light brown eyes, small pupils due to the needle. They call that "pinning," right? "Look, that guy shot me up seven times, no marks." "The needle is not afraid of me. Sometimes I think that everyone is afraid of me. That's why I go to the needle. The needle is not afraid of me." The bruises on her arms are like black eyes from a lover's quarrel. Black eyes up and down her arm. "I probably deserve it anyway." Everybody gets what they want, everybody gets what they deserve.

► ► ► ► ► ►

Fuck, I wish there was something I could do for you. I saw you on the street the other day. It took me a second to recognize you. I tried to get your attention. No luck, you looked so busy and so hurried that I didn't really pursue. I wanted to so bad. I wanted to have one last look at you. I don't know, I think that it's going to be the last time I'll ever see you. Believe me, that's not the way I wanted it. But when I saw your face, I just knew that it was going to be the last time. All those people calling you, the dirty children at your feet, the holes in your arms, the monkey on your back, licking your ear. You, filtering the air through chainsmoke, stacking lie upon lie to get to the truth. I saw you for the last time. I stood alone and said goodbye.

► ► ► ► ► ►

Dancing in the inferno. There's so much to cry about. There's a place. I swear there is, where no one gives a fuck about how much you don't care and how much you don't spend or how much you gave, took, bled, hated, loved or wanted. Eyes look upon you, the faces twist. You're surrounded by laughing hyenas. I don't know what I need, I don't know what you need. All I know is what I want to give you. The place of which I speak is right here, always has been. Your everything means so much to me because I am sad a lot of the time and when I find something of yours that I can take and bring to my place the look on your face makes me laugh like a hyena. And when I find something to give you, that makes me laugh even harder. This whole place is my place because I said so, because you want it so bad. Stealing from thieves.

► ► ► ► ► ►

Tight rope walking on soul
The fuckers will strip you of everything
Until you're just like them
Nothing
They want you to be nothing
So someone may mistake their pile of shit
For something other than shit
Well
When I close my eyes

I see an annihilation machine
The machine is so good, so clean
Takes no shit, makes me feel good
Makes me see right into their eyes
Right into your eyes
It feels so good to be strapped in and riding down the trail
Seeing things pass me by
One of these days I'm gonna drop it, stomp it, tie it up and beat it and burn it and leave it. Nothing from nothing leaves nothing. Nothing to take, nothing to give nothing to lie about. And that's the way uh-huh, uh-huh, I like it, uh-huh, uh-huh.

► ► ► ► ► ►

I'm gonna get up in the morning... almost sounds like a blues song, I'm gonna get up in the morning shake off my hangover as best I can. Stagger into the living room, flip off my parents and let my father cook me some food. I'll tell him about the coke I did last night and how much I don't care. He won't kick me out. He's a fool. He loves me. I don't love. I hate everything. The phone rings, it's one of my vacant friends. We have a short vacant conversation. I am vacant man. I am vacant, man.

► ► ► ► ► ►

I was playing at this party the other night. This drunk dude gets in my face. He keeps trying to get my attention while I'm playing. Between songs he says, "I want you to impress me dude." I took his Bud and poured it on him and then I bounced the can off his head. I don't know if that impressed him or not. I just don't know what to do in those situations. I was in the partying mood. I didn't drop the guy, did I? I gotta be careful, I might be starting to get civilized or something. After the show, I was outside changing into some dry clothes. I hear some people talking, "They didn't do Nervous Breakdown." "They're pussies, let's go home." That always makes me wonder why I do this shit. I must be out of my mind.

► ► ► ► ► ►

Sometimes I feel like I'm walking into a storm with my hands tied and my eyes blind folded. I feel like I'm throwing myself into the arms of a maelstrom. The stinging rain, the screaming wind. The swirling and snarling elements attempt to destroy me. The maelstrom seems like a welcome friend to walk along the trail with. When I think of the stagnant, frozen vacuum glacier that I left behind. Yesterday is not my friend. Yesterday is a suction ghetto. Yesterday wants to pull me in, pull me down and starve me. Yesterday is a rotting bird on my shoulder, a leash, a trip cord. Thinking of yesterdays makes me hurt inside. Deprives me of now. Sometimes it's a pain that feels so good. Like remembering a time that I felt wanted or loved, when I'm lonely. Crippling the crippled, pushing a drowned man under the water one last time. I must set my desperation and my starvation forward. Yesterday is not my friend. I must run for the rising sun. Past suns will freeze me. I must look forward to the rising sun. I must keep running until I burst into flame.

► ► ► ► ► ►

I should have walked away when I had the chance. I should have listened to myself. I should have believed in myself. Things get unsure, it's so easy to look to others for what I need. I know better now. I know where to go. I know who I can trust. I know who I can depend on. I slander myself with truth. The game has gotten so twisted that the truth offends. Lies are a more desirable medium of communication. That's cool. I don't need them and they don't need me, that's for sure. These days truth is a slap in the face, a put down. Something you would never do to a friend.

► ► ► ► ► ►

It gets so cold inside. In my dreams they all die. Annihilation. Extermination. Incineration. In my dreams they all die. I am exterminating from the inside, no one hears the screams. No one holds the keys my to my dreams but me. The assassin of my dreams comes to destroy from the inside. The assassin of my dreams exterminates without mercy, without judgment. I am the assassin of my dreams. I am the exterminator of my thoughts. I am the rust that corrodes my will. I am my worst enemy. I am my best friend. I am my end.

➤ ➤ ➤ ➤ ➤ ➤

Walking in a dark tunnel. The darkness is brutal. On occasion there is a brief and incredible illumination. The light is so brilliant that it blinds me. Back to total darkness once again. I can look into my own eyes now. It took years to attain this view.

Now I walk alone in the dark tunnel. The darkness leaves everything to imagination and insanity. The blinding light. I don't understand its origin. I used to question it. Now I roll with it. I'm alone in this dark tunnel. I think if my tunnel was invaded I would die.

I have been walking in this dark tunnel for a long time. I learned that dark is dark and cold is cold. Other than that I have not learned a damn thing.

It's a big place. You can walk down and down and never hit bottom it seems. Sometimes I stare at myself with my eyes closed. I don't see a thing.

Sometimes I think I have gone too far. I look at things and they don't seem like they used to. Walking in the dark tunnel is like a downhill river. Fast and silent. That's what drives me insane. The never ending silence. I don't know if it's the total absence of sound or if it's a roar so loud that I am deafened. Now that I have seen nothing and heard what cannot be heard, I can't feel the same about things. Things that I used to look at with awe and wonder now seem dull and lifeless. That's just the trip I'm on.

▶ ▶ ▶ ▶ ▶ ▶

Labels on records. Why not labels on booze? For example, a label that ran like so: Warning: Use of this product can cause vomiting, blurred vision, loss of control, loss of memory, severe headaches, dry mouth. Prolonged use of this product can lead to a dependency on this product. Prolonged use of this product can lead to the destruction of self-confidence. Prolonged use of this product can lead to the total destruction of self respect. Prolonged use of this product can lead to the destruction of the soul.

▶ ▶ ▶ ▶ ▶ ▶

There's lots of time. Time all over the place. Time for everyone. In order to make time really yours, you have to steal away. You have to kidnap yourself from the time takers. When I think of the hundreds of hours that those thieves have taken from me I wince. I've had a lot of useless hot air pushed in my direction...when I think of the word fool, I apply it to myself for the torture I have put myself through. You have to steal your time away. Hold it close to you like a precious jewel. There is time for everyone. Making time is not enough anymore. You've got to rip it off.

▶ ▶ ▶ ▶ ▶ ▶

Tampa outline: Show starts. People grabbing me, trying to pull me in. A guy keeps punching my knees. I clip him with the microphone. Guy fucks with me so I kick him in the face with steel cap shoe. Feels like kicking a melon. He keeps it up. I break his nose with it. He bleeds and smiles. People keep getting on stage. Ratman and Joe Cole eject. During 2nd to last song of the set, skins pull power in side fills. Ratman investigates and they kick the shit out of him. His face mangled, the music stops People spit on me. Chants of "Bullshit" "Black Flag Sucks" People tell me that I suck, I'm a pussy, faggot and that they want their money back. I sit behind the drum monitors. Dehumanization/dehumanized. They are lumps of shit. If they're all destroyed, so what.

▶   ▶   ▶   ▶   ▶   ▶

I watch the roads, the highways and the streets. They teach me things. The concrete that paves the roads teaches me about wear and tear. After endless cold the concrete cracks. I watch the cracks. I memorize the lines. I study the decay. In the relentless summer the concrete bends and expands. Sometimes it crushes the curbs and chokes the roots of trees. I study the distortion and suffocation. I observe closely a substance that's pushed to extremes in either direction. I know some things about cracking up and I know some things about expanding and crushing. I have always seen streets as rivers. Automobiles as river boats. Streets as rivers. Ever since I was very young when I would watch the heat waves come up from the tar and melt into the wheels of the cars. Streets as rivers. River man. Endless ride. I crave up river. I study the cracks in my face, they teach me things about myself. The cracks in my face teach me about others and about being pushed to extremes. Streets as rivers. As a boy I always played by the riverside, the things I saw taught me well. Sex, blood, needles, guns, hookers, faggots, pigs, hippies, muggers, lovers, killers and parents. The rain washes the blood away. Public servants remove the bodies. The faces change, the rivers remain the same. The rivers are eternal. The hearts of these rivers are pitch black. They beat not for love of life or not for love of death, but because of life and death. I am a riverman. The rivers don't judge me. The rivers are kind enough to let me taste the death inside, allowing me to taste the life in me. Passage up river affirms my existence. I have looked into the eyes of too many living dead to believe their talk for another minute. When I hear them speak of their idle dreams when I watch them torture each other, I laugh, learn and move upriver. The black water calls my name. I have no choice but to answer.

► ► ► ► ► ►

I found out what there is for me. Nothing. Nothing I can see. There's only things to learn from, and forces to make myself aware of. My brain is on a different wavelength now. Names, faces, I don't remember them. They don't matter. More and more, day by day, I break from them. There are no answers, just a lot of questions. No, scratch that. I don't have any questions anymore. No questions, nothing to explain. I can't talk to them. They have proven that to me over and over. I used to think that I could talk to her but sometimes I don't know. Sometimes when I talk to her I think that I'm being quietly laughed at. That's how I felt today. I held the phone in my hand and stared at it. Finally I just hung it up and walked away. Those phone booths are almost like coffins. I wonder if anyone ever gets buried in them.

► ► ► ► ► ►

I always compromise myself when I have to take the shit that people choose to lay on me at the time. That's when I sell out. That's when I use the word "pathetic" to describe myself. I smile and look like a jerk when I should be extracting my fist from someone's mouth. I feel like a piece of shit when anyone who's in the mood feels free to come up and do their thing to me. Yes, that's when I sell my ass out. That's when I am pathetic. That's when I'm the stupidest person I know. It's like going to a bad neighborhood, walking down its streets with money taped to your clothes and being surprised when you get robbed.

▶   ▶   ▶   ▶   ▶   ▶

I have a great deal of self-hatred like a lot of people. Sometimes I find myself in certain situations where some prick is wasting my time and enjoying it totally. With each of these occasions I find that my self-hatred and self-contempt grow. I curse my stupidity and weakness. I'm too far gone to redeem myself in my eyes and that makes it worse. I am what I hate. The shit drives me to distraction. I got my eyes. They feel like rivets pounding into my skull. To be made of lead, that's what I want sometimes.

▶   ▶   ▶   ▶   ▶   ▶

Everyone is alone. No one has real friends. Everyone has doubts about their friendships. Complete trust doesn't come from love. Complete trust comes from desperation. It's a declaration of desperation. In that way we're equal. We're all riding on that lonely train.

▶   ▶   ▶   ▶   ▶   ▶

Sometimes, I think of myself as this guy holding onto this propeller that is going full speed. My body twists and turns as I hold on for dear life. Pulled along. In motion but not really in control.

If I close my eyes I can see my self and this propeller go ripping by, the propeller cutting itself a path through dense underbrush and tree limbs. The propeller does fine. My body gets mangled as it slams into tree trunks, branches and bushes.

I need to make friends with the machine. I need to understand the power, to harness it and direct it, not be dragged along by it. I need to become one with the machine. I've got to stop holding onto the monkey's tail. I must get on the monkey's back.

► ► ► ► ► ►

Fucking weather. Give me a week's worth of nights like this and my problems with the destruction of my peace of mind will soon be over. Good. I can't take too much of that at once. I've been here a couple of days now.

The tour took a few days off. I would rather have played tonight. We won't play for another three nights. I'm sitting here in this black heat. I close my eyes, movies play in front of me. Thoughts go to Washington DC. Those crazy hot empty nights. When the hot nights hit, that's the first place my mind goes. I can see my room. I can smell it. Now I think of a hot Texas night. Playing for people who are drinking beer and spitting on me. Load out the equipment. Tired. Heat. No sleep. Beating off in the men's room of a gas station. Beating off under the florescent light, closing my eyes, trying to blot out the stench and the heat and the leeching light.

► ► ► ► ► ►

I remember when we used to travel through fields of glass. Cutting our hands and mutilating our bodies. We laughed and wiped away the blood and the dirt. On Fridays I would watch the sun go down through the window of my work place. I could almost smell the fields that glittered and waited outside for me.

► ► ► ► ► ►

The roar of airplanes arriving and departing from LAX, the drone of the north-south traffic on Pacific Coast Highway, the occasional siren. Even closer and even louder: all the birds squawking in the avocado tree in front of me. The drone of the washing machine, the phone ringing in the house across the way. I hear what sounds like a fist sized fly above my left shoulder, I flinch and look up. It's a hummingbird. Seeing the hummingbird makes me think of the title of a Henry Miller book *Stand Still Like The Hummingbird*. Now I see. A hummingbird can be perfectly still to your eye but in reality the hummingbird's wings are beating so fast you can't even see them. Stand still like the hummingbird, got it. Like I said, I can still hear summer, it's way off. Makes me think about how after I die, the following summer will not notice my absence.

► ► ► ► ► ►

I can see it in your eyes. They're wet like a dog's. You're looking for a leg to climb to keep you from drowning. Your hands reach out, clutching for something solid to hold onto. You're weak and in need. You want something to hold so you can have something to blame. Don't reach out to me. I'm drowning too.

► ► ► ► ► ►

I'm talking about ultimate deceit. I am talking about unparalleled treachery. Bottomless lies. Depths seen that are previously unimaginable. Darkness and shattering despair that could break bones. Paranoia and horror that could stop the heart. All inflicted upon one's self by one's self. The soul turns schizophrenic and goes hopelessly insane. The body is dragged like dog meat through endless and tortured forays into darkness. Hopelessly insane. What about being hopelessly sane?

► ► ► ► ► ►

Self-abandonment
Throwing yourself out of the car
Deserting yourself in the middle of nowhere

All the wars, prisons, death row gas chambers and plagues
Stacked on top of each other
Can't reach that low

▸ ▸ ▸ ▸ ▸ ▸

I stare at my hand. I put the hand through the most excruciating scrutiny I can muster. I open and close the hand. I bend each of its fingers one after the other. I stare at it so long that I no longer see it as my own. What a beautiful machine. I study the scars on the top side. I think of my hand as a machine that works for me. I could put a gun in it and the hand would shoot it. I could kill someone. I could kill myself. What if I should someday lose control of my hand? What if my hand should decide to choke me to death while I was asleep? I look at my hand again. Filthy monster, bony scarred spider, killer, filthy deceiver hand. I think about chopping it off to protect myself. What about the other hand? Would they conspire together to kill me? Would I raise the knife with my left hand to cut off the right, blade scant inches away from the hand when the left hand would make a sudden lurch and redirect the blade into my heart? I now look at both the hands as potential killers. At any moment they could grab a sharp instrument and wound me, smash my skull, gouge my eyes out and I would be helpless to stop them. I would have no choice but to watch my hands mutilate and finally murder me. I don't want to go to sleep ever again. I don't trust them, I can't. I cannot turn my eyes away from them knowing that at any moment they could turn against me. I live in the same body as my assassins. I am my worst enemy.

▸ ▸ ▸ ▸ ▸ ▸

My soul is big and as pure as the sun. My master's mercy is like horse piss, rubs salt into my wounds. His money breaks my back.

He gives me work, it destroys my mind and crushes my hands. He has a name for me. It's not what I call myself, he doesn't need me. He takes advantage of my needs. He knows I'm a hostage to hunger. He knows my fear of pain. My life is his. He gives me life. If it weren't for him I'd be dead. He is my reason for living.

► ► ► ► ► ►

Art? Fuck art. Fuck me, fuck you, fuck all of it. Just do it. Whatever it is. However it turns out is the way it is. Poetry? Fuck poetry. Fuck poets, fuck poems. If you're going to write, then shut the fuck up and write. Just like that Mexican dude in that Clint Eastwood movie when he shoots that other dude, he says, "If you're going to shoot, then shoot, don't talk."

► ► ► ► ► ►

I hate that "blunt honesty" shit
Honesty isn't blunt
Honesty is cool
Lies are blunt
You want to hurt someone?
Lie
I do it all the time

► ► ► ► ► ►

I was thinking to myself as I was entering a toilet in the Arizona desert: Think of the sun beating down on smooth polished steel. What about frozen steel? Frozen steel, like a black sun. Radiating cold, cold power. Cold energy. Frozen steel. Rigid impenetrable. Liquid steel, not hot or cold, tepid. Hard as steel because it is steel but bendable, able to adapt to the shape of its surroundings. Smooth, hard and aware. Ready for anything but having the strength of the steel to keep distance and perspective. Or to lose it if need be. That's what I must be, liquid steel.

► ► ► ► ► ►

Watch her smoke that cigarette while she sits at the bar. Watch her talk as that smoke wiggles up and down. She can talk and smoke at the same time. Doesn't that turn your ass on like a motherfucker? Think of her kissing you between puffs. Dropping ashes on your leg as she gives you head between drags. You're talking to her and she says, "Wait a minute, will ya motor mouth?" She pulls out another smoke and lights up. Imagine fucking her, she's on top, riding you. She's not even looking at you. She's looking at her nails while she takes a long drag. You call her name, she stares at you and says, "What the fuck do you want? Aren't you ever gonna come?" Imagine putting on steel cap boots and kicking her as hard as you can, over and over. Imagine kicking in her skull. See the smoke from a million cigarettes come out from her eyes. Imagine smashing her mouth with your fist. Imagine jamming a carton of smokes down her throat. Look at her at the bar smoking, letting cocker spaniels buy her drinks and light her cigarettes.

► ► ► ► ► ►

People are pigs. They want to make you soft. They try to kill you with small talk. Death to the annihilators of time.

► ► ► ► ► ►

Take my no man's body and point it towards the sun. Going home. You got me feeling like a hole dug in the ground. I got to fill up the hole. I fill it up with dirt. You got me feeling like a hole dug in the ground. I open up my window and I take a look around. I see killers looking back at me. Killers walking in the sunshine. Dirt hole man. Dig it. Dirt hole man. Pass me by. I got nothing to give you. I'm digging myself. I dig myself. I dig my hole alone. Don't want anybody in my hole with me.

▶ ▶ ▶ ▶ ▶ ▶

Your smile sends beams of sunlight through the window of my shaken asylum. It burns my eyes, my skin burns, my hair burns, my body wheezes and cracks like burning timber. I crawl inside my head. Wrap my coffin trip around my eyes and feel the pain. On the outside it's a hot sweat man burning alive. Twisting in a killer's skin. Wishing for ash but never getting any farther than animal pain. Prisoner to gravity. Prisoner to flesh. Glued to ground with shovel in hand running around in circles looking for a hole to fill with dirt.

▶ ▶ ▶ ▶ ▶ ▶

Paste people shuffling past me like corpses too stupid to die. Their clothes hold their guts in. Fear holds in the rest. Running like rats. Scurrying through the waste paper and filth to their holes before the sun goes down. They got umbilical cords of sewage wrapped around their throats. Choking on life and nursing their wounds. They'll tell you that they're loving every minute of it, just like prisoners come to love their captors. Just like roaches in a roach motel. Tasting the poison and telling you it's wine.

▶ ▶ ▶ ▶ ▶ ▶

Dreaming about the past is like squeezing a match that has just been blown out. The fire is gone but it still burns you and causes pain.

▶ ▶ ▶ ▶ ▶ ▶

Your weakness is money in their bank

▶ ▶ ▶ ▶ ▶ ▶

Today I watched three hours of rock videos with the volume turned completely off. For three hours beautiful girls rubbed my cock from outside my pants while their eyes looked at me and said "Not a chance". Didn't make me want to buy records, made me want to go outside and start stabbing people. Made me want to walk the streets for hours until I saw an incredibly beautiful girl, made me want to break her jaw with my fist. Made me want to kick her with my boots, made me want to stamp her head until her brains came out. Didn't make me want to dance. Made me want to join the Marines.

▶ ▶ ▶ ▶ ▶ ▶

I haven't seen him in eleven years. He comes up to me. Somehow I recognize him and even remember his name.

"How are you doing?" He asks.

"Working and playing." I tell him.

"I see pictures of you everywhere. You're famous. I can't believe you remember me." I shrug my shoulders and smile. I do remember him. He's a good guy. It's cool to see him again.

"I was in a band in college, we were shit. We broke up." he says.

"What do you do now?" I ask him.

"I got married. I work in advertising, it sucks." he says.

We shake hands and he turns to leave but before he does he says, "You know man, it's so good to see you again. It's so good to know you're around. I'm shit, I sold out. I fucking sold out. You're a vestige. No you are, you're a vestige. It's good to actually know someone like you. You're real. If you ever need a place to stay, call me." He hands me his card. I shake his hand

and nod my head. He leaves and I drop his card on the ground and put my shoe over it.

► ► ► ► ► ►

Get in your car. Drive into the desert. Straight into the desert. Smash your car. Taste your blood. Crawl like a snake over the wreckage. This is the greatest thing you've ever done. Examine the mutilation of your life, your shattered existence. You did it yourself. You are the boss. You're the master of your destiny. Fuck destiny. That's just a pile of trash. Destiny, no such thing. Get in the car and strap yourself in. Drive into the desert and wreck yourself. See your blood and bones and brains on the dashboard. Shut up and fuck me. Shut up and kill me. Shut up. Strap in and drive.

► ► ► ► ► ►

Sitting here looking through the bars at you. Dodging the peanuts. I watch your face fall in disappointment when I don't stoop down to eat what you've thrown my way. You watch every move I make. You fear the way I grin at your children. You see the cage you've made for me and on some days you've even felt that you should be in it. You've seen it as a pedestal and you think you'd like to try it out but only if you could leave when you wanted to. I like where I am. That's what confuses you so, that's what makes you so mad and that's when you start giving me things. I'm on the receiving end of everything. Sticking my hand out and catching your fear and hatred every day and grinning right in your face from behind the bars. Freedom is my prison. The way I have to live to be free has turned me "criminal." I refuse to be anything but free, and for this I serve a life sentence under the watchful eyes of judgment. Freedom is prison. Real freedom is like Death Row strolling down the street. I watch them run to their locked cage apartments. Bolting the doors, loading their guns, punching time clocks, blowing their brains out. They treat their freedom like a light, they turn it on and off. Living like rats. Telling me I'm dirt, pointing and whispering and laughing out loud to try and take their minds off the fear that runs their lives. Making freedom a guilt trip. Faking life to get to death as smoothly as possible.

▶ ▶ ▶ ▶ ▶ ▶

Poughkeepsie, NY Toilet: I'm standing at the urinal, taking a piss. I see a man coming at me from the left side. He's got a camera. He reaches around me and snaps a picture of me taking a piss, or more likely, a picture of a hand gripped around a meaty tree trunk of urinating flesh! Well anyway, I finish with the piss, turn around and grab the man by the lapels of his leather jacket and slam his head into the wall. I take his camera from him and ask him how it works. He points to a little red button. I click off several pictures of the floor. I should have smashed it on the floor but I didn't. I just handed it back and left.

▶ ▶ ▶ ▶ ▶ ▶

I don't want to stay out of the sun. I want my skin to turn to leather. I want the elements to take their toll on my body. I want all mutilation, tattooing and other bodily damage to be deep, massive and clearly visible. I want to do everything the hard way. I want to walk alone in the desert. I want to walk alone in the steaming jungle. If the ride becomes smooth, I'll create catastrophes to keep it rough. I want to claw forward. The past is my enemy. The present is all there is for me. I want to love completely. I want to hate beyond conviction. I crave deep breaths that feel like inhaling fire. I will never run from pain. I'm crawling in absolute darkness, underground, waiting for the summer heat to drag me away into the depths of madness. Every year the phosphorescent summer comes burning like a hell hound on my trail. It sticks its thumbs through my collar bone and shakes me senseless, and I dance, sweating, clenched and jointless. I'm waiting to swing and dance and sweat and scream.

► ► ► ► ► ►

He's here to sell pot. I knew it before he pulled it out. I could tell by the way he hung around the place as we were loading in the equipment. He made small talk with some of the locals in that eager disinterested manner that gives them away every time. Now he's backstage, slight beer belly, scraggly hair and sneakers. He tries to talk to me about tattoos and I cut him short by telling him I am not interested in the purchase of any pot thank you. He shuffles away to find some other people to sidle up to. He looks like he's the coke type too. He's got that weak wormy cutthroat thing about him. I feel like kicking him so I can hear him nervously laugh and say some chicken shit line. I feel like picking up the folding chair I'm sitting in and bashing him with it, so I can hear him say, "Hey man! what the fuck?" while I shrug and smile.

► ► ► ► ► ►

I haven't fucked in over four weeks. I got my calendar out and checked. That's almost all I've been thinking about the last few days. I think I forget how it feels to fuck. That's what always happens. Beating off doesn't help me much but it does often make me laugh. Some jerk standing around with his dick in his hand looking all messed up, trying to remember something he's trying so hard to forget.

► ► ► ► ► ►

I'm in this club, sitting in a room, trying to get some time to myself. There's this drunk woman staggering around being loud and obnoxious. She starts talking to me while I'm trying to read. "Oh don't bother with trying to understand what I'm saying. I'm so messed up on gin I don't know what the fuck is going on." She rattles on, spraying my cheek with her saliva. I feel like giving her a quick shot to the head to get her away from me but I think I had better not. A man comes over to her, looks at me and glances an apology and leads her away.

Later on, walking into the room, I see the two of them cutting up coke on a plate with a butter knife. The man looks at me and shrugs, "It's shitty stuff, this little bit cost me fifty bucks. I already lost that at the door." I ask, "You're putting on this gig?" And he says, "Yea, me and my wife here. I'd turn you on but this is all I've got. I swear." "It's really shit," his wife assures me. I nod and watch the man roll up a dollar bill to do the coke with. He does the line and hands the dollar bill to his wife. She does hers and then sponges the rest off the plate with a moistened index finger. "We both went to jail for this stuff," says the man. "Once it's in your blood, you just can't get off it. We've tried, believe me." His conversation trails off into some shit about how their lives have no direction and how I have it lucky and how they don't feel like living sometimes. Much later I'm loading equipment into the truck. The man comes up to me with a small child. "This is our little boy." I nod and keep loading the truck.

What a life that kid has ahead of him. Hey kid, your parents did time in prison for drugs. Your mamma is showing me her tits and stumbling stupid drunk, just another drunk. Your daddy cuts lines of cheap coke real good, has he taught you to do that yet? Has he turned you on yet? Have you ever asked him what it's like to sit in a cell and dry out? Well, you can always ask your mom. They're gonna teach you a whole lot kid, and if you don't watch out, you'll end up a chip off the old rock. Your parents are killing you. You know what they told me about you. They said that since they had you they are in shackles. Your mother looked at me and asked, "What were we supposed to do, have an abortion?" You're a pain in their ass kid. You're unwanted. There will probably be times when you wish you were an abortion. You'll think to yourself. *If they hate life so much then how come they had me?* Your parents are weak. They're gonna drag you down to their level, they always do.

► ► ► ► ► ►

The man who has all of nothing:
Life pulls me down the drain
Sleep throws me into a black hole
My body spins and sinks
Sex makes me feel like a servant
Love makes me feel like a slave
Hate puts me in a prison cell
Freedom terrifies me

► ► ► ► ► ►

Looking for that Solid Sender
Virgin boys dying in the steaming jungles of Vietnam.
Watching the streets fill up
With come and blood
The sun hangs high and dirty
The music is insane
The clocks stop
Hot fuck war children claw the streets
Show their teeth
Howl, moan
Rut and slash
Find senselessness for the first time.

► ► ► ► ► ►

I'm sitting on a green lawn watching the sun go down. The sky is clear blue. To my right is a cherry blossom tree in full bloom. Its red and white tones cut a sharp contrast against the sky. The colors are so vivid, I can do nothing but stare, scarcely able to believe them. then I think of some acne-faced white boy walking scared shitless through a jungle in Vietnam. He sees a freshly slaughtered family lying face down on the trail, their limbs twisted in unnatural forms. Large parts of their bodies torn away by bullets. He sees green and red and other colors. Years later he sits on the lawn and listens to the birds in the cherry blossom tree. I wonder if his colors look like mine.

▶ ▶ ▶ ▶ ▶ ▶

Five mile man on a ten mile trail: Shaking hands with a snake asking him if he's my brother. The starvation mind. Incineration camp. The disease runs wild, joining hands. The disease spreads. The disease triumphs and celebrates and does the annihilation dance. The bodies fall and stack. The bodies pound the streets The disease spreads. The disease triumphs. Shaking hands. A friend to all men. Bodies pile high. They blot out the sun. The living burn the dead. And the ashes settle. And disease triumphs.

▶ ▶ ▶ ▶ ▶ ▶

All around me knives pressing into my flesh. Beady eyes staring me down, up and down, in and out, all around me. Clever lies. Lies that make me feel so good keeps me on the line. Keeps me swinging on a braided chain. Keeps me climbing a hope rope. Choking and pulling.

▶ ▶ ▶ ▶ ▶ ▶

I was given the glittering odd keys to the highway trail. I hold them in my hand as I walk along on the crusty edge of the horizon. I'm a five mile man on a ten mile trail and my bones are starting to burn underneath my flesh as I walk towards the sun.

➤ ➤ ➤ ➤ ➤ ➤

I call her on the phone. I try to talk to her. The words don't come out very well. I tell her that it's hard for me to talk to her on the phone. It sounds like I'm bothering her from the way she talks to me. I don't really have anything to say, I don't even know why I called in the first place, maybe I just wanted to hear her voice. I tell her that when I get back home in a few days I want a few hours alone before I see her. I tell her this because it's very hard to come down from the trip I'm on. It's very hard to just walk out of one world into another. I tell her that if I can get a few hours to myself to just catch my breath then I'll be better off. This seems to make her mad. I tell her not to take it wrong and it's not that I don't want to see her right away. It's that when I do see her I want to see her and be with her without a bunch of stuff swimming around the back of my head. She says that maybe she should just wait for a few days, will that be enough time? She doesn't know where I'm coming from. I can't explain. I say goodbye and I hang up the phone. I sit down and wrap my arms around myself and squeeze tight. Sometimes I think that I'm from another planet. I used to feel lonely at times. Now I just feel <u>only</u>. That hurts worse but it makes me see things very clearly. I have no one but myself to identify with. I do my best to communicate all things with her but I don't do a very good job. When I try and fail, I feel farther away from her than before. That was the feeling I had when I hung up the phone. The distance. I only have myself. Now I don't know about how I'm going to be when I get back there, I really don't know, it's so hard to come back.

I don't expect her to understand anything about me. I'm a soldier and I travel through the jungle. I know what I know and I'm the only one who understands my trip. I hate having to explain myself, it's like having to build a house out of air. I have no explanation to give to anyone.

When I go away and come back after a long period of time, I have to get to know her all over again, it's hard on both of us. When I come back, I'm a different person and sometimes I think that when I come back from one of these trips, she'll be tired of all these different people calling her name.

▶ ▶ ▶ ▶ ▶ ▶

I sit. I don't make a sound. I wrap my arms around my torso and squeeze. There's only one number. The number one. Two people can't be one. That's a lie that people use to try to escape themselves. I'm one and I'm all of one.

Inside I'm running wild killing and swinging from a chain. Outside, they're throwing sticks and stones, trying to teach me a lesson. Showing me the meaning of pain. Showing me the meaning of weakness. Beating my brains out and telling me that they're helping me, trying to make me better. Trying to make me mindless so I'll fit in. I'm laughing in their face. Every day I wipe my ass with their minds.

▶ ▶ ▶ ▶ ▶ ▶

I see breeders in the alley. The male carrying one of the offspring. They cross the street, another one of the offspring follows behind on foot. They look like a funeral procession. A little death trip parade. Breeders. Someone, somewhere, would probably call me obscene for saying that. Breeders, living the good life. Breeding pets. Breeding little minds to twist and fuck up. Calling me obscene. The son of a soldier. I jumped out of the line before his plane crashed into his driveway. Breeders. Obscene. They get so angry when someone kicks the dream, get all uptight when someone pulls at the seams and sees the holes in the ship's bottom. I walk by and give it a shove and watch the feathers fly. Breeders in the alley, staring at me, aiming guns in their minds.

▶ ▶ ▶ ▶ ▶ ▶

I walked through many plastic temples. My feet got swollen from sharp glass and spider bites. The inhabitants screamed at my back as I left. The temples were never the same. My existence is sheer defilement.

▶ ▶ ▶ ▶ ▶ ▶

This is a soul sucking place I live in. Everyone around here is some kind of scientist, running around under the sun. Looking for an asshole to rape. I'm not looking under rocks for a place to hide. I'm not looking for a place to live or die. I'm not looking for escape or a way to buy in. I'm looking at you.

▶ ▶ ▶ ▶ ▶ ▶

I'm walking through a thieving jungle. Killing myself. Living in the big house of the elements. One day I took a look in the mirror and saw the lines in my face. I started laughing. The sun, the rain and the fuckers are taking their toll on my carcass. Pulling my flesh tight over my bones. I see what's happening to me. I know what's going on around me. I see the rats running wild in the temple, I see the flies crawling on the dead man's face. I see my eyes sucking into my sockets. I know what's happening to me, and I don't want to miss a second of it.

▶ ▶ ▶ ▶ ▶ ▶

Coming down kicking through the hole
I got no opponents I bring no news

I leave no victims
No trail of broken hearts
No tracks that you can follow or would want to
I have no brains
That's what you told me
I'm a self serving loud mouth jerk
I got nothing to say, so I say it very loudly
Right to your face
I'm not responsible
I have no brains remember?

► ► ► ► ► ►

You got buttons. I push them all the time. You're better than a video game. You got triggers. I pull them all the time. And you tell me I'm on a death trip? You got bars that you live behind. You and all your monkey friends. I don't roll shit into little balls and call it anything other than shit in little balls. So if I seem a little brainless to you, that's cool.

► ► ► ► ► ►

Walking down the basement stairs trail. No one around. Not even my shadow. This is where it gets real good. Real good. I don't care if they don't know my name. I don't care if they don't listen to what I say. I wasn't talking to anyone in particular. I hear the screams through the apartment walls. I hear all the choking sounds. Murder dogs ripping each other's throats out. Doing ceremonial dances around large piles of garbage. Making signals with their hands. Looking straight ahead. I'm watching from a long way off. I walk the trail and I laugh at the blood, it's all doggy guts to me. Put it in cans and feed it to your family and other people you don't know.

► ► ► ► ► ►

I want to help people, all people. Especially people in need. Like if a junkie needs help tying off, I want to be there for him. If a guy wants to shoot his wife, and he's short of bullets, he can turn to me. If a kid needs some helpful tips on how to kill his father, I'll be there with pro-tips to see him through. Everybody needs a helping hand here and there. Hey man, I want to be there. If you ever need your wrists slashed... reach out. I'm there for you.

▶ ▶ ▶ ▶ ▶ ▶

Two strangers meet somewhere, the location doesn't really matter. Neither one talks to the other, no conversation is needed. They go to a room to fuck. They fuck without talking. Each looks away from the other while they do their thing. They finish as professionally as possible. They separate and sit on opposite sides of the bed with their backs to each other and dress. They finish dressing. The one closest to the door leaves first. The other waits a short time and proceeds out the door.

▶ ▶ ▶ ▶ ▶ ▶

I would show my kid videotaped footage of myself and the kid's mother fucking on the night the kid was conceived. I would then show him a video of the child's mother giving birth to him. Years later, he will show his kid a video of himself shooting me in the face.

▶ ▶ ▶ ▶ ▶ ▶

There should be films shown in classrooms of males and females masturbating in all kinds of different ways to help kids along on their way. Get people that the kids respect, like the members of Motley Crue. How about Ruth Westheimer, she's supposed to be so open about everything. I would like to see how Bruce Springsteen does it, or how about Sheila E.? Mike Jackson! Beat

It! Linda Evans rolling around the floor of her estate with her hand jammed up her night gown, that would be ripe. The kids need a break these days, they're kept in the dark about so much stuff, they get into drugs before sex. Too much TV violence these days. I say give 'em real guns and let them go out there and check it out for themselves. Teach 'em that old immigrant zeal.

▸ ▸ ▸ ▸ ▸ ▸

The boy with the world in his eyes: He seemed totally aware of everything around him and to everything he took a gentle fascination. I say gentle, what I mean to say is that he was affected by a nature scene the same way he would be affected by a multi-car collision. He saw death as part of life, intertwined and beautiful. People thought that he was odd and disturbed. The way he would smile when someone would come to him with their problems. I never thought him odd at all. I saw him more as an open door, a man at one with the elements. On some days, I could look into his eyes and I would swear I could see all the way into his soul. On other days, his eyes were clouded and dull. It was on days like these that he spoke of feeling very old inside himself. He told me that sometimes he wished he could get out of himself for awhile. I never really understood him. I would ask him what he was about, he would smile and tell me I had someone a lot more important than him to learn about. When I would ask him who that was he would laugh and say nothing. It took me awhile, but now I see who he was talking about.

▸ ▸ ▸ ▸ ▸ ▸

The world hangs on a gleaming chain
Turning black blue
It spins like a sick dog running in circles
I see the whole world spinning around
It makes me sick to see the trash fly through the air

I dreamt that the whole thing burned up
All the little ants ran around with their hair on fire
Screaming as the whole lying shit house fell to the ground

▶ ▶ ▶ ▶ ▶ ▶

The dirt children, dancing in the city streets. Ghetto winds
blowing through thin summer cloth. Running with flowers.
Running with knives. Driving the new day insane before it has a
chance to say its name. Ambulances screaming necks into
rubber bands. Dying leading the dying to the repair shop.
Broken skulls and broken hearts dragged through endless days
and nights of heat that shows no sign of releasing its lovers from
its death grip. Summer heat handcuffs its prisoners to their
sweaty carcasses and watches what happens as the day melts
down on their brains. I have hallucinations of vultures. I see
them perched on every tree limb. They wait so patiently. I feel
honored by their presence.

▶ ▶ ▶ ▶ ▶ ▶

I've got a roach crawling on my hand. Should I kill it? I don't
know, let me think. It was the first thought that popped into my
head. I raised my other hand to crush it but all of a sudden I
stopped dead in my tracks. I thought about all the people who
think of me the same way I think of this roach. All the people who
see me as a filthy crawling piece of vermin that should be
destroyed. Hah! The roach is my brother and long may he
prosper!

▶ ▶ ▶ ▶ ▶ ▶

Sitting in the electric house watching the spiders crawl up and
down the wall. Feet on the floor. I'm not going to move an inch,
I gotta brainstorm that's giving my head a ride. The eyes of all the

pictures on my wall are staring at me. Sitting in the electric house wired to the night. Strapped to the electric chair watching the spiders crawl up and down the wall. This is the endless night. The one I had always wanted. Got a handful of dice rolling big numbers, killing time. The spiders are laughing at me. The world is laughing at me. The words are flying back and forth. This is the electric house. I am the watchman at the electric house strapped into the endless night riding low and covered. I saw her with a flamethrower walking my way. She was screaming about the addiction and how hard it is to pull away. She said that she was bailing out and that she was going to leave a trail of fire. I said if she had any guts she would leave no trail and burn alone. It's so hard to burn alone, but if you want to burn completely you have to burn alone.

▸ ▸ ▸ ▸ ▸ ▸

Sitting in an alley watching the sun set. Its light coats the bricks and the concrete with dirty burned out red. Makes me think of bloodshot-eyed drunks lounging in these flooded gateways. Imbibed on the stench of rotting garbage and stale urine. They lean against the brick and feel their thirst kick and claw at them. A monkey on his back. A child who's never satisfied with his toys. A monkey with brass knuckles.

▸ ▸ ▸ ▸ ▸ ▸

Warm Kentucky wind blows past me, the sun sets perfectly. It always seems that the breezes blow sweeter in ghettos. The birds chirp happier, the flies buzz louder. I watch this old dude in stiff working clothes walk around a trashed out cement parking lot like he was contemplating some lush meadow. All the beer cans and pieces of broken glass make it look like the place is a ghost town. Tomorrow morning the sun will be high, perched like a smoldering god. Its rays will bludgeon the bricks and I'll be gone from here.

► ► ► ► ► ►

I am the dark train. I am the long ride. Me and the highway taking the long way around. Long Dark Ride. Whistle blows in the dark, drives me insane.

Bang!

Knife Street

Knife Street
Everything you want:
Cocksuckers, killers, diseases, love, war
People are geniuses here
They have found all kinds of ways to destroy you
They are also your friends
They want to fuck and kill you
Talking big and then shooting you full of holes
Full of death
What the hell do you want?
Don't stick around here for too long or you'll get it
It all starts and ends here
All your dreams get raped here
The human will be overcome
The human will be destroyed
By other humans who couldn't handle their minds
Who couldn't handle their own balls
You're going to get it
In your mind
In your ass
In your veins
In your mail
In your soldier's hearts
It's hot
It's burning
It's real
Your mother raping your wounds
It's time for you to get the real feel of things
I want to see what you have been doing in your nightmares
You got sold out
You thought that they liked you
They are scientists
Checking out their new drugs on you

And you like it
It takes you away and gives you back to them
You're always getting delivered
The ozone layer breaking doesn't scare crack dealers one bit
More blood
More good times
More high roller games
It's all coming to a head
You're riding the big wave this time
You will be right in time for this one
That's why you are going to get destroyed
You never learned restraint
Never had the guts
You will learn mercy
It'll be encoded into your DNA
While you bleed and shit your pants
Here's a hole
Put your dick into it
Put your money into it
Like a circus ride
Get on the monkey's back and get taken for a ride
The garbage truck is coming
Throw yourself and your kin on board, you're going home
You made it straight and flat and now it's killing you
I'm laughing, it's not me
I don't exist, remember?
I didn't do the right dance
Never mind me, this is your party
I am the wall flower
Un-addicted
I don't think you're tough
I think you're on drugs
I think you swallowed one of their super vitamins
And now you're running wild
I see you driving by, car stereo blasting thunder

Painted face cracking like a clown's
Shake hands with the thirteen year-old who sells PCP
Look at the black eyes
His father's eyes
The nights in the black room full of fear
Cutting his teeth
Learning a new and harsh language
Now he brings it to you
I see them, you
Lining up to be skinned
Seeing if they got what it takes
Getting their wings, getting them clipped
*"We come from the suburbs to get destroyed. There's nothing like
it out there. We come here to see all the freaks and the violence. Hey,
who needs movies? Last week me and my friends wasted a fag and
we got his ears to prove it, you wanna see? I got them right here.
Wanna beer?"*
Knife Street always waiting
A mecca of understanding
*"Bleed on me, puke on me. It's all been done before. I don't care if
you live or die on me. I'm here for you, here to serve you. Here to
suck you right through your shoes. I got all the time in the world."*
So it speaks
The Beast is always hungry
I can hear it at night,
Howling, telling me to get up and dance
To come into the fire
Get wet until the blood turns to dust
Rehab to rehab
Front door drugs, back door drugs
You can always score again
Junkies getting back into harness
After being free from the monkey for so long
So good to be back home
You're falling now, calling for help

They come running to give you more poison
Digging your grave deeper and deeper
The fourteen year-old boy who sells you his dick
The burning bum
The long lines
You never get enough
Your stamina is amazing
Bullets, lots of bullets
Where do you go?
Call the hot line
They're waiting to destroy you
The flowers explode
The cunning mind of a junkie
The art of lies
The blade that cuts so well
You bleed invisibly
The howling sun to take you away
Look into the eyes of the whore
Endless and burning
More truth than you can take
Run to the bar
It's time for more poison
Tie one on, it's the weekend
They said that it's ok
Your shoes covered with vomit
Are wings to take you higher
You earned this
Open up, relax
The more you relax the less it will hurt
It's taking years, this appointment
Do you ever wonder why you never get better?
The killers are lonely
They wrap the disease around you
They built the fire on the outskirts of town
Salvation vacation null and void salvation

The wind up and the pitch
Coming down from speed
She sees all the things for what they are
She never knew how ugly it all was
The drugs helped
They got her in touch with a lot of the bad voodoo that she had
been missing. She told me that it was a lot better for her now that
she had a handle on it all. She said there was a lot of creeps out
there. *"The more you do, the more you want to do. The more of
these people you meet, the more you like them. They become your
family. They take you in, they look after you. They sell you things,
they cut you deals. They help you with your habit. Without them
it's too hard to survive being hooked. I guess when you get into it,
you have to get into it all the way. It's my life now."*
Slam monkey slam
Grinning bloody moon
Are you ready for the big one?
The super abortion?
Like a crack dealing uber insect
24 houraday mother comin' for ya
You're like that guy
That living-dying god, Evil Knevil
Taking anything
A handful to get you on the trail
A handful to get you down it
High school life
Drug time, big time
A time of discovery
Like getting the shit kicked out of you for the first time
The first joint, Death's handshake
Welcome to the Loser Club
Sample goods from our duty-free shop
It's your duty
It's part of growing up to be a good machine
Rock out on this trip

No one has ever taken this ride before
All those things that you heard, about how they took too much
Killed themselves
Turned into hallway legends, super freaks
Terminal subterranean-minded slow boys and easy girls
That will never happen to you
They didn't know what they were doing
They didn't have the right stuff
Old wives tales
Like thinking that you can fly
Like forgetting how to breathe
Whoops, no sweat
A lie
You're the super thing
You'll never fall, you'll never die
The old wives rolling on the floor
Choking on blood and laughter
Fingering their scarred sex
Praying for you to get on with it
Join the club take a step down
It feels like up doesn't it?
Fly like an eagle fuck head
You look sexy with a tag
on your John/Jane Doe toe
Slabbed at the city morgue
Chillin'
Boogie chillin'!
I can hear you revving your engines
The highways are yours tonight
Get the Andy Warhol action
Twisted accordion car, pedal to the metal
Let god put on the brakes
Attention thieves: The meat is here!
The veins are swollen
Come forward out of the darkness

Show them that they matter
Do what you do best
Go for that genetic imperative rock
Make'em into headlines
Get your paycheck and head for the hills
Castration starts in the womb
Pollution starts in the home
Let's make this a big year for disease
Let's take it over the top!
Always go to the source for your information
A lie is best when it's fresh
The bum in the pool of blood
He is scraped off the sidewalk and taken away
The Mexican attendant hoses off the remains of the dead nameless
They are in love
They share everything
Nights of sex and sweat
Needles
Lies
A need to keep the monkey happy
The monkey wears a three piece suit
Works the high road
Keeps his blood clean
No monkey on the monkey's back
All for you
It's all coming your way
Like the fall preview that never stops
The smell of heartbreak comes running at your face
Spring makes you cry at night
Thinking of the way it used to be
The good times
Times that you know nothing about
Times you got out of a book, out of a movie
A rose out of the beast's mouth
The night rapes and confuses

We got the technology
No one gets out without getting a taste
Look at the survival rate
So far they are perfect
"We would like to thank you for making this the biggest year in our career. Without you being so god damned helpful, there is no chance we could have done it. Thanks to you, it works. We take you and take you and you keep on taking it and taking it and we don't see how you can do it but you do it and we thank you. God bless."
This glorious violence
How long can you keep it up?
I love the fury of the dying breed
It never gets as active as it does right before
The whole thing shuts down
It loves the conviction of a loser
Only a loser has any
I love the lies of the well-adjusted
It's not the truth, but an amazing substitute
It does the job
If it doesn't, you pay someone else to make it work
I love the music of your dying world
The sound of people crawling up their own asses
The children barely escaping the destructive confusion of their parents
Learning crime as survival
Dodge the hand
Duck the needle
Sidestep the drunk who gave birth to you
Monster to monster in your image
Hello, new meat!
Alcohol's volcanic love bite
The youth scarred, sharpening their teeth
Getting ready to try out all the new things that you taught them
They always do it better
Up the ante
Make your parents proud

Letter from jail:
"Dear mom and dad. I made it. I am in the roughest ward of the whole prison. I have tried to kill myself three times, and all three times I have been stopped by this one guard. I am working hard in shop class saving my money so I can buy him off and kill myself without hassle. I know I can do it."
Denial
It's always someone else with the problems
Some poor jerk
Never you
Stay away from those who kick the real jams
It's too real
You make me sick
It's ok
You will taste the blood
It will be too late to do anything about it
Your angry words
Can't you see that you aren't at war with me?
You don't know me
Don't give yourself that much credit
It's all yours now
You are the one who will have to be responsible for all this blood
The saddest song ever written
Will be written by a human
Probably some white dude
Talking about what's happening right now
I'm not always sure of myself but I am sure of you
I'm sure you will do all the things that you set out to do
Do it well
How much do they want?
They want it all
Like the football coach said,
"Make it hurt now so it won't hurt later."
Never seems to stop hurting
Take care of it with the pain killer

The weekend approaching
Ready to spit blood fire gasoline
Obituary writers lick their lips in anticipation
"It's really hard for us obit guys. We do a lot of sitting around it's not as bad as it used to be. In fact, it's getting better all the time. We love the holidays. It's a real call to arms for us. Don't take this the wrong way, but we all cheer in the office when the reports come in. 'Die baby, die!' we always say. Not that we are into people dying, but hey, it does give us a chance to flex our fingers if you know what I mean. So yeah, we like it when someone gets smeared out all over the highway. But it's only because we like to work. You know what I mean?"
The Bud trucks are starting their engines
The bars are oiling their taps
The whores are sharpening their blades
The pigs are cleaning their guns
Getting ready for the good times
FM radio barking out the commands
The religion
The love call for the death trip riders
"Rent a limo for that weekend concert night out. With all the police on the road, you know you're going to get busted! So party hard and leave the driving to someone else. Don't get busted! Ride in style."
Can you hear it?
In the street lights
In the stores
In the roar of midday downtown
Locking and loading
Pumping up the insanity
Get busy
So many stories
All lies
No one really ever goes to jail
No one really ever gets raped
Do they?

If it's not you, then who cares?
Some strange celebrity
Rape victim number two million
*"Hello and welcome to Rape Rap, the call-in show with a differ-
ence. We take male and female callers that have never been raped,
that's right, never been raped and we hear their questions. We give
advice on how to prepare for the first one. We advise those who
have never had intercourse before, how to relax so penetration will
be as painless as possible! At Rape Rap, we say, hey, lets get it out
in the open so we can deal with it! You're not alone on this. We are
here to help. We can even arrange rape sessions. Tell you the hot
locations to get raped. How to dress to attract the rapist that you
have been having those nightmares about. It's free and lines are
open. Call in now!!!"*
Do you ever look at your hands and see blood?
Good times
Punches in the stomach
All for you, by you, to you, from you
You scare me
I'm running
On top of the bar she is dancing
Underage and unsure
The beast is getting hungry
It's the same old thing
She is from the mid west
Looking for something different
This will have to do for now
It won't always be this way
But for right now,
She can pay the beast
To let her live and drink the water
Good drugs in the water
Help you to sleep
Kill the pain
Kill the madness

Get on with the television show
The guy got wasted because he loved men
Another man killed him
It's a man's world
You ladies wouldn't understand
You just better get used to the stupid violence
Buckle up
It's a man's man's man's man's man's Knife Street
Get in the car and duck down
The killer intent of the boy hooker
The world's hardest hustling night act
A cure for every cure
We will get you yet
Using the word nigger out loud
Under the breath
"Oh honey, you have nigger on your breath."
Cars going by
Mario Andretti killers
Master of love call out
You would like to think that
They are another breed
But you are the same kind
Me too
That's why I'm running scared
Away from the party
I'm thinking about
Tearing my face off
While I still have one
Baby born without finger prints
File it under missing person
So many of them
Shapeless remaining nameless
Boogie till you vote
No more poison
No more pain

That's not the way it goes around here
You want humanity?
You have to pay the price
Have you paid your dues?
Have you gone up on the cross yet?
The hard dirty blood of justified action
Fellas, it doesn't get any better than this
Fella with a beer in his hand
Fella with a gun in his mouth
Waiting on the god with the paycheck
All the time, they're trying to be angels
Seeing if they can fly
They get scraped off the ground by the other gods
The ones who didn't make it to the bank on time
Didn't make it to the morgue
Not you?
Oh yes, you
Pay them to love you
Pay for the lie
Be nice to me
Don't kill me
Another has been eaten by the Beast:
*"The war was something that we could never get too far away from.
We decided to make it our lives instead. You know how it is, they
tell you it's going to be one way and then when you get there, whoa
boy, are you in for a surprise. That's it. That's our lives. This war.
This disease. You're never going to get out of it, why don't you just
get into it? I could show you some nifty dance steps. Hey wait,
don't go over there. Those guys will shoot you. Stay here with your
own kind."*
Broken knuckle blues
Real love songs
Sung by the men with no real teeth
Lived by the ones with the old stare
The broken hands

The white noise television sets
Old wars screaming through the night
A lot of vomit
A lot of hard blood
The kind that comes out,
A bit at a time
Hanging on like bionic ticks
No lust for life
It's just love of disease
The ones that have become addicted to the disease
The survivors
They got smart and learned how to kill
I can see it
Evolution happening right before my eyes
Babies born with broken knuckles
Already addicted to violence
It's good but it's going to get better
The hot nights on the roof
Sex and desperation
Thoughts of escape
Pure fantasy
Don't let the master catch you thinking for yourself
There will be crime events in stadiums soon
Have a ghetto in dodger stadium
Turn two gangs loose in there
Give them the weapons they want
Let them do what they do best
What they have been taught
Allow them to follow their genetic imperative
The crowd will go wild
The fans dressed in colors
Everybody who hates their mate, raise their hand!
All of those who have been thinking about killing them testify!
At night I go out and listen to the beast
I hear it sharpening its fangs

Eating whores, jacking speed
The beast is out tonight
Filling them with hate and soul power
"If I were you I would take it to the street."
The ambulance drivers are like those pit stop teams
There to get rid of that pesky bullet and get you back into the game
"Ok. You're all patched up. Now get back out there and give them hell. We don't want anyone to think that you're some kind of slacker right? Right! You have a job to do like all the rest of us. Hey, if it wasn't for you guys going out there and getting shot, stabbed, slaughtered and mutilated, us guys would be like that guy in the Maytag ad, right? You're hot. Now here's some free bullets. Get out of here. You're a maniac."
He drove your daughter all the way home in the trunk of his car
He shoved a coke bottle up your dad
He did a lot of things
There's no time to list them all here
But you can go check it out
It's a pretty heavy duty achievement list
A man on a mission
A real work ethic happening here
A hall of fame for murderers
It's called Channel 7
All the stars come out at night to suck and eat you
Get to the finish line
The dead line
The white line
The fine line
Think of what that is
What separates you from them
Television
Money
A car
The color of your skin
The year you were born

Fences
Green lawns
Ignorance
Apathy
Fear of: life, death, bullets, work, confrontation
What you are
What you are becoming
Having to deal with yourself for the first time in forever
Like kissing a new stranger
Not recognizing the breath
A destructive stranger coming to call
Coming to ruin your life
Knife Street passing through you like a train
On your hands and knees in the back of the limo
Choking on the poison
Villages burning
These sad tortured skies
This ugly heart
The black blood
Feel life's pain
A curse for you
Roll with it
Swim through it
Disco abortion
It's alright if your name isn't signed to it
Do you have a lover?
Look into its eyes
Feel the pain
How many times have you lied today?
Knife Street pushing through your chest
Light up another smoke
Finger your lucky number
Await the gas
Gas light
Arc light

How will you handle the final shove?
The final love?
The big joke fist?
The big rock down your throat?
The bitter taste
Overwhelming
Do you feel it rising?
Oh baby, I can feel it
Give it to me
I don't care who's looking
I don't care what happens
Sex like a suicide pact
The last lie will be the best
That's the way to do it
Save the best for last
And then you fall
Diseased and breathless, cold and friendless
Sullen and endless, distorted and selfless
Broken beyond repair
A bad machine with bad habits
Make your eyes look backwards
Through your mind
Try to find the face
The first face
Of the million who took you for everything
Try to remember the place where the first violation occurred
Was it a good time?
Did you get your money's worth?
Do you feel the rope around your neck?
Do you see the man on the corner?
Smiling and holding his hand out?
Is it real or is it you?
Is that a window or is that a mirror?
Is that a limousine or a hearse?
Did you win, lose or draw?

Are you fearless yet?
Have you seen enough to where you can't see anymore?
Can you laugh at everything yet?
Our ancestors had bigger tear ducts, but smaller brains
Locked in tight, making love to the machine
Modern gods:
Smith and Wesson
Jack Daniels
They help you see who you are
How much you can take and how low you can go
In the dead of the night I can hear every alarm in the world
Ringing
Buzzing
Screaming:
Don't get destroyed
Don't get taken
Don't get choked on your emotions
Get your arm out of the machine
Get the monkey off your back
No one listens to alarms
The sound
So loud
So clear
Goes unnoticed
Pathetic
Addict
Hand in the machine
Somewhere,
There's got to be a prayer for you
Somewhere, a bullet is flying,
Looking for a home
A roach is giving birth
Thank god all is not lost
There's still something they can take
Your soul's not enough

Your mind was too easy
Are you into this or not?
Stop hiding
Give it up
You're blocking
Watch out
You might get busted for resisting unrest
Last week she got visited by a man with two heads
His blood rushed to both and he did what there was to do
She's a comedian of sorts now
She doesn't talk but she sure walks funny
You're getting pushed
Shoved
Smile and love it
It's all on file,
And soon we'll all know the truth about you
What little there is of it left
You're like us
A million pairs of hands
Reach out to you from the subway
Calling to you:
Get up
Get into it
Get involved
Shake the man's hand boy
Shake your father's dick boy
Shake your past
Shake the recurring reality
Shake the rage
Hey, cool it man
You're shaking
Both eyes open one eye blind
Turned the other cheek so many times,
He broke his neck and died
Pity

Could've gotten a few more years out of him
Do you ever hear the drums
The call of the warriors?
Do you ever feel like you're walking through someone else's movie?
Like you don't belong?
It's ok
You belong
You're locked in so tight,
The first time you get out will be the only time
And the drag is, you'll know what hit you
You'll have two hundred shares of it
Just understand this:
You were never one of the beautiful people
Sweep away the ash
Separate the cinder from the bone and teeth
Separate the humanity from the scum
Understand the impossibility of separating something from itself
That whore staking out that corner
Hands on hips
Wide stance
Hungry
New food for the new flesh
War stories fill the air
Find the jungle in the city
Soon, everywhere will be the bad part of town
Coffee, tea, or a shot?
This time it comes down hard
In brutal, choking, easy-to-read user friendly language
Beautiful
Terminal
Action
It's gonna be a party y'all
You learn from criminals
Too chicken-hearted to identify yourselves
To choose what side you're on

You choose it or it chooses you
Hunts you down
Lines you up
You know, there's no place like home
With all the things that will get done to you
By you,
You might as well say goodbye to the home front
Take a spin through the old streets
Take a friend
Show your friend where you got raped
Show your friend where you saw that man get shot
Don't show your friend where you used to jump and play
Don't let anyone know you ever did anything like that
They will use it against you
All the things that happened,
They don't count
Remember your mother's embrace
Things are breaking down
They are lying at your feet
Get your galoshes out
Don't get any on you
This game will not tilt
This fire will only stop when there is nothing left to burn
What a beautiful inferno
A siren song
Knife Street dying
The big cleansing
Iron sanity
From the ruins, a bigger, better one will be built
We know ourselves very well now
Fire up the engine
Put another child on the grill
Get psyched
Get ready
Get set

The beast is screaming
Filling your ears
Telling you to come forward
There's no place to hide
On Knife Street

American Hardcore

Checkout at the market. There she is baby in one arm, five year-old at her feet. Purchase: Six of Bud, fifth of Old Granddad, pack of Kools, potato chips (bar-b-que), tampons. The cashier checks the bruises on her arms rings it all up she is short, she puts the tampons back. Priority.

◇　◇　◇

Yelling. Crushing noise level. Terror then he hits her. She cries. Things get quiet. Then it starts again. Locked in his room, the boy sits on the floor next to his bed. That's the place he goes when they go at it. Mother and alien. This man/boyfriend. The one who watches television and drinks long cans of malt liquor in the dark. Sometimes the alien is there when his mother isn't. The alien doesn't talk. The alien drinks, beats mother and watches television. The boy knows that he is lucky the alien doesn't beat on him. Aliens beat on his friends. He sees them at school with their bruises. He figures that aliens are here to make life hard as possible.

◇　◇　◇

He steals his father's pot and sells it at school for beer money. He gets drunk whenever possible. Fucks shit up. Cuts classes, comes into third period high, steals shit from stores at the local mall. Wrecked his friend's father's car. Listens to FM radio. Watches television. Found a video of his father screwing some blonde chick his age. Knows the alarm codes to all his friend's houses. Plans to be in a rock band some day. Has ripped off a guitar in preparation for this.

After Burn

Rhythm of decline
All night long
Do the choke dance
Get it right
You find yourself in the land of the lost
You fit in
Disappear into the background
The soundtrack blaring
Relaxing in the ghetto
Picking the glass and plaster out of your hair
Some party
Everything smells dead
Perversion
Distortion
Decadence
Low tide going lower

◇   ◇   ◇

What happened to your body?
You used to be so good looking
It looks like a storm ripped through your eyes
Looks like you were wrung out
Pasty dry skin
Sagging
Paint peeling
What?
No shit
Crystal meth
That shit tore you up
You look like you've been fucked,
By the army, the navy and the lower east side
Damn girl, you used to be so fine

◇   ◇   ◇

I see you walking through the ruins
Broken child lost
Blown apart and schizophrenic
Where are they now?
Your friends I mean
Let's sit down here and watch the sun set
You're right, there used to be palm trees over there
Yes, they were destroyed
Here's a word for you son,
Can you say "ghetto?"
Good, all you have to do to keep away the evil spirits,
Is to say it to yourself, everytime you inhale

◇ ◇ ◇

I used to love you
I still do
So selfish
I love the old you
The you that doesn't shoot drugs
The you that didn't get beat on by men
You laugh in my face, and call me a fool
But it's true
I still love you
Sometimes, I can see the old you
When your eyes flash
When you look almost alive

◇ ◇ ◇

He sits in the folding chair
He stares at his hands
All the scars
Fist to face
Fist through glass
Fist through wall

Fist
Fist
Fist
Where to now?
Glory is an echo
He listens to the others tell their stories
They all sound the same
He thinks to himself:
Rehab isn't a road, it's a tread wheel
He looks at the men he's sharing the wagon with
Faces hollow
Seen ghosts
Seen Vietnam
Seen Korea
Seen Beverly hills
Seen too much
Too many times
They sit in a circle
Confessing
Coming clean
Wagon wheel
Lonely, holding on
Still addicted to addiction
The florescent lights make them look injured
Soon, time to go home and wait until next week
Get back together and sing the old songs

◇   ◇   ◇

Awoken from a dream
He looks out the window
Three a.m.
What happened to the last two years?

◇   ◇   ◇

Running away
Curling up
Hiding
No use
Just abuse
He conceals his pain and horror
Life could be so great
Without them
He got raped
By his mother's boyfriend
You think I'm joking
I wish

◇　◇　◇

The disease died
Broken hearted
There was no one left to infect

◇　◇　◇

There was a time
When things weren't so
And the air was
And people were
When you could go about at night
And not hear
Gunshots

◇　◇　◇

27 to life
Staring him in his face
Hanging out with him in his cell
Following him to the shower
Putting him to bed at night
He's got a lot of brothers
Friends as a gesture

On the edge of violence
The thing that keeps everyone together
He doesn't want to be a faggot
It's hard
No woman in seven years
What the hell was it like?
How did it feel?
There they are
The walls
There it is
The time
There it goes
Life passing

◇   ◇   ◇

My Dead Friend
(sung to the tune of three blind mice)
My dead friend
My dead friend
See how he lives
See how he lies
He got himself to the halfway house
He's half way there and he'll never get out
You should hear the trash
That comes out of his mouth
My dead friend

◇   ◇   ◇

She was raped by her uncle
Her father left home
For another man
She is confused
She is sixteen

◇   ◇   ◇

He never told anyone about the beatings
The time his father broke his arm,
He yelled so loud,
That the neighbors called the police
Now he lives with strangers
They're alright
He had the closet door taken off its hinges
He doesn't let anyone touch him

◇   ◇   ◇

Listen!
Hark!
Machine gun music
In the sky
Police chopper
Electric warrior
Round up from above
Random gunshots
Somewhere in the palm trees
I sit in my hole
Safety in #1
At night LA glitters like a woman
Who got punched in the mouth
And got told to get her ho ass back to work
Listen!
Hark!
I think I hear an angel!
Oh, it was just a pig

◇   ◇   ◇

What was that shit they all said to you? I forget. You told me the
last time. Yea, that's right. They said that you were going to turn
into a robot if you kept smoking that shit. What was it again? Oh
yea. That's wild, cigarettes dipped in Lysol. Man, I bet you could
hear the brain cells cooking. What was it like? You don't

remember? Do you ever have dreams? What do you think about? Man, you're scorched! No wonder they call you "Terminal."

◇　◇　◇

How many years on the job?
How many kids at home?
What's her name?
No, your wife's name
What is life?
How many drinks after work?
Where did your life go?

◇　◇　◇

I'm lost. I don't understand. There are a few things that I can remember. I have dreams of him touching me. Dreams of his tongue. I swore to myself that if anyone ever touched me like that again I would kill them. The dreams never stop. I am afraid he will be there to rape me again. I know I do it to myself. Why? Do I hate myself? I rape myself in my dreams. I torture myself daily. I murder myself at night. I let him into my dreams. I've tried to have boyfriends. I don't want to be alone. I like boys. It's hard to deal with it when they want to touch me. I know that there's nothing wrong with what they want to do but I can't do it. They call me bitch, castrator, tease. They don't understand. I am so scared and alone. I wish someone would hold me. I'm so cold. Why doesn't anyone understand? I can't talk to anyone. Sometimes I want to die. I feel that I will go through life with no one to love me. The only one who ever told me that he loved me was him. Maybe that's why I keep having the dreams. Please God, let there be someone to love me besides him. Someone on the planet to love me. I see the looks on people's faces. The world is cold and mean. People are wild and dangerous. Someone to love me. Please don't let me go through life like this.

◇　◇　◇

I miss you. I know that I keep saying that and I know that you're getting tired of me writing you all the time but I can't get over the fact that you're gone. I know that you only live across town but it's hard driving by that house you share with that guy and knowing that all the time he's using you. You know that he's using you don't you? You never did listen to me. I have some friends that hang out in this club that he goes to. I am told that he hands you some pretty heavy beatings. I hear that he sells you to his friends. I am afraid to go over there and knock on the door and talk to you because I am afraid he might kill me. Are you using drugs? You never needed to when you were with me. Can I see you again? Will you call me? Will you at least call me? I miss you.

◇   ◇   ◇

Turned subterranean ruthless. A new education. Humans stuffed. Living museum pieces turned inside inside. In-bred. Wrong shoes on wrong feet. Stumbling into work. Lying to keep it together. After awhile the pain goes away. What sets in? Earner of the new scars. The new promotion. The new flesh. Sold by the pound. Worthless. Breathless. What happened to romance? Someone raped it. Turned it into a movie. Turned into Never-Never Land. Always waiting. For the crash, the earthquake, the break in, the drive by shooting, the football game. Waiting to see if the man caught on. Hurry. Sneak in a quick beating while the machine isn't looking. Get some action before the shift starts. Before it's too late. Before they come home, before the sale ends. It's all final. You can stay alive a little longer if you have credit. Put your blood in a washing machine, it's dirty. Kill the man who's breathing your air. Be the first. Be the last to leave. Survival is like a video game. Love is like the lottery. Pain is like the boss. Truth is like the wife. Fun is the pot of drugs at the end of the hall. The reward is yet to come. It's in the end zone. The full color wine cooler ad come to life. The spotlight is a very small circle. Who are you letting into your circle? Who is the enemy? Drink your fill. Get your kicks before it decides that it causes cancer. The next world war will start across the street.

◇ ◇ ◇

Everybody is somebody else's freak
Think about it
Sit at home with the television on
Watch some people burn shit down
Thousands of miles away
"Look at those freaks. Aren't they are something? Must be rough over there."
Outside a killer is checking you out
Thinking to himself about the freak propped up in front of the television set
That's you
Everybody is somebody else's joke
You laugh all the time
You're always up for a laugh
Point your finger and laugh
Put it all below you
Meanwhile
The monkeys are laughing at you from their cages
From their glass boxes
You laugh back and throw excrement
You go back and forth and laugh and throw
But it gets to you
You wonder what's so funny
What's the matter, can't take a joke?
He is laughing his ass off
You do look funny with a gun at the side of your head
And his cock in your mouth
Who is the freak now?
You're one of those bad trips

One of those things you read about
Don't bite
You might get shot in the head
I don't know if you get what you deserve
All I know is that you get it
Sleepwalker with the "boob job"
Yea get one of those
You'll need it
Otherwise fuckhead won't fall in love with you
When he grabs the top of your head
And tells you to get busy, just think of it as an investment
Get yourself well-oiled
For the life long sell out
Drive down the blvd.
Look at the young boy working the corner
Look and laugh right?
It's not you
You couldn't touch a reality that fierce to save your life
Look at the freak
Don't look for too long or he will rip that smile right off your face
Hand it to you
And then he'll start laughing
You're a ripe apple on a low branch
You're a filet in a shark tank
You were born human
Perfect for gang rape
Mutilation
Prostitution and glory
Everybody is somebody else's excuse
Perfect
All you need to get by
A point man
So you can have a reason to point a finger
To be able to escape yourself one more time
That wasn't me

I was drunk
You know how it is
That's not my fault
I was in love at the time
The pressure of the city made me do it
I took drugs to get away from my father
I drank to get away from my boss
I go to the bar to loosen up from the hassle at work
I hit my wife
Because the car wouldn't start
Because our son won't listen to me
It's not me with the problem
Someone else will take care of my sins
Some medicine will be invented
Someone on television will say something
Everything will be alright
And since I can stop any time I want
Don't tell me how to run my lie
I'm free
I heard that in a song on the radio
The cesspool of love
Festering swamp
Hear the blues song
The one about the man sitting alone in his room
Waiting
Hoping
That maybe she will come back
It's because of her all this pain
All this sweat
Like heavy thoughts
Like:
I don't want to live
I can't live
There is no sunshine
There is no life

There is nothing
Without her
So when that woman comes staggering back in
There will be a hot fist of love
Waiting
It's nothing but the blues
Keep your blues to yourself
Unless you want every pore, every hair, every thought you possess,
Bought and sold at the speed of light
Blood, dust and an empty six
Spent shell casings
A broken television
A bent spoon
Dirty sheets
Broken glass
The smell of rotting beer
Stale sweat
Dreams of nowhere
You want mercy?
A break from the plague?
Arms to hold you?
A kind word?
Then get out of the 213 area code
It's all the blues around here

Death Song

I stand at my window and listen
I hear the sirens
One after another as they wail by
Sirens gunshots and helicopters
All the time in this neighborhood
I am lucky
I live in a good one
The Beast has been wounded
It crashes through the underbrush,
Roaring and snorting
The Beast is so heavy and has been running for so long
That it will take years for it to fall
Meanwhile we wait in all kinds of spaces
Watching television,
Marveling at the criminals
The ones that have the most charisma are the ones that we root for
Glad it wasn't us
The Beast is howling tonight
Trying to pull the shrapnel from its joints
Blood and rust
That's all that will be found of me,
When they come to see why I didn't pay the rent
They will say:
Yea, he was part animal, part machine,
But that wasn't enough
Tell what's her name to get in here and clean this up
To make it through the death song,
The right stone throw
The right dance through the mine field
It's all in the walk
And how you stand up to intimidation, humiliation and violence
The Beast is shuddering at my blues song
Showing its teeth

One thousand suicide glory thoughts later I am still here,
It's still here
The cars are crashing tonight
Blood and rust
The last few nights there have been gunshots across the street
The fact that the police never come doesn't mean a damn thing
You see what I mean?
Last week I was in the midwest
Omaha, Nebraska
There was real rain
Heat lightning
The sky was swelling
Electric snakes coiled and struck
Darting in and out of warrior clouds
They looked like they were going to explode
I asked someone if this would be a good place to move to
He said no
I asked why not
He told me that nothing ever happens here
It's a hollow faceless song that this place leaves you singing
All alone to yourself
As you clap spoons on the kitchen sink,
To keep time with the crime
Hey that rhymes
As crime goes by...
As I sit in a doorway,
Thinking
This girl told me that she wanted to join the circus
A real circus
I asked her
Since when is the one on Hollywood Blvd. not good enough?

Black Sabbath

So much litter out of place
It's time to put it in its place
A mind is a terrible thing
A dream is flashing like a polished weapon in my mind
To the summer ambulance
Siren songs
The two girls
Drunk
Fighting outside the club
Broken glass under the crime lights
Fuck these streets
And the bastards who put them here
All these experiments
Like how much blood will it take to drown you
All the while I know
That I am a hero in the making
A walking legend
Superstar status is my domain
If I had a car big enough,
I would drive all of you right off the edge
But there is not the time to play games
I walk the streets looking at you
Listening to you living your garbage cowboy coward fantasy
This place is going to look a lot different
After I get done decorating
Too bad you won't be here to see it
I am an angel
I am a soldier
I am on a mission
No one knows but me
The streets talk to me
The sidewalk looks up at me and makes faces

It mocks me
When I breathe in the stench fills me
Tries to consume me
Tries to destroy me
It will not destroy me
I am here to clear the air
Look at this place
Look at the filth
Look at the decadence
It forces you to pick a side
Either you destroy it or you become it
Every moment of the day it stares you in the face
Taunting you
Destroying you
And you let it
Tag
You're it
You're shit
It is too late for spiritual awakening
Fuck that hippy shit
It's too late for social change
You can't educate a flock of sheep
Can't you see that's what they want
They want you to turn away
They want you to lay down
Like a lamb for the slaughter
Like a chump for the sellout
There will be no revolution
There will be no uprising
There will be no race war
How could anyone be that stupid?
How could anyone believe that bullshit?
What a joke
I know a lot about jokes
I see them all the time

I spent years with some living jokes
You should see them now
Fat
Stoned
Cowards
Living death
Men of action turned into weak pieces of shit
They could get my respect again
If they shot themselves in the head
At night I walk the streets
I take mental notes
I take inventory
The filth
The garbage
The stench
Liars
Freaks
Clowns
My mission becomes clear to me
My life focuses into a laser beam
My purpose
My life
My vision is pure napalm
I am here to clean
There is only one way to clean
You have to incinerate
You must cleanse with fire
You must turn disease to ash
Or it still lives
Things have gone too far
The strong are destroyed by the weak
Decadence has set a precedent
It has become a way of life
Not the way of my life
Shit is shit

I am here to burn it
Can't you see?
I am beyond your timid lying morality
I don't believe in equality
That is to say
That I don't think that if you're alive
That's all you need to get by
The man who sells drugs,
Is not equal to me
The man who rapes his son is not equal to me
They cannot hide
Guilt trips will not shield them from me
I don't believe in human rights
I think you have grown fat and evil
Hiding behind your human rights
Reveling in filth
The balance must be brought back
When I walk the streets in my neighborhood
Drunks come staggering from bars
Guns go off
Police helicopters fly above
Yet nothing happens
Some show
Let's cut the drama
Get rid of the display
The ritual is nowhere
It's hollow
The nights are made of tin
Cheap
Bitter death
I will show you my world
I will bring it home
My beauty
The summer nights of fire and truth
Can you see it?

A dark hot night
The whine of engines from above
The treeline explodes in fire orange
The air fills with the smell of gasoline
The air strike
Like a flower erupting in rapid birth
Filth turned to ash
So beautiful
Decadence lies bleeding
As I walk and plan
I hear angels singing
Black Sabbath songs
The soles of my shoes are thick
Keeps the blood and urine at a distance
The mind I occupy is iron
My time is now
I see them
Maybe it is you that I see
Singing the song of the loser
Your endless, diseased song
The end is coming
And I am the one who is bringing it
I am the punchline
I will defoliate before it's too late
You spend millions on rehabilitation
Rewashing the brainwashed
There's no such thing as rehabilitation
How big does a lie have to get before even you can no longer
avoid it?
You shit in your bed
You wait for someone to come
And clean it up
Well, here I am
Ready to throw out the baby with the bath water

War Pigs

Terrified
You
Sucking the television set
Wishing reality was video
Humiliated
Raped
On the lookout
Pick a side
See the man equipped with the zero remorse factor
And the anti-personnel device
That's a gun that kills you
Look at your friend feeling up your wife
Don't just stand there
Do something
Call the pigs
They will help
You better get busy
Everybody has a war
Where are you at?
You're not going to sit this one out
You have to get hot
Look hard
Find someone to hate
Better yet
Don't hate anyone
Just kill them for the hell of it
Like that last hit of X you took
Flash the peace sign
Go to one of those marches
Pick up a sign
Yell some shit about saving some animal
Then go home
Lock and load war pig
You never know when you have to get real

Lord of This World

Look at the gun
Fortune teller
No fiction
The best truth you will ever get
Loaded and walking cold
Looking for a friend
Searching for love on these mean streets
Look at the gun you dumb fuck
Like a pig sweating you
Do you have one yet?
Make the gun dance
Learn the language
Dance the new slow dance
Better than a computer game
I can see it now
You on the ground
The smell of your shit
The sound of the sirens
Talked tough to the wrong guy
Trying to look good to your date
He laughed and cold smoked your ass
He speaks the language
He knows the new dance steps
Make the gun prick up its ears
Pray
And be prey
Or
Get loaded
Lord of this world
Riding the bus
Talking sweet to the ladies
Looking at you and smiling
Knowing full well

Bullets don't care
Choke
Look out your window
History is being jacked

Electric Funeral

Alone in the room
Over did it
Ended up a blues song
Everybody loves you now
They all want to say that they knew you
Lucky women got to know the real you
Don't worry
None of them will ever say anything
About how you were too high to fuck
The moron from Motley Crue
Telling you he is sorry for being a killer
He is all better now don't worry
He is still wild
But not as wild as he used to be
Look at the Hollywood bitch
Face sagging to her tits
She used to look like something human
Three of her exes died this year
Pounded into the soil by the needle
They had a party for him
Played his records at some club
Told stories about how wild he was
He is not so wild now
Another electric funeral
Take that one for the road and sell it
Make a t-shirt
Put on a hard face
Talk like you seen some shit
What a joke

Tomorrow's Dream

No more streets
No more cities
Paths line the forests and plains
Between villages
People laugh
They tell stories to the young ones
About how the old ways fell in on themselves
How the streets burned
Melted into the sewers and disappeared
How the ugly ones took too much, too fast
How they choked on humanity and illusion
And went the way of the weak
At night while the city stabs and pimps,
Some watch and wait
Keeping themselves sane and clear
With tomorrow's dream

Tiny Master

You Rock & Rollers
Cowards
Harnessed
Castrated
Tame
Timid
Weak
The craziest thing you can do is overdose
Useless disease spreaders
Defanged
Declawed
There ought to be a law
I see you prancing about
Your entire thrust, a commercial
You freaky stepping stones
MTV
You took it to heart
You're taking the whole trip down the drain
Neutralized
Swimming in a sea of used bath water
That's what your music is like
Lukewarm
You cowards
How could you do it?
How could you approach the beast,
And not be a warrior
I don't care what you think you are
Or what your managers and cocksuckers tell you
We both know what you are
You are going to cry when you hit thirty
Those tattoos turning blue
Your hair dye running
The lines in your face

The pose slipping
How will you clutch
All of a sudden you will see
That you blew it
You fell for it
You will get sold out so hardcore
That not even your re-hab counselor will be able to help you
And to all of the suckers
That you took with you,
I don't give a fuck for a sucker
A nation of suckers
A world of suckers
Your people
I am the war that you will not win
I am the hard sell
Money doesn't do amotherfuckingthing to me
Word

Golden Boy

How do you like the new golden boy?
Magic parasite
On the corner
Made to order, soon to die
Suckingsuckingsucking
1-2-3-4 criminal arise!
Lick the ashes from the wounds
Lick the blood from the mouths
Smack your lips
Pack your piece
Hit the streets
Real rock and roll
Get up early
There's a lot of new flesh to mutilate
The fields of bodies
Lost, selfless, slaughtered daily
You can do so much when you're stupid
When you trust
When you open wide and say I do
Back to the golden parasite
Love affair with millions
Bloodletting in the home
Amazing what you can do when you put your mind to it
Terrifying what you will do when you can't control it
Day after day paying sick homage to the god
The golden parasite
Walking on coals, doing 1001 dances
Expending
Fighting off the urge to end it all
Didn't you know it's already over?
That's how it goes with the parasite
The golden sucker
The sexy mind fuck

Death's cheerleader
That's our boy
I keep waiting for you to drop
I keep thinking that I'm going to read about you
And how you fell
But it never happens
I don't know where it all came from
I want to tell you about a man
I watched him sweat bleed and scream
Through hot lit nights of brutal human tests
Sometimes I thought he was going to explode
Or burst into flame
He scared me, inspired me, pushed me upwards and onwards
Like there is any other way to go
I watched him die
I saw it happen right in front of me
He gave up
Curled up
Stepped off the line
Now he sits behind a desk
Stoned
Overweight
Paranoid
Evil
All the things that he sought to destroy
He became
The golden parasite shakes his fist in triumph
And racks up another one
I think of him sometimes
Wondering when he will pull down
One last shot at reality
Goodbye goodbye
Sweep your ashes out the door
Yea kill yourself
But not here

Ok, you can do it here,
But could you wait for a commercial break?
The golden parasite
Gleaming in the sun
Hell yes turn it up
But don't get out of line
Come on in
Get destroyed
That wise ass kid
Six months in the womb
Somehow the little bastard got a fax machine in there
Worked out a three movie deal
Sued his parents
Complained about the food
Said that the PCP she was doing gave him the worst headache
Things are different now
The water tastes funny
Easier to get a bullet than a good cup of coffee

ART TO CHOKE HEARTS

5-25-86 Destruction Blues. I'm in the shed. It's 2:30 a.m. At 4:00 a.m. I leave to get in the van and drive to Gurneville, California. I will spend the next six weeks on the road.

I look at my desk. It's a door bolted to the wall. On the desk: an orange, a bell pepper, a Black Sabbath tape, scissors, pens, cups, a pot of cold coffee almost empty, letters, change, parts of manuscripts, Tylenol, Chloraseptic, thumbtacks and glue.

Above the desk is a shelf with a row of pictures tacked to its edge. From left to right: Jesus Christ kneeling and looking skyward, Arthur Rimbaud, a Christmas card with a swastika on it, a picture of me and Greg playing in New York last year, Edgar Allen Poe, a Swans sticker, Jesus Christ, Madonna and Adolf Hitler together and a picture of the Grateful Dead.

I look down. Underneath the desk is my girlfriend. She's asleep on the floor. I watch her. I like watching her sleep, her face is so peaceful and composed. I listen to her soft breathing and I think about how I'll miss the feeling of her breath on my neck.

I'm tired. I can't sleep. I can never sleep on the eve of a tour. I'll be able to doze off once I get in the van and get on the road. All the coffee I drank this evening is making my stomach burn.

I look back at my girlfriend sleeping on the floor. I study her face. She has a black eye from our show in San Diego last night. Some girls beat her up. She has cuts on her nose and chin.

I have done this so many times, sat in the shed and waited the last few hours out until it's time to go. I get up to go to the main house to take a shower. I'll be on the road soon. Leaving is always a relief wrapped inside a goodbye.

⏴ ⏴ ⏴ ⏴ ⏴ ⏴

Sacramento CA toilet: I pity the man who has to clean the men's room at this place. He'll walk in and here's what he'll see: the sinks are filled with spit, blood, broken glass and paper towels. (The stench is overwhelming.) The floor around the sink is covered with more of the same. The urinals are filled with broken glass and paper towels. One is stopped up and there are a few quarts of urine sitting it its bowl, right up to the rim. The toilet stall is covered with wet toilet paper. The toilet is crammed to the rim with shit, rolls of toilet paper and the cover to the thermostat. The toilet seat has been torn off and is on the coat hanger on the door to the stall.

I can see him now, probably a Mexican getting $2.35 an hour. I can see his face, expressionless. He takes a deep breath and shakes his head and grips his mop.

The boys who messed up the place will never see him. He'll never see them. He's thankful for the job. He starts his work.

◄ ◄ ◄ ◄ ◄ ◄

Darwin on LSD. Darwin on speed. Throwing rocks around. Knocking the cities to the ground. Wondering why it even lasted this long.

◄ ◄ ◄ ◄ ◄ ◄

It's all moving
The girls are moving
Their hips are moving
The cars on the street are moving
The sun is moving
It's moving all around me
Inside
Nothing is moving
It's dead in here
When I see everything moving all around me and feel the dead stillness inside me I feel like I'm the axis of the madness I see. I feel like I am the seeing eye of a shit-filled hurricane

◄ ◄ ◄ ◄ ◄ ◄

I'm one in a million million. I'm a drop in a sea of faces. I'm just another one walking down the street. I've been following you. I've been watching you. If you said you saw me any one time, any one place, I'd know for sure that you were lying. You pass me by, you never turn your head. I never catch your eye. That's good. I don't want you to notice me. I'm a stranger looking at you. Your life revolves around me. I am the axis upon which you spin. I'm a stranger. We've never met. I know your cell number. I know your real name, the one you use when you're alone. There is no door you can shut to keep me out.

◄   ◄   ◄   ◄   ◄   ◄

Some nights I look into the crowd and I want to see them all destroyed. I'd like to have a flame thrower and just fire right into them. Burn their hairdos right off their heads. Every night I play I listen to them yell at me, telling me what to do. Telling me to sign this and shake their hands. Telling me what they think of me whether I want to hear it or not. They poke at my eyes, pull my hair and punch me while I play. Fuck that shit. Flame thrower full bore into them. I'll watch them burn. My face will be expressionless. I'll feel good.

◄   ◄   ◄   ◄   ◄   ◄

A sun hangs quietly in the back yard
I put my hand out and feel its warmth come down
To the North
The sun hangs just the same
It shines down on the tower guards of San Quentin

◄   ◄   ◄   ◄   ◄   ◄

Walking broken streets. Crippled broken song in my broken, free but now down and out. Idle minded. I've been in park for so long now. Waiting for some stranger to pull out the key to put my wreck to rest. Driven so many miles of nowhere to get somewhere only to find out that I was here all along.

I've been here all along. Walking lone, giving the time of day the time of day. Taking a deep breath and taking a long look into the mirror. Seeing the man who sees me clearer. Seeing the man who sees me dearer than my mother ever could. It's time to dust off my death machine and give this man what he really needs.

◄ ◄ ◄ ◄ ◄ ◄

The summer had fully unfolded. It stretched out full-length and pressed its smooth muscles against mine. The air was thick. It surrounded me like invisible prison bars. Every night was dedicated to delirium, dreams of confusion and confinement. I walked in and out of steaming jungles. I would rest in damp, cool shade. Sometimes I thought I would not be able to get up because the rest would make my bones ache so bad. There was a constant din in my ears. A world of sane, soulless pigs surrounded me. Sounded like a war. In this madness I found a quiet place. A place where I could hear my breath. The quiet place. Silent sun. Heavy air. Shimmering jewel eyed woman in my brain. No confinement. An infinite pass. Insane beauty. I thought if I made a sound the whole thing would collapse right down on top of me. I guarded the quiet place. I kept it clean, told no one about it. Even now, the directions to the place stay with me. I've been thinking about that place a lot these days.

◄ ◄ ◄ ◄ ◄ ◄

My father would take me to restaurants sometimes. Every once in a while the lot would be full of cars, the only place to park would be the spaces reserved for the handicapped. My father would park there. As we would get out to go in, he would look at

me and say, "Limp!" and I would fake this limp and we would
go in.

◄　◄　◄　◄　◄　◄

A heavy thought walks in my brain like a cold, slow lead
lightning bolt. Confusion and madness scream and dance in
my death trip white matter. I'm carrying something that I can
barely hold onto. I don't know where it comes from, but it feels
like a gun in my hand. One shot. Like a perfect drug. One shot
gets you off, man.

◄　◄　◄　◄　◄　◄

The truth is a loner. The truth drives people away from me.
Keeps my house empty. There's not much money in the truth.
It's kind of plain. It's not very popular around these parts.

◄　◄　◄　◄　◄　◄

Sitting on a park bench alone. Sun's out. I got no shirt on and
the sweat is streaming down my back and stomach into the
waistband of my pants. People coming out of the office across
the street look at me long and hard. Overweight women in ugly
clothes clutching oversized pocket books walk out of the door.
There's a stiffness to their gait. Sit in a chair for hours, get up
and walk to the car to sit down again. The legs forget about
standing up. Men with soft bellies, razor-burned necks popping
out of uncomfortably tie-locked shirt suits look at me as they
come out. Their eyes squint when they hit the light of the sun.
Fluorescent is a lot easier on the eyes. They check me out as they
get their asses packed into their cars.

Behind me there is a pay parking lot. I hear two black
dudes yelling at each other.

"Hey faggot!"

"Fuck you nigger faggot!"

"What? WHAT?"

"Come here nigger!"

Then I hear the sound of shoes scuffling and fists hitting flesh. I hear some more yelling and then car doors slamming and then the screeching of tires.

A beat down looking whore walks by, looks at me and spits and keeps walking. One of her heels gets caught in a crack in the sidewalk and she falls on her face. She gets up slowly and turns around to see if I saw her eat the sidewalk. I smile and give her the old thumbs up. She makes a face like a snake and goes wobbling down the street. A car pulls up and a guy asks me how to get to the university. I shrug and tell him I'm a stranger in this town.

◄   ◄   ◄   ◄   ◄   ◄

Snake head pops of a hole in the burnt black ground
It surveys the annihilation with eyes that never close
Almighty annihilation complete
Fire is the holiest disease
Fire is the panacea
Fire destroys life
The destruction is the cure
Fire is the cleanest and mightiest disease
Annihilation man, bring the fire
Cure this sick place
When you say annihilation
You've said it all

◄   ◄   ◄   ◄   ◄   ◄

Chicago O'Hare Airport Toilet. O Lord. Thank you for the big quiet men's room in the D concourse at O'Hare. It was great. I was the only one in there. All the urinals and toilets were lined up and ready for action. I went in the first stall I could stagger over to and locked the door behind me. A real toilet! The last time

I shit was about twelve hours before in the bushes at an outdoor Grateful Dead concert in Wisconsin. I had just pulled up my pants and was picking my first step to carefully avoid stepping in my own waste when this hippie girl walked past me. I flashed her the peace sign and scampered through the bushes. I looked behind me to see her standing where I was just squatting. She looked up and our eyes met through the bushes. No it wasn't love. But anyway, here I was enclosed in steel and tile. There was an empty quart bottle of Black Velvet by my foot. Boozing in the men's room, bourbon and shit. People from Chicago are tough. I flushed a few times because it sounded so cool reverberating off the walls at 2:06 a.m. I left the stall feeling like a slightly used man. Amen.

◄ ◄ ◄ ◄ ◄ ◄

We play, they clap and yell. They pound my feet with their fists and get mad when I say, "Cut the shit." Playing away we're all having a good old time and they're raising their beers in the air and trying to light cigarettes while all these people are pushing and shoving and it looks like a riot in a subway car. A song ends and they start yelling what goddamn song they want to hear over and over as if I didn't hear them the first or fifth time. Some yell and scream titles of songs that we just played. Fine. We're rolling and it's cool and during one song a beer pitcher flies through the air and nearly removes my balls and at the end of the song I say, "Hey excuse me sir or ma'am who threw the beer pitcher at me, you're probably just mistaken, empties should be returned to the bar, preferably by hand, no air delivery needed. You have to watch those pitchers because if you hit us they hurt and uh..." What's the use talking? They don't listen. So we finish the show and we leave the stage and a guy jumps up to take a drum stick. He grabs it and jumps back onto the floor. I go up to the edge of the stage and say hey man, gimmie that stick, they cost money. The guy says come on man, just one and I say what the fuck do you think this is, Van Halen? I grab the stick. Some drunk Marine tries to kiss me. I get away from him and sit on the side of the stage. Some guy sees me and points to an empty bottle of water that I was drinking from and says, "Hey, can I have your bottle?" and I say, "Hey, go shoot yourself." He says, "What?" and I say, "Go to the parking lot, get a gun, and get the goddamn lead out. Now leave me alone." He leaves. These people come up to shake my hand and have me sign their whatever and one asks why I told the dude to go kill himself. I say that I'm not Bruce Springsteen. I'm not running for office. I'm a sweaty, foulmouthed motherfucker who cries and beats off all the time. I have a bad attitude, a great ass, and a tremendous jaw line. I'm cold and going to go put some clothes on. Good night.

◄ ◄ ◄ ◄ ◄ ◄

I'm sitting in a small room with one window. The sun's almost down. I'm thinking of a parking lot I used to hang out in a long time ago. The sun would set against an old brick wall. The sun's light made the bricks look purple. I like hanging around in places where there's no one around. I can't get that parking lot out of my head. The shards of broken glass looked like jewels when the sun would shine on them. The dirt and the garbage and the polluted air. The fag magazine, pictures of a bunch of skinny guys with cocks in their mouths. The syringes and little piles of cigarette butts. It was a cool hang-out scene. I nearly got laid in a car in there once but the girl said it was too cold outside.

◄ ◄ ◄ ◄ ◄ ◄

Being back here: it's hard being back here. I feel like a bullet that's just lodged itself in a wall. Ready-set-stop. I can't explain it to anyone. I tried with my woman but it didn't work. The only thing I could tell her is that when I come back from being out there I feel that if I'm not careful I'll break everything around me. I told her that things and people seem fragile and weak. Weak, that's what infuriates me. I walk around and I feel like kicking. I want to lock myself in this room for as long as it takes. That's what I want. I want to see no one. The people in my brain are bad enough. The real thing brings out the worst in me at this point. Flame thrower in the shopping mall. Five Mile Man on a ten mile trail—not a chance.

◄   ◄   ◄   ◄   ◄   ◄

I see it plain as I can see my hand. It's all swinging to the right and coming straight down. The pigs and the masses are in fear of each other. The pigs fear the hatred and the threat of violence towards their own flesh. The pigs make people feel like criminals before they have committed any crimes. The people are being watched and they know it. People fear the police. People hate police.

It's almost impossible not to get some kind of ticket if you are an automobile owner. When you get a ticket you have broken a law. You're a law breaker. You're a criminal.

When a policeman looks at you, you immediately question yourself as to what you're doing wrong. If you keep on doing what you're doing despite his stare, you feel different about what you are doing. When (if) he leaves, you feel relief, or maybe a rush from your act of defiance. Maybe you question yourself. You start to feel criminal. You've got the stink on you now.

◄   ◄   ◄   ◄   ◄   ◄

When I die I want the body to be cremated outside in a public place. I want the body to be stripped bare so everyone can see my naked disgusting corpse. I want the body to be kicked and mutilated by strangers as it was in life. Then I want the whole thing covered with gasoline and lit on fire. I wish I could be there to see it burn, to smell my own flesh cooking. I don't care about the looks on their faces or the way it makes them feel because it's my body. Okay, that's a bit harsh. Maybe it should be a party instead. Get a keg, some tunes, maybe even some coke. Invite some critics to the event. Tell them it's some kind of "performance art" type thing. Tell the assholes that it's some kind of statement. What a way to go. Couldn't get laid off it but what the fuck.

◄ ◄ ◄ ◄ ◄ ◄

Monkey man handcuffed to a wrist watch. Guts burning, late for the bus. Sweating through his shirt as he runs down the sidewalk to catch up with time. If he was asked if he ever thinks about his life he would probably tell you that he doesn't have the time, he gave at the office, doesn't want to get involved.

◄ ◄ ◄ ◄ ◄ ◄

He stretched his arms straight out from his sides like cockroach wings. He stood grinning in all his debasing, absolute glory. Beyond hate. Beyond you. Brother to fear. Brother to starvation. There was no end in his sight.

He once said: I can drive anyone away from me. Someday I will learn to drive people away from themselves. That's what I want. I want the whole world to kill itself.

He was a one man celebration of penetrating filth. He was the King, the real King. I watched him walk away just as they were putting the final touches on the palace they had made for him. I understand he came back later and torched the place, laughing and spitting at the people who stood at the edge of the fire.

◄ ◄ ◄ ◄ ◄ ◄

Men's room etiquette. I'm at a show. It's almost time to play. I go into the men's room to you know, do it before I have to go out and you know, do it. Almost every time I go in there, the place is packed with guys. Sometimes there's girls in there too. Most are in line to use the facilities. Some of the guys are in there just hanging out, smoking, drawing on the walls and having a good time. Why any one would like to hang out in a toilet is totally beyond me. So like I said, I go in there to do my thing and get the hell out of there so I can go play. Almost every time, the fellas at the front of the line will let me cut in front of them. As I piss into the urinal, some of the fellas will slap me on the back and say stuff like "Get wild man! Do it! Tear it up tonight!" And I do. I piss as wildly as I possibly can, but the tear it up shit I totally disregard.

◄　◄　◄　◄　◄　◄

Climb out of the wreckage
Run with me through the burning fields
You're playing games
Running circles in your mind
You're locked up
You're a door slamming man
You're tied up
You're a hog tying pig
Watch me walk away

◄　◄　◄　◄　◄　◄

Black soul boy. Black soul girl. Walking hand in hand through the black soul world. Wordless and numb, burned out and hollow. So dead inside. Mutilation is the only chance for escape. Annihilation is the only chance for survival. They're not going to make it, they're in love. The garbage crunches underneath their shoes as they kiss in the park. I'm going for their throats and then I'm getting the fuck out of here.

◄　◄　◄　◄　◄　◄

End Creator. the only thing I remember is that he walked away.
That's the only time I saw him, walking up the brick alley with
his back to me. The sun was low, burning purple red, looked like
the walls of the apartment were bleeding onto the alley floor.

◄ ◄ ◄ ◄ ◄ ◄

If you're walking all alone
All the way alone
You're walking with me
If there's nothing in your hand
Then you're holding hands with me
I'm with you every step of the way
What happens to you happens to me
All the way for real
Alone
Riding it
Feeling everything there is to feel
Laughing at the blood and the madness
Brother to insane
Brother to alone
Brother to one
Pain is free
Pain runs wild
Pain slips into the house of love
And has a high old time underneath the sheets
Then coils like a snake and waits for the next go round

◄ ◄ ◄ ◄ ◄ ◄

The car crash. The bodies inside making silent history. The girl.
Her head smashed into the steering wheel. Her beautiful face.
Her skull. Her forehead caved in and purple. The girl next to her.
Her body. Her gentle eyes filled with glass. Her unborn child,
twisted inside, neck broken, back broken, small mouth open, full

of black congealed blood. The four year-old girl in the back seat, neck broken, legs wrapped around each other broken several times. Her little arms wrapped around her as if she was freezing. Nothing moves. The car and broken bodies wait for the janitor to come and clean them up. A crowd gathers around the car and looks in as if it were a space ship that contained visitors from another world. Ten minutes ago no one would look at them twice, but now, they command a captive audience. The corpses in the car must have done something incredible because everyone's asking the person next to them if they saw what happened. The police come and tell everyone to go home. Those that can walk do. Those that are dead will need assistance.

◄   ◄   ◄   ◄   ◄   ◄

Desert man incinerator
Bugs crawling
Spiders crawling
Snakes crawling
In the desert
Smashed up cars
Human life destroyed
Dead silence is pretty quiet in these parts
Burning bodies at night
Burning metal at night
I piled the junk up high and burned it down
Melted it down
All human life destroyed
Me and the brothers
Watching the fire burn
All human life destroyed
I can smell them cooking
I'm smiling
It's a ruptured gutted trip I'm on

◄   ◄   ◄   ◄   ◄   ◄

Sitting in a chair in the sun warming my bones. Airplane drowns out the blues record. Time is slipping through my teeth. Every second. My head is nodding in time with Lightnin' Hopkins foot. What am I doing here? I feel like an old man in the garden watching the spiders. Glory is a worn out place. A fast train that leaves your life echoing in its hallway.

◄　◄　◄　◄　◄　◄

Hitching a ride in the desert. The car pulled over to the side of the road to pick up the hitchhiker. The hitchhiker opened the door and said thanks a lot man. The hitchhiker pulled a gun from his pants and pointed at the driver's head. The driver held his hands up. The hitchhiker gave the man a pair of handcuffs and told him to cuff himself to the steering wheel. The man did. The hitcher laughed and started to sing. The hitcher tore a sleeve off the man's shirt and stuck it into the gas tank of the car. He lit it and walked away to a large rock to watch.

◄　◄　◄　◄　◄　◄

He grabbed her hand and they ran. They ran through the rain. They ran through screaming ghettos. War sounds were all around them. They ran through burning fields. They came to a place where they knew they would no longer have to run. It was all over then, everything that they had was gone. So much for peace and quiet.

◄　◄　◄　◄　◄　◄

Little boy left for hardly fifteen minutes. The sitter had gone to the store for some cigarettes. When she got back she saw the fire engines in front of the house. She saw the smoke. She found out that the boy she had been watching over had lit his little brother's crib on fire with the matches she had left on the table. He had heard that the only child gets more attention from the parents, more love and extra dessert.

◄ ◄ ◄ ◄ ◄ ◄

The family man had a dog. A German shepherd. He kept it in the backyard. Every once in a while the dog would get out and I got to see him. What a poor excuse for a dog, his fur was patchy, his legs were weak. He looked awful. I regretted having thrown those rocks over the fence into the yard so I could hear him bark and make the family man turn on his crime light. I thought the dog was some huge beast that was ready to kill anything that got into the yard. I was always hoping that the dog might chew up one of the kids. I stopped throwing rocks into the yard. The dog finally died. Now there's a smaller dog living in the back yard. He never gets to walk around in the front yard or anywhere else except the back yard. He barks like a neurotic cop. One of these days, I'm gonna get a sling shot and wipe that little bastard out to put him out of his misery of course.

◄ ◄ ◄ ◄ ◄ ◄

A black man is walking along the beach in California. Some white youths come up and ask him where he's going. One asks him if he has a passport. The youths say some other shit to the black man. The man just stands there looking at the ground. Finally he looks at them and asks: "Do you really get off doing this?" One of the youths repeats what the man said in an exaggerated black slang. The man's eyes go back to the sand again. He looks up and asks if he can leave now. One of the youths says he can. The man backs up a couple of steps and walks around them. The youths watch him as he heads up the beach. They make some jokes. They sound hollow and forced. So does the laughter that follows them. They go back to their blankets and resume their conversation about girls.

◄ ◄ ◄ ◄ ◄ ◄

A great shot. When I was about seven I used to play in this park across the street from the apartment where me and my mom lived. One day I was in the park playing alone as usual. I was on the swing. This black kid came up and grabbed one of the chains and tried to shake me off. I stopped as quickly as I could and got off. The boy pushed me and I backed away. He picked up a rock and threw it at me. The rock missed. I ran away back toward the apartment building. I turned around to see if he was chasing me. He was standing where I had left him. He had another rock in hand and was winding up to throw it at me. I knew he couldn't hit me from that distance but I kept running anyway. The rock hit me square in the back of the head. I saw stars, blood was all over my shirt and neck. I turned around again, he was running the other way. His friends would never believe him in a million years but he and I both knew it was a great shot.

◄ ◄ ◄ ◄ ◄ ◄

See the violence in his eyes. See the city come down around your ears. Paranoia at one hundred miles an hour. Stinging dirt and hot rain. Beating off into the sink. Thinking about suicide every time. Slapping at flies and needing a shave. Looking for a girl. Finding a fight instead. See the violence in their eyes as you walk into the bar. Listen to how hard they laugh and drink. Walk home at night broken and alone. Feel so empty that you think you're going to cave in. See the heat in his eyes. Watch the man argue with his girlfriend and try to pull her out of a cab. Keep walking. Hot night right now, right here. All you have is what you are. All you want is much too much. All you get is so much less. All you feel is nothing. All you see is darkness. All you know is senseless. All you can do is ride.

◄ ◄ ◄ ◄ ◄ ◄

Hot night wind blows all around me. I take a deep breath and imagine I'm in a polluted desert. I walk alone on the sidewalk.

The street lights look like little moons as I make my way. Damp, everything is damp. I can smell myself, I must be here. Crickets and cars, otherwise just the sound of my breathing. No one on the sidewalk. I'm the only one in the whole world right now.

◄ ◄ ◄ ◄ ◄ ◄

I'm going to walk through the night. I'm going to walk for as long as it takes to clear my head. I'm going to walk until it all makes sense to me. The night will wrap itself around me. I'm going to walk and curse the oncoming sunrise. I'm going to walk and sweat and think to myself. I'm going to try to get it straight. I'm going to walk until the night quits on me. After that I'm going to walk backwards and try to figure out where it all went and why it left me behind.

◄ ◄ ◄ ◄ ◄ ◄

I walk the streets. The dirt fills my lungs. I'm just another face. I pass you by. You don't see me. Skin stretches across my face. I'm desperate. Nothing you could put your finger on, nothing you could see, nothing you could touch. Nothing to see in my eyes. Everything makes me insane. Dirt and heat fire my driving desperation. Thirsty and insane. You pass me on the street. I make no sound. Sometimes I have to shake my own hand for not grabbing my head and screaming about the thundering war that's pounding in my ears. This is called maintaining. I put my ear to a brick wall. I can hear the hot animal machine sounds. I wait for the night to come and take me away. I'm on a hot street in thin shoes. My clothes make me itch. They all turn into policemen as they watch me pass. Beady hungry little eyes — pig's eyes. They squint through sunglasses. They see the world from a different place. A place more tinted, more air-conditioned that mine. More prone to breakdown and the need for maintenance.

◄ ◄ ◄ ◄ ◄ ◄

I sat on my bed
I didn't move
The room was hot, the air was still
Almost 3:30 in the morning
I wanted to kill myself
I was getting all pumped up to do it
I ended up getting the floor sticky with blood
I took a razor and carved designs into myself
It didn't hurt
I felt like I was flying
The blood smelled good
The boss saw the scars on me the next day
Started screaming at me
Calling me a freak
I remember his eyes swelling up
His spit hitting me in the face
I thought I was going to lose my job
I was lucky he needed me
I always considered myself luckier than he was
I may be a freak
But at least I'm not a twice divorced alcoholic

◄ ◄ ◄ ◄ ◄ ◄

Dreams smash into me. Hot flickering night hot in asylum fuck smashing into flesh swastika fist death trip rusty loser thirsty crawling flesh bullet machine machine machine meathouse on off switch left on left alone swastika bullet straight shot juice under hot on off bright lights switch left on switch left on bullet swastika faster slaughter house bullet straight ahead light on the other side mass appeal suicide hot animals killing each other crawling like roaches multiplying in endless death grip fuck lock smashing kicking biting a bullet is the end the answer the cure for all ills bullet god answer man hot insane animal light switch left on.

◄ ◄ ◄ ◄ ◄ ◄

Businessmen in diapers. Having big fat mammys to look after them. Men in three piece suits crying in restaurants. Mammy puts the dirty boy on the counter at Denny's and changes him in front of everybody. No one even misses a bite. This happens all the time.

◄ ◄ ◄ ◄ ◄ ◄

No time for me, only time for everyone else. They think nothing of wasting time. They think nothing. I'm getting out of here. Taking a vacation on my life. Trying to kill me with their bullshit. They get me good. But I've got a plan. Oh man, I've got plans. They'll turn around and I'll be gone. They'll be looking. Where did he go? I wanted to tell him something. I wanted to put a noose around his neck. I wanted to drag him around in my shit for awhile.
Oh well...

◄ ◄ ◄ ◄ ◄ ◄

Christmas day 1985 Global practice place
The phone rings
Global. Yea it's true, okay, right.
The phone rings
Global. Yea, somewhere in Arizona. I'm not sure, I don't know about a funeral date. Call back in a few days, okay?
The phone rings
Global. Yea man, it's true, who told you? Yea, we're all tripped out about it. It's real strange being here on Christmas day and all... see ya.
The phone rings
Global. What paper? It doesn't matter. What do you want? No, D. Boon was the only one killed in the accident. I don't know much about how the others are doing. Call back in a few days.
The phone rings

Global. Hi Mom. Did you hear? Oh, D. Boon is dead. Yea, he was in a car wreck. There were two other people in it too. I don't know what their status is. I gotta take care of these phones. Bye.

◄ ◄ ◄ ◄ ◄ ◄

Make him watch
I want him to see everything
I want him to remember it all
Cut his eyelids off
Make him watch
Make him see
I want him to see it all burn
I want him to remember everything

◄ ◄ ◄ ◄ ◄ ◄

Summer exhaust fume music. Summer night music. The sun goes down. The long dark incineration begins. I burn alone. I call out from my cell. I want someone to burn with me. I call out through the dark heat. I look out the window to see if she heard me. Crawl in with me. Burn with me. Incinerate this dream with me. Summer night music makes blood run down the walls. I lie alone. I burn. I want. I wait. I grind my teeth and destroy myself. I burn.

◄ ◄ ◄ ◄ ◄ ◄

I was riding in a truck. I closed my eyes and I saw myself walking to my apartment at night. I looked up at my window and I saw that my room was on fire. I got closer, I saw that there were three of me standing in a human ladder up to my window sill. I climbed up and I looked into my room. I saw myself inside. My body was on fire, and waltzing around the room. Even though I was engulfed in flames, nothing else in the room was on fire. I watched myself dance around and around the room. Finally the body lay down on the bed. The flames went out and there I was, lying on the bed, naked and heaving. I looked around me and I noticed that I was on the ground. The human ladder was gone. I opened my eyes and I was in the truck. The road filled my eyes. I rolled down the windows and breathed in the hot air.

◂ ◂ ◂ ◂ ◂ ◂

The guy at the counter said that I had gotten the job and I was to now go downstairs to meet the boss, get my apron and get briefed on the rules and regulations of the restaurant. I went downstairs to meet the boss. I walked to the threshold of the door and knocked gently. He looked up from his desk told me to come in and sit down. He asked me how bad I wanted the job. I told him that I really liked the place and I thought that I could really...he cut me off and asked me what I would do to get the job. I didn't know what he meant. He told me if I wanted to get the job, I would have to give him good head. I couldn't believe he told me that. He looked at me and said that he didn't have all day, if I wanted the job I was to get down and suck. I needed the job. I got down and I did it. I got the job. I went home that afternoon and told my mother that my uncle was going to be a hard guy to work for.

◂ ◂ ◂ ◂ ◂ ◂

I like explosions. I like obituaries. I like anything that gives the game a twist. Maybe it's time for terrorism, maybe it's time for a race war. Maybe it's time for the cards to fall where they may. Give them all guns and let's see who the real Lord of the Flies is. Maybe I'll get my brains spattered all over the place. I've taken that into consideration. What the fuck. All I know is that it's going to come down. Take a look around. The lines are being drawn. The captains are choosing up sides. The weak are falling into line. It's all around you. It's all I can see. There is only annihilation. Salvation is a bad joke and a good lie. So many people are standing out on the porch waiting for the man.

Take a look around. Look at the filth. Look at the freak show. Look at the mindless fools who surround you. You watch them try to pull you down. Still the chaos. Put an end to the madness. Get a hold of yourself. Grip the throat of your soul and get a hold. Still the chaos with a cool lead hand. Look at all of them. Take it all in. Don't lose your head, that's where all the good stuff is.

There's no sense to the mindlessness that surrounds you so don't try to make any of it. Don't let the weakness of others drag you down. There's only one way and that's forward. There's only one sin and that's weakness. To get by, to get past all the cheap backstabbing bastards, you must annihilate. Hail the annihilation. Repeat.

◂   ◂   ◂   ◂   ◂   ◂

They stripped me of my clothes. I stood naked and shivering in front of a large hole dug in the ground. I turned around and looked down. I saw my mother's corpse below me. Naked and mutilated. I moved over a bit so that when my body fell, it would land next to hers. I felt lucky to have seen her one last time. They had been lying. They told me that she had been dead for several hours. They told me in detail how they tortured her. I looked down at her body and I no longer felt cold. They told me to turn around. I looked to either side of me. We were all lined up naked and pale in the early morning light. The soldiers raised their guns and fired. Our bodies jerked and fell into the hole. The lucky ones died quick. For myself and some others, it took hours. How we wished for death! Other bodies fell upon me. I lost sight of my mother. Finally I died. I thrust my head between two corpses and suffocated. Amen.

◂   ◂   ◂   ◂   ◂   ◂

The four of them got out of the car. The husband, the wife, the kid and the dog. The kid spills his soda on the back seat as he's leaving the car. Whack! The husband hits the kid. "You little jerk. I just had that cleaned!" The wife leans over and says, "Why did you do that you idiot? He didn't mean to do it!" Whack! He claps her one too. The dog tries to bite the husband's leg. He kicks the dog in the ribs and sends it packing. The wife and the kid stagger to the house and make it inside. The husband comes in right after them. He's limping from kicking the dog so hard. The dog runs away. The wife makes dinner. The kid goes to his room and plays with his toys. The husband gets a beer out of the ice box and sits down to take the weight off his foot which is now starting to swell.

◄ ◄ ◄ ◄ ◄ ◄

When I was seven years old I went to a public school. At lunch time I would hang out in the yard and watch the older boys fight and play baseball. I remember one time these two guys got in some kind of argument about something. I don't really remember what it was all about. The one thing I do remember was one of the guys pulling out a pencil from his pocket and trying to stab the other guy with it. The kid blocked the pencil and it went right through the kid's hand. For a second, the kid stood there looking at his hand, he looked as if he couldn't believe his eyes. Right after that he started to scream. A teacher came and took the boy away. I never found out what happened to the kid who did the stabbing. I did see the kid's scar after it had healed. He was a cool guy. A few years later he saved my ass at a public summer camp that we were both at. Some guy was going to beat my head in with a tree branch and this guy came over and talked him out of it. I gave him my bus token and most of my lunch. Seemed like a good trade at the time.

◄ ◄ ◄ ◄ ◄ ◄

I kicked the wailing wall in the balls and walked away. I went to the funeral and checked it out. All these people paying their respects to dead meat. Come cry with us they said as I walked away. Yeah, right. I was thinking how funny it would be if one of them didn't have the money to pay the man at the graveyard's parking lot. Everything has a price don't you know. Come cry with us they yelled. Come cry with us you bastard! One of them threw a rock at me. Another screamed. Soon the dead meat was all forgotten about. They chased me out of the graveyard and out onto the street. I ran away, I thought they were going to kill me. If they did, I bet they wouldn't be at my funeral. It would be great...right as the priest is giving the big send off, the coffin lid rips open, the dead guy sits up, looks out, screams: WHO INVITED YOU?!

◂ ◂ ◂ ◂ ◂ ◂

Their child drowned in the sea. The lifeguard brought the little body to shore and put it on the sand. He stood up after there was nothing more that could be done. The lifeguard asked where the parents where. The crowd that was gathered all looked at each other and shrugged. No one stepped forward to claim the child.

Ten miles away at a bar in Manhattan Beach the mother and father toasted each other and their new found freedom and happiness. They were in love all the way. One said to the other "Let's settle down and have beautiful children." At this they both broke into laughter and ordered more drinks.

◂ ◂ ◂ ◂ ◂ ◂

I'm not you. I don't want you around me. This business of constantly having to explain myself is going to stop. My trip is my trip. Your trip is not my trip. You want to talk about weakness, talk about your own. I am a selfish man.

There's nothing more egotistical and fake than selfless-ness. I am selfish. I am self. It's all I have and it's all I want. Your love doesn't keep me warm at night. Your love won't drive me to the edge. Your hate moves me just the same. You can't give yourself to me. Even if you could I wouldn't take you.

◄　◄　◄　◄　◄　◄

War sound track. I need to hear war sounds while I fuck. Otherwise I feel dead. I can't come. I need to feel good. If I'm impotent tonight, I will beat you. War is hell. I can find no love in the eyes of peace. Please give me war. I want to love you. I want to kill you. I want to hate you. Let me hate you. Let me love you. Let me in. Let me stab you. I want to love you. I want to kick you. For the rest of my life over and over. In the eyes of love. There is no love. War now so I can have you. You are what I want. After we come, let's go out. Let's kill some of them. We will rape their wounds. We will destroy them. We will incinerate them. It's only them. Annihilate them. We will love them to death. We will violate them completely. We will turn them to ash with our love. Our love will be the salvation. Our love will be our answer to all the questions. Our love will be the guiding light. You and me baby. All the way. Tonight.

◄　◄　◄　◄　◄　◄

I will incinerate the Pepsi generation. I can't tell you anything about Shakespeare but I can tell you the whole thing is going to burn. It stinks and it's going to melt. Take a look around, the plague is starting already. It's rotting from the inside. Every day it gets more rancid, it festers. Looks like a bunch of maggots in a garbage pail. Boiling and crawling with life. Ready to explode. I say torch all their cells all the way from Beverly Hills to Palos Verdes. Stand on the roof of your car and wave goodbye to the beautiful people.

◄　◄　◄　◄　◄　◄

Earlier that day I had agreed to meet up with a friend. I got to the place five minutes early. He had gotten there earlier than I had. He was sitting down on the sidewalk, talking to this skinhead. As I approached, my friend got up and greeted me. The skinhead looked me over and smirked slightly. My friend said seeyalater to the skinhead and we turned to leave. The skinhead said, "Could you spare some change towards my next twelve pack?" My friend was going through his pockets looking for some change. I looked at the skinhead. Bald, black T-shirt that had a pair of boots on the front with "skinhead" printed underneath the boots, blue jeans, and a pair of boots, just like the ones on his shirt. He was pale and fat. He wouldn't last a day in Hitler's army. Wouldn't last half of that in any black street gang. He looked at me for some change. I smirked slightly. Me and my friend turned and left him sitting there in his own juices.

◄   ◄   ◄   ◄   ◄   ◄

I'm in the hot room again
I am a time junkie
I am a user
Like all addicts, I come to the point where I ask myself
Who's using who
I take a look around and I see what I do
I look in the mirror and I see what it's doing to me
And I come to the conclusion that we got a pretty good thing going

◄   ◄   ◄   ◄   ◄   ◄

It took me a while to appreciate it, but now I am thankful for every event that dehumanized me. Every instance that stripped me. They were good lessons. They taught me a lot about myself and the people around me. The human is the lowest form of life on this planet. If I am less than human, then I am more than human. "Only human." I hear that one a lot. I'm standing in the hallway. I'm naked and shivering, they are laughing at me, pointing at me, trying to make me feel some way, trying to make me feel the way they would feel if the same thing was happening to them. They try to provoke me to do something that they can punish me for. They're trying to make me mad so I'll do something they'll understand, something they'll be able to react to. They're only human. They want me to feel less than human. They think that this will make me weak, they don't know that at that very moment I'm becoming more by becoming less. Now I have an understanding of the term "only human" that's different than the one they have. They use it as an excuse so their weakness will be seen as something beyond their control. I see it as a sewer to climb out of, a real "manhole." I am brother to the roach. I am brother to all that crawls. At least they have the smarts and the guts to run.

The roach is a higher form of life than my species. No morals. They value only life with a tenacity that is astounding. No judgment. They count only one life as their own. No love, no hate. They're running rings around me already. Public enemy number one. You can buy the means to exterminate them at the place you buy your food. Whole corporations dedicated to their total annihilation. And they're so cool. They don't even give a fuck. Let's see you top that one.

◄ ◄ ◄ ◄ ◄ ◄

I stand in the mirror and stare at my face. Sometimes I think that something's going to rip out of my forehead. I'll suddenly be overcome with an overpowering feeling of claustrophobia. It took me a while to understand but now I know. I'm locked in solitary. Sometimes I feel like my face is pressed up against the roof of my skull. My head becomes a bad place to be. I used to think that there was someone else in there with me. I couldn't

believe that I would do all this to myself. Now I know that it's all
me and it's all in here. Sometimes I want to be driven out of my
mind. Like a vacation. I know it will never happen. I accept what
I'm becoming. I watch myself like I'm watching a movie. Inso-
lent mutation alone in my room. It's a cool ride.

◄   ◄   ◄   ◄   ◄   ◄

Summer isolation insanity machine. Napalm in the womb.
Bloodshot eyes crawl the streets looking for something that's not
dead. Watch me terminate this command. Watch me terminate
this impotent dream. Watch me annihilate this vision. Dog eyed
soldiers walking straight lines up the alleys of their assholes.
Dark and getting darker. It's time to destroy the lie. Watch me
slash and mutilate their womb. Whip it 'till it's thick. Melt the
streets. Stack them up and burn them. Let'em burn the sun to
cinder.

◄   ◄   ◄   ◄   ◄   ◄

I feel like a soldier in my convict brain
I look out the window into the street
Thieves killing thieves
People in line waiting to be victims
Wanting to get hurt so they can feel involved
I can see the love in their eyes as they lie bleeding
Wounded in the big game
Victims are heroes for a minute and then they're just victims

◄   ◄   ◄   ◄   ◄   ◄

Summer's almost over. I feel like running backwards into it. I
can't believe the bastards are leaving me behind. The nights are
cooler now, almost sane. The people are walking the streets with
a weary step. Three weeks ago they were running to the liquor
store or to their bedrooms to fuck or fight. School starts and the

wild dreams go back to sleep. Suicide rate will go down. Marriage and death rate too. It's winding down. I can still hear the echoes of the sun, the screams and the laughter. The light is growing dim. The roar is softening. Summer's almost over.

◄ ◄ ◄ ◄ ◄ ◄

I find myself in all the dark places. Can't see their eyes, can't make out their faces. I'm getting followed around again. Self doubt puts a hand on my shoulder, says, "This is nothing son, you know it gets a lot colder. Time is running by you and all the time you're getting older. If you're looking for the end in my eyes then come with me because it's right around the corner." I wanted to forget all the names when the plane went down. I had to find a place where I couldn't be found. Everywhere I looked they were looking too. They said, "Hey man, what a trip you know I never thought I'd meet you." I'm getting followed around again. It's all inside, walking around seeing myself in their eyes, looking at myself to see the one that I despise. It goes on and on.

◄ ◄ ◄ ◄ ◄ ◄

I'm getting used to the idea of not being in Black Flag. The band was great. I see now that it also acted like a security blanket. I thought it would never end. Now I see that all things end. I'm not trying to sound heavy or anything but it's true. It all ends up. I don't want to ride on any reputation of any past. I want to make it on what I'm doing now. This is a new start, a new reality. I'll have to change a lot. If I don't I'll be the worse for it.

What a trip. Today, in that office, I assumed that they all had heard about Black Flag. They didn't know me from a hole in the ground. Could be the best thing that ever happened to me. It's time to get to work. All energies must be put to moving in a forward direction. There can be no backsliding into depression. It's all cool if I can keep moving, working and growing. I will show myself what I can do. I'm on my own now, somehow I think I'll be the better for it in the long run.

◂ ◂ ◂ ◂ ◂ ◂

They say rehabilitate. I say exterminate. They say educate. I say eradicate. There's no such thing as rehabilitation. Nothing can be undone. No institution can understand. That's why they get built. Brick walls look impressive. The well-fed fear-bred think that the law knows what they're doing. There's never been a correctional facility that ever corrected anybody's anything.

Brick walled confusion looks impressive on the outside. Looks like someone knows what they're doing. They preach from a book they didn't write. They preach from a book they don't even believe in.

◂ ◂ ◂ ◂ ◂ ◂

I have a criminal mind. I have a criminal need. I have a criminal dependency. I need others to exist. I need a little help from my friends. I get help all the time, from the strangest places. Every suicide, every plane crash, car accident, overdose. Everything helps me. I'm getting stronger every day. I'm feeling better about myself all the time. I spent so long in rehab. I think I'd kill for the chance for someone to like me. Before the medication my mother put me on, the only person I cared about was myself. Now I see that others matter. Now I see things a lot differently. I think I'm growing inside. I was told that I'm a criminal. I believe them. I believe everything they tell me. Like I said before, I have needs. I need something that you have. Give it to me before I rip your fucking throat out.

◂ ◂ ◂ ◂ ◂ ◂

The summer's almost over. I can feel it. The way my muscles are tightening up. It's almost dead. I'm not. I'm still here. I didn't do what I said I would do. I told myself that this was going to be the summer that I was going to destroy myself totally. I didn't. I'm still here. I failed. Now another winter will come and I'll live through that too. For months I'll be chained to life, locked in solitary. It will be months before I have the chance to incinerate myself. All the houses will turn cold, no more insanity. I love myself so much that I keep torturing myself with life. It's like some kind of fucked knife. It cuts but it won't kill. That's my weakness. I can cut but I can't kill.

◂ ◂ ◂ ◂ ◂ ◂

I got up at 5:02 this morning to take a piss. I looked out the window at the rock house. There they were, three of them, hanging out waiting. Sometimes they resemble sharks, the way they walk, their heads moving from side to side, taking everything in. Sometimes they resemble mosquitoes, the way they hover around for hours, leaning on a different part of the wall every five minutes. A police car came by and shined its light on them. They retreated to the back of the parking lot. The pig bailed and they came back to their spot. I went back to sleep.

I got up at 9:00. I looked out the window at the rock house. There they were. Not the same three, a different three. That's kind of like the changing of the guards I guess.

◂ ◂ ◂ ◂ ◂ ◂

I need to feel pain to feel involvement. I need to see reaction in some one else's eyes to be satisfied with what I've done. I need to know what you think of me so I can form an opinion about myself. I need to do things that are hard to feel individual. I need to feel that I am an individual. I can't do it alone in my room. I need to do it in front of as many people as I can. I need to see them react so I can know that I did something different. I need to be the center of attention for awhile, all the time. If I fit in I feel as though I have failed. I see it as a shortcoming, a sign of weakness. So obsessed am I with this need to be different, I will deny myself things that others want that I want as well so I can say, "That's not my trip." Pathetic.

◄   ◄   ◄   ◄   ◄   ◄

11:00 a.m.: I look out the window at the rock house. There's an unmarked police car parked out front with its front end going the wrong way down the street. A few locals sit on a low wall on my side of the street and watch. Minutes go by, the locals shift restlessly, one starts throwing punches that fall short of his friend's face by inches. Across the street, a boy with a pick sticking out his Afro sits on the hood of a car that's parked next to the pig. He looks like he's waiting for someone in the house. A moment later a pig comes out and talks into his radio and then goes back into the house. A moment later the pig and another one come out of the house. One has a knife in his hand. He gives it to the boy with the Afro. The boy starts throwing it into a piece of wood that's lying on the ground. He picks it up and shakes it at the pig in the driver's seat. I look at the blade, it's sticking a few inches through the board. The boy grins at the pigs and puts the knife back into the sheath strapped to his side. The pigs leave. Everybody gets up and goes into the house. It was as if the whole block was holding its breath while the pigs were there and now that they're gone, everything's cool again.

12:00 p.m.: I hear helicopters overhead. The dealers look up like they're expecting rain. The chopper comes down so low I swear that it's going to land on the roof. Eventually it goes away and life returns to normal again.

6:00 p.m.: A blue Datsun pulls up to the rock house. White guy driving, black guy in the passenger side. They get out, the black guy goes in the house. The white guy sits outside on the wall in front. He looks real nervous, he knows that all the locals are checking him out. He looks like he's waiting in the lobby of the dentist's office to get his teeth pulled. Finally his buddy comes out and they split.

◄ ◄ ◄ ◄ ◄ ◄

I think that beer ads should depict young people throwing up in parking lots of fast-food places in the Midwest. I think that limp wristed fags should be in Marlboro ads. I think that Trojan condoms should do television ads. I think that MTV should have rock videos that use color footage of Vietnam casualties being loaded into helicopters. I think that punk rockers who piss on the rolls of toilet paper in the men's rooms of clubs should be taken to Watts and dropped off without bus fare. I think that David Letterman should be busted for cocaine and sent to the East Village of New York to take up heroin addiction. I think there should be John Holmes bubble gum cards. Gary Gilmore should have had his own line of tennis clothes. I think that all the street people in Los Angeles should hike over to Bruce Springsteen's house en masse, knock on the door and ask if they can use the bathroom. I think that Vince Neil of Motley Crue should have to do his time on the main line at LA County so he could learn the real meaning of "Soul Love." All the co-eds at UCLA should be dosed with crabs at least once a week for as long as it takes. Humboldt County pot should be the official weed of the US Olympic team. There should be a TV series called "Famous Suicides." All heavy metal bands should be made to give a large portion of their earnings to AIDS research. Joan Rivers should be tied up and teased by a famous transvestite, perhaps Joan Collins. There should be a magazine called "Modern Terrorist." ....To be continued.

◄ ◄ ◄ ◄ ◄ ◄

Every morning she gives birth. She lays on her side, panting and heavy lidded. They crawl out by the millions, naked and confused. They stare bleakly into the rising incinerator. She kills them one by one. She eats them, her mouth is bloody. Her teeth and claws are encrusted with dead flesh. She destroys them day after day. The flesh of the dead feed the unborn, and it goes on and on. She's a blank faced loveless, soulless hunger machine. She's a steel winged abortion mother. She houses a ghetto womb in her belly and no one gets away.

◄　◄　◄　◄　◄　◄

Nine in the morning I get woken up by the assholes from across the street. Nine in the morning and they are already out there giving each other a bunch of shit. Today's heap is about how one motherfucker owes the other mother six hundred dollars. Right underneath my window they're screaming at each other.

Now that I'm up, maybe I can see some real action. This is better than TV, at least this is the real thing. No action! They just sit there bitching at each other at the top of their lungs. Why can't they do this shit on the other side of the street? Why do they have to come on my side to do their arguing?

Now they're really going at it. Why can't one of them kill the other and get this shit over with so maybe I can get some more sleep? Why doesn't the guy just pay up and get the fuck out of here? I think I would like the shooting thing better. One of those assholes blowing the other away would be so great. The cops wouldn't even come. It's not payday and they're not interested in anything except money and power. I wouldn't call a filthy pig ever, what a sell-out that is.

Wouldn't it be hilarious if I went out there and walked up to the two guys and told them that I was trying to get some sleep and could they take their drug-related disagreement somewhere else? The looks on their faces in that split second before they kicked my ass would be classic. I could tell all the nurses about it.

Even cooler than that would be to take a gun, walk outside, go up to the guys and say, "Hey, you're fucking up!" Shoot them both, look across the street at all the other guys hanging out and say, "Does anybody want what these two got? Huh, I can't hear you? How come you're not screaming so loud now? What the fuck is your problem?" Then I shoot out the tires of their motor scooters and go back into the house.

◄ ◄ ◄ ◄ ◄ ◄

Tuesday night. I hear a pig's radio outside. I look out the window, there's a youth getting talked to by a pig. The only part of the conversation I can hear is the pig's, the boy is talking too low. "Where did you get that bike? You know we get about fifty arrests a month out of that apartment building, fifty arrests. Felonies. People go to prison. Where did you get that bike? Okay, we have two warrants out for your arrest. Put your hands above your head." I hear the click of the handcuffs. The boy is put in the car. The bike is put in the trunk. The car drives off.

◄ ◄ ◄ ◄ ◄ ◄

The air is cold. My head is shaved. I have a number. I'm watching my breath as I wait my turn. Twenty-five year old corpse. The guards laugh and smoke cigarettes. Twenty-five years what! All this and then onto death. I will be gassed and then burned. My body will go to a concentration camp in heaven. I will wait my turn and then my body will be gassed and burned again. I will spend eternity burning in a camp.

◄ ◄ ◄ ◄ ◄ ◄

Don't resist. It will only be worse for you if you do. Put your belongings in this trunk. Wave goodbye to her. Kiss the little one. Sign your name here. Shut up. Don't resist. Get on the train. Sit down if you can. Sit down. Shut up. Let's ride. Don't look back. They will be looked after. Don't resist.

◄ ◄ ◄ ◄ ◄ ◄

I only feel good when I'm taking orders. I only feel good when I'm down in a hole covering my eyes. I only feel good when I say please. My name is whatever they feel like calling me. I feel good when they put the blinders on. I feel good when they tell me that I'm feeling good. I need to feel like they tell me so I can live. I need to feel good to live. If I can't feel good then I want my life to end. That's my philosophy you might say. That's what I've been told. I believe everything that I am told to believe. I think that not believing everything you're told to believe is a sign of weakness. I have been told that the weak will be destroyed. I feel that in obedience there is strength. When I serve them I grow stronger. Every minute I allow them to run my life my discipline grows. They know better than I do. That's why they are where they are. This is what I know, what I believe.

◄ ◄ ◄ ◄ ◄ ◄

I'm sitting in a car that's speeding down the streets of Houston at about three in the morning. The two girls up front are talking about the two speed freak friends of theirs they saw at the show. I'm in the back with a drunk, mean looking woman whose tits are falling out of her dress. Every time I look over, her eyes meet mine and she looks like she wants to fight or fuck but fight more likely. The two girls are up front telling about how this girl can't hardly bend her arm because the black and blue lump is so big. The other girl says, "Yeah, it sure is gross, made me want to puke when I saw her in the toilet." Then they start talking about the guy who sells her the stuff and also goes out with her, says that he's always on it and his arm is all fucked up because he doesn't give a fuck where that needle's been before. They say he steals and has a band and deals and also has a job to try to keep it all together. I make some comment about how it keeps him mighty busy. They ignore me. The mean girl looks at me again and I figure that I'll just keep my mouth shut and hope to get out of this car in one piece on account of how the girl who's driving is all fucked up and no one really seems to care that she just ran that red light back there. There's a guy sitting on the other side of the mean girl, he starts talking and I find out that they go out. He tells how he got in trouble at work when the boss saw the bruises on his body. I lean over and ask where he got the bruises from and he points at the mean girl. I say, "Oh." and shut up again. The girls in the front start teasing the mean girl and her man about their sexual goings on and one asks if she is still into that "S&M shit." She says that she is very much still into it and she's going to get into it just as soon as we drop them off. The guy nods his head like it's no big thing. Fucking hot night out tonight, hope I get some sleep. I find out that the two speed types live in the place that I'm going to be staying in tonight and I'm thinking fuck man, there goes another night of sleep down the drain, what a drag. I'll tell you something though, not like it has a whole lot to do with what I've been talking about, but for a while there I thought that mean girl was a guy with a lot of make up on before her tits fell out of her dress.

◄ ◄ ◄ ◄ ◄ ◄

Cleaning up after the crash part 3. Oh man, I saw it on the news today so don't tell me it didn't happen. I saw it on TV. That big plane hit that little one right over Cerritos. What a trip, seeing all that luggage and burned up shit all over the place. That engine sitting in that front yard, outta sight! The guy on the news said that at least five people in their houses were wiped out when the plane crashed. Imagine sitting in your living room watching TV and a large commercial airplane lands in your yard. Would you trip out or what? Would you think you were on your kid's drugs or what? I started flipping the channels to see the other news broadcasts. This one channel had a close-up of one of the body bags, looked hot. The guy on the news said that there was luggage and limbs for blocks. If I wasn't three thousand crummy miles away from Cerritos today, you know I'd be out there, partying down like fuck, and looking for some spare parts to take home.

Budweiser should do one of those "For all you do" ads about those who clean up the bodies at a scene like that. It would be great, full color footage of these guys picking up arms and heads and wiping their sweaty brows. Then the shot would cut to the guys getting off work and going down to their local hangout with all kinds of blood and brains and shit all over them. They go into the place and there's all these pretty girls hanging out, they all hold up their mugs of Budweiser. The ad line comes up and that gutty throated guy comes in and says some line about hauling out guts and limbs is a tough business but someone has to go out and do it, and then of course, the "For all you do, this Bud's for you" trip comes at you.

Sure I'm happy about this plane going down, it wasn't me was it? Would I be writing this if it was? So, you know that I'm gonna be reading those news magazines with all the color pictures and I'm gonna be all cocky and shit, laughing and talking a bunch of shit because I'm gonna be riding back to Cal on a train.

◄ ◄ ◄ ◄ ◄ ◄

You get into a town and it squeezes you like a wet hand squeezes a bar of soap. It pushes you right out. You have to sneak in and find yourself a little place when no one's looking. That's what all the cheap places do to me. All the places with money are the places that are the cheapest. Slaves raping slaves, blowing the whistles on payday, forgetting their names forever. That's why I keep creeping along through all the creeps. Don't think that it's naiveté, it's just refusal to burn out. It's optimism to the rhythm of a motor engine. The beat of the heart sends my whole picture show into random motion. Just as I need to breathe, I need to move. I can't let the tears crush me all at once. I can't let the night freeze me out in one foul blow. I know myself well enough now to know that I need to keep bleeding. I need to keep the wounds fresh so I can sing the only song I came in at the beginning of, as the road passes through my soul and under the wheels of my existence.

◂ ◂ ◂ ◂ ◂ ◂

I sit down. I see the walls. I take my thumbs and screw them into my eyes. I shut down, I pull in. It hurts but there's no pain that I can find that's anything like it. My brain is caving in. I don't have the sense to get out. I can't feel shit. Cut me, kick me. I need to feel. Rip my eyes out so I can see.

◂ ◂ ◂ ◂ ◂ ◂

Home chokes me like a noose. Every time I go away I can feel it. I feel like a man who's just gotten out of jail. When I get back, it's good for a few days and then I gotta get out again. Home is a lie to me these days. Telephone whore liar calendar checking liar lover at arm's length lying dinner table trip. That's where I'm at and no one can tell me that I'm wrong. I'm nothing. I'm no one. I'm home. Easily reachable. I feel like a target waiting for some fool to take his shot. My scales are clean and I'm getting weaker by the minute. I can taste it and it makes me sick. Like I said, I'm nothing. I'm home. Only when I'm on the move do I feel good. I need to feel good, this other shit is a lie and I can't hold it up any longer. Here with all the other fools. I see them standing against the wall waiting for someone to come by and hire them to go out and work for not enough an hour. Not me, no way. But close, real close and getting closer every minute I stay here.

◂ ◂ ◂ ◂ ◂ ◂

I woke up early to try and get a good start on the day. I was up for a little while, a few hours, and then I fell asleep. I don't remember any dreams. I just remember all this shit that made me wake up over and over. It was something about a thread. A thread that you pull out of your shirt and the entire garment falls apart. Like if one was sticking out of your head and you gave it a tug, all your brains would fall onto the floor or something. That's the thing that I kept thinking about. I could see a cloth pouch holding something and then the thread gets pulled and all this stuff falls out.

Then I started thinking about killing myself. I think about that a lot these days. The thing that upsets me the most about these thoughts is that they come to me in a much more rational way now. It's no longer this crazed wild man urge, it seems like a simple way to deal with what's ailing me. I no longer fear this feeling. In fact I feel a lot better for facing up to it. I don't want to be here sometimes you know what I mean? I know everybody feels like that sometimes, everybody. I'm not looking for attention you know, I'm not. It's just that it makes so much good sense to me, good solid sense. What I mean by that is it makes sense when I'm alone in my room and I can think it to myself and I know that I'm right for me and I have no need to tell the world. I think a lot of people feel like this. I've been around, I'm not trying to say like, "Hey man, I've been around!" I'm saying that I've seen a lot of people and I see what people are up against. I've seen the same things that you've seen. I'm not trying to come off as any great philosopher but in my small way I've seen a lot. I've seen enough to know that this is a mean fucked up place that we are living in and I don't see any good that will come from my sticking around. That's the way I feel. I don't always feel like this. Sometimes I feel good. Sometimes I forget all the shit that swims around in my head. It's cool but the drag is that it's always temporary. At the end of the day I'm back to these thoughts.

◄ ◄ ◄ ◄ ◄ ◄

Walking to the store. The first thing that hits me as I go out into the light is the smell. Dog shit all over the grass. I walk down my street and watch the homeboys watch me. I have to look right at them, I can't help it. They piss me off when they stare. I feel like shooting their little heads off. I turn onto the main street and walk past the family planning center. A worn out street dude looks at me and waves and nods his head like he knows me, that random recognition always leads to the hit up for some change. I keep walking. There's bums and garbage all over the place, it looks like some low-grade war was being fought. Bum soldiers. They look battle torn, bloodshot eyes, slow stumbling walk. They pick through garbage like they're picking over corpses. I keep walking. The store signs are mostly in Spanish. Little Mexican children run by me screaming and chasing each other. I see a bum in a doorway, his stench is so strong that I can smell him from almost ten feet away. His fingers are yellow from cigarettes. I breathe in, it's like trying to breathe in a rock. My breath just seems to stop like it doesn't want to go any further. I turn the corner and go into the store and get what I need. The lady at the checkout asks me how I'm doing and I know she doesn't really want to know so I don't say anything. These people always make me want to destroy. All I can think of is the flamethrower and the destruction. I leave the store. The side of the shopping center is the place where several busses pick up and let off. Run-down people of all types. They look like they're on their way to work, they all have that bottomed-out hopeless look. The more beaten down they look the longer the shift is I bet. I pass the bum again and again I get that smell. I turn my head to the street and I see a beautiful girl on her bike. She has long blond hair and a blue tank top, her hair is streaming behind her. As she goes, I look back at the bum and then back at the girl, what a view, what a trip. I go to the bakery to get a loaf of bread. There's a line out the door. I squeeze in and pick out some bread. The line is made up of two distinct groups, old Mexicans and old Jews. The Mexicans look like they have worked the night shift of every shit job there ever was. They are silent and they wait patiently. The Jewish folks are very talkative, they make a bunch of comments about how long the line is and how strange that is for this time of the week. They look like they have just gotten off a Miami golf course. The men have their pants pulled way up past their waist. I finally get out of there and make my way back to the apartment.

◂ ◂ ◂ ◂ ◂ ◂

Have you ever thought that the night could be hungry? Like it wants to eat you up? That's the feeling I get sometimes. I don't want to move because if I do that I won't want to stop and I'll get all wrapped up in some crazy shit that I won't be able to deal with. But the night it seems, is always there, waiting around, looming over me. It's the feeling I get when I'm in this room at night. I want for something but I don't know what and I feel so isolated but at the same time I think I could run right through the wall if I really wanted to. No matter what I do I think I'm wasting time when I should be getting on to the real thing but I don't know what the hell that is. I tell myself that something's coming. I don't know what, but it's coming....but it never does and I knew that it wouldn't in the first place. But to think that something's coming makes me feel like living a little more. Sometimes I don't feel like that at all, living I mean. Sometimes I crave something so big that it will be big enough to really knock me out, or do something. I sit here and I can hear all this noise and shit outside and I wonder if any of it's for me, if any of those noises are supposed to be telling me something. I listen intently. I don't want to miss the right one. What a drag, but I don't know what's dragging. The night is the only constant. But that doesn't help much right now.

◂ ◂ ◂ ◂ ◂ ◂

I wanted this to be the real thing. I wanted it to finally be the real discipline. The discipline that I had been so well preparing myself for. I needed something to be real. I saw all things around me falling apart, all people caving in. I asked myself how long I was going to live this lie, how long I was going to let myself down and blame someone else. Finally I kicked through the wall. It was like a junkie that busts through the scar tissue that keeps him from hitting. It was like slashing through the womb with your teeth. It's the lies that are killing me. The lack of discipline. I was killing myself and I didn't even see it. I couldn't feel it. The painless days are over.

◄   ◄   ◄   ◄   ◄   ◄

Living on hope is like being locked in a prison cell and the sun is shining so brightly through the window that your eyes become blind to the bars. As soon as you're blind and drunk on hope, they gotcha.

◄   ◄   ◄   ◄   ◄   ◄

I'm leaning over the railing
Trying to steer clear of the bad nights
I can't get my head wrecked again
I got my head pressed up against a hot wall
I'm trying to push through
My head is killing me
I'm hunched in a corner
I'm trying to blend in with the scenery
What a hung over lie that is
I'm lying low undercover
I'm trying to hide from myself
I'm winning and losing at hide and seek
I'm stopped over the toilet bowl
I'm looking for a sorrow to drown in
Sometimes I wish I wasn't such a good lifesaver
I'm lying underground
I'm trying to rest easy
It's no good

I can't fake it
I'm alive until otherwise ordered

◄   ◄   ◄   ◄   ◄   ◄

I went to a show last night. I went to help out the sound man set up his system. What shitty bands. What a poor excuse for music. I looked at the crowd all night. There was nowhere else to go. All I could do was sit there and listen to this shit. I cannot count all the times that I wanted to take a flame thrower and fire it into the crowd. I wanted to incinerate the whole mess. That's what it was, a fucking mess. The only thing I liked the whole night besides all the people leaving was the pig's guns. I liked their clubs too. It would have been great to have rammed one of them down their throats. The show was at a university. Those kind of shows are always a joke. There's something about colleges that really sets me off. I guess it's all that idiotic knowledge going on. Like sheep getting trained for the slaughter. When I walk down the halls, I always get the strangest looks from the students. Makes me wonder if they would survive a war on these shores, or even an afternoon in a bad neighborhood. If some bad shit ever did go down, I bet they would make good prisoners of war, patient, obedient. When I walk the halls of these schools I feel that these guys are really getting taken for a ride, on their parent's money, I guess that's the way it should be.

The music, what a mess. All of it was so hollow. The opening band was called Guns and Roses and they blew the headliners off so hard it was pathetic. Even the applause after a number was hollow, well that makes sense. The audience and the performers go hand in hand. Seemed really depressing that this is the stuff that these people are playing in their rooms at night. What a shitty world to go home to. I was so glad when all the people finally left. It was a joy to load the equipment out and get out of there.

Some music might be alternative for a while, but if it is any good, it gets sucked into the big scene, and then that's when they get their pants pulled down in front of everybody. There's nothing like a little success to dissolve anything good about a band that had little to start with. Most bands have so little to start with these days. There's this thing where alternative bands get to be real shitty and not get pinned to the wall for it. That's the funny and stinking thing about the music business, it's all bullshit, on every level. You just have to find the pile that smells the best.

I choose to do what I want and not get in the light with a bunch of faces who are in competition with each other for the trophy. Gone are the bands that want to destroy and fuck the place up. This place needs fucking up.

◄ ◄ ◄ ◄ ◄ ◄

I want a gun. The heat is making my brain stick to my skull. I'm thirsty. I want it so bad that I could crawl up the wall, grind my nails into the plaster. I wish I could kick my own head in. I wouldn't think. I wouldn't know shit. A bare bulb in the ceiling, that's my brain. Hot and hollow. I wish I could scream the walls down. I can't scream. I can hardly move. Hot prison man. If I wrap my arms around myself tight enough maybe I could collapse my ribcage. No I'm not getting out of here. I'm not getting out of this night. I'm not getting out of this brain. The brain I'm in. Prison, bastard, fucker, self-mutilator. I'm all those criminals. If I could somehow turn it all around. If I could somehow breathe life instead of death all the time. Then I could get out of here less painlessly than all the rest. I don't have the guts to go out like you.

◄ ◄ ◄ ◄ ◄ ◄

We have a little war going on here. I just heard an ambulance go around the corner. What will it be tonight? The son who kicked his mother down the stairs? The father who beat his wife to death with the telephone? The baby who got forgotten by his mother because the drugs were real good today? You never know. You never know and you never get to know unless it's you and if it's you, well, you don't want to know. Maybe tomorrow it'll be me. I'll fuck up and walk on the wrong side of the street and then someone will teach me a lesson and the ambulance will come for me and I can be the star for a while. Oh, there goes another siren. Holy shit, they're dropping like flies out there. Tomorrow is just another day. You pack your lunch in a brown bag, make sure your gun is loaded and get your ass to work. You don't want to be late.

◂   ◂   ◂   ◂   ◂   ◂

A man sits in a jail cell serving a life sentence. He doesn't want to live anymore. To live the way he must live now means no women, no safety, no life, no nothing. Just the rest of his life sitting behind bars waiting to die. He wants no part of it. He wants to die, better death than God knows how many years in the hole. Everyday he looks for ways to kill himself. The guards took everything they could think of so he couldn't do it after he tried to hang himself with his shoe laces. The guards love when they get a guy who wants to die. They know they cause the man great amounts of pain by keeping him alive. They have no concern for his life, they enjoy the amounts of suffering they can cause a man. They pride themselves in the duration of the man's suffering. The know full well that at some point the man will find a way to kill himself. Imagine seeking death as fully as you would seek to regain your freedom. You would do anything! Imagine wanting death so bad. Imagine death as freedom. Wouldn't you hate the men who kept you from your death, your freedom? All night, you would lie in your bed all alone, thinking about your death like you were thinking of your lover far away. You would miss what you never had. You would find a way to kill yourself. You would, you would die somehow. Some die inside, the guards can smell that a mile away, they can tell when a man's dead from the inside. They give up. They leave the man alone, they let him get fed to the sharks.

That's how I feel some times, dead from the inside. I look into the mirror, I look dead, my eyes look tired and gone. Sometimes when I walk down the street I think that no one can see me, that's when I wonder if I'm dead. I feel like a bottomless pit. Like a big garbage hole. You can put stuff in but it never gets full. In fact you never see any of what you put in again. Kind of like in one ear and out the other, but down and out of sight. That's where I'm at right now. I'm nothing and I'm passing time without the guts to make a move in out up down or otherwise. That's the name of my tune. That's the ring on my hangman's noose. That's my Death Row hallway walk. I'm fake, artificial. I think at one point I had it. I had it down but now I'm a swinging man. A cold breeze from way down the hallway blows my dangling body back and forth from day to day. Life has nothing in it worth living for, not in my mind. I tried all the things that were supposed to make me feel more alive and they damn near killed me. I was lucky once.

◄　◄　◄　◄　◄　◄

If what I say alienates you
That only means you're alien to me
You and your fragile reality
You mild dissatisfaction
Your artificial subtlety
I love the way you look at me
Your well-rehearsed disbelief
You think I made all of this up?
You must be out of your mind
I never had an original thought in my life
I got it all from you

I owe it all to you
You walk outside and close your eyes
The truth hurts when it catches up and bites you on the throat
Nothing will incinerate this vision
Nothing will stop this train

◄ ◄ ◄ ◄ ◄ ◄

I'm always right when it comes to me
I used to think that people got in my way
Until I realized how little they have to do with what I'm doing
I live in one man's land

◄ ◄ ◄ ◄ ◄ ◄

I'm riding on the bus. I hear these youths sitting in the seats behind me. They're talking all this shit about how they were at this party and the one is going on about how hot this girl was when he had her in the hot tub and how soft she was and how her boyfriend in the other room was getting all jealous and shit. The other guy says that yeah, he knows that the girl is fine since he was with her last week. Then they start talking about all these fights they had gotten into last week, tripped me out. They were talking about how one dude got it with a chain in his head and how another got all messed up and had to lie to his folks saying how he had taken a fall down a flight of stairs. All this shit is going down right behind me. I was too scared to look around at these guys. I thought they might kick my ass too. The thing that was funny about it was the Californian accents they had. They're telling all these way out tales of sex and violence and it sounds like a bunch of rich surfers. So I'm hoping to fuck that these heavy mothers get off the bus soon before they get any ideas about knocking me around. About two stops later they get up to leave. They filed past me and didn't give me even a second glance. You bet your ass I checked them out. I couldn't believe it. They were fat kooks and they were wearing these new wave clothes

that you could tell cost a lot of money. The last one to get off the
bus is the one I can't forget. Thick glasses, big butt, with a denim
jacket that said "The Cure" written in magic marker on the back.
What the fuck is wrong with these people? The Cure? I'll bet
those kids raid their parent's liquor cabinet and get out the Lite
beer. What ever happened to juvenile delinquents? It's too late,
I think. There ought to be law. Any one under the age of twenty-
five will not be sold any weak alcohol products. It's going to be
malt liquor, whiskey or nothing. Anybody who wants to pur-
chase Lite beer will have to be over forty and have the identifi-
cation to prove it. Right.

◄ ◄ ◄ ◄ ◄ ◄

The palm trees make it all look like such a lie
They make the streets look like they're part of a movie set
Bums and palm trees
Garbage and palm trees
Urine soaked hallways, puke stained stairways
And palm trees
Like a postcard
There should be a postcard
That shows a dead street gang member
Lying in a pool of blood
His dead body resting at the foot of a palm tree
The desert ghetto
Dogs lifting their legs and pissing on palm trees
Palm trees lining the front of a star's home
Anyone can have them
Limbs of Barbra Streisand's severed corpse
Thrown all over her front yard
Her fat head resting on a palm frond
Her crossed confused eyes looking up
At the warm California sun

◄ ◄ ◄ ◄ ◄ ◄

The bums in Venice should get together and form a gang. They should get some patches to put on the backs of their filthy jackets. The initiation would be to shit and piss in your pants, without changing them, for a year and a half. They could rumble with other gangs of derelicts in parking lots by the pier. They would square off and bum change off the tourists. The gang who had more dough at the end of the night would be the winner. Not to mention the most fucked up by the dawn's early light.

◂ ◂ ◂ ◂ ◂ ◂

Have you ever got the feeling that there's no time left? Or maybe that it's running out faster than you think, faster than you could possibly imagine? Do you ever get to feeling like that when you're lying in your lover's arms talking a bunch of shit that seems to make sense at the time but not really because you know that tomorrow you're not going to feel that way? And you know it all the while and still you go along with it for some reason and you don't know what that reason is but you never stop to question it because you're too wrapped up in some shit that's making you blind?

Do you ever get to feeling like that when someone is stringing you along to your death by wasting your time with bullshit and lies that feel good? Do you ever get that feeling? Do you? Ever at all? Do you think that you'll be here forever? Do you ever think that wasting time is losing time? Do you ever think that losing time is gaining on your death? Not death that doesn't touch you, like in a movie or in a magazine or some fucking cause that you give your filthy money to, but your death. The real death, the one that takes your life. Do you ever feel like there's no air to breathe? Like things are getting tight and heavy in your chest? Do you ever get that feeling in your guts like it's going to be over sooner than later and sooner as every hour passes, as every minute, as every second goes by? Do you ever feel like the air is being sucked out of you? Do you ever feel like running until you burst into flames and explode? I do.

I've got a stopwatch strapped to my brain. Got a death trip man screaming in my ear. I got a part animal part machine vision digging its spurs into my side screaming, "Faster, you idiot, the sun is coming up!"

◂ ◂ ◂ ◂ ◂ ◂

Hail the oncoming light. Breathe in fire. Hail the oncoming light. Rip your flesh. Soul on fire. Soul on fire. Soul on fire. Hail the oncoming light. Time is running out. Time is running away. Time is incinerating the sun. Time is burning my soul. Time is eating my brain. Time is killing me.

◂ ◂ ◂ ◂ ◂ ◂

Do you ever get the feeling that there's no way out? Everything around you closes in. The walls that have all of your favorite pictures become your enemies. It's suffocation. Every thing, every thought, every movement, everything becomes a knife slashing at your face. You start to think that existence is a dirty trick. A sucker punch. You're a punched out sucker waiting for the air to not be so hard to breathe. You have to look out because you're walking into coffin walls all the time. You turn around and something says: don't breathe, don't think, don't move. Don't do anything to remind yourself that you're alive. Maybe then you'll be ok. Ok for now or as long as it takes your heart to beat once. Don't close your eyes, don't do it. Don't even blink. You don't want to miss a second of it.

◂ ◂ ◂ ◂ ◂ ◂

Public person stripped bare, divested, defiled by eyes, defiled by recognition. Pigs revel in their filth. They never go home alone until the one night they find themselves so alone, then they fall apart like a disintegration machine. You better face the alone before it's too late, before you become a whore. Before you become addicted to the voices, all their little voices, all their beady little pig eyes staring. Whore! Whore to their needs. Self abusive. You tie off and pass the needle without using. You're too busy listening to them. Watching out for them. Killing yourself for them. You get what you deserve. You choose to serve them. It's like stealing from yourself. But it's okay because you're not worth shit so it's no great loss.

◄ ◄ ◄ ◄ ◄ ◄

My brain is a low rent district. Look at all the folks that are moving in. Look at them, do I know you from somewhere else? Can I come over when the power goes out? What if I need to borrow some sugar? And all the while I never knew that all these folks liked me in the first place and I don't think they do but it seems like the rent is good even if the place is noisy all the time. All these neighbors, boatloads of them! Will I have to move out of my brain so I can get some dreams for my self? That's what I'll have to do. I'll have to get out so I can sit down and get some shit done and I tell you I don't mind all these folks fucking up around here but I wish they wouldn't piss in my gene pool.

◄ ◄ ◄ ◄ ◄ ◄

That's right, that's right, you remember me now. I'm that guy with the gun, that's right, the guy who killed all your friends the other night. Well, I came across the street just to tell you assholes that I have bought a new gun. Let me tell you it's a real beaut. It's a rifle and it has a big scope and the salesman assured me that it would blow big holes in your ass from the range I would be firing from. So I thought it would be real cool of me to come on over and tell you all that if you make any of that bullshit racket in the middle of the night I won't be coming out making a big fuss like I did all the other times, I have a new trip, I'm just going to shoot you from that window, right up there, you got that? I'll be seeing you through my scope, assholes. Good night!

◄   ◄   ◄   ◄   ◄   ◄

In the evenings the noise outside escalates to the point where everyone is yelling at each other. I keep waiting to hear that gun shot, that scream, that siren, something to tell me that someone has blown their top. It never comes. I wish there was a schedule I could look at. I would stay home so I didn't miss the men taking the body out of the apartment across the street or the two men squaring off in the middle of the street to kick the shit out of each other. That would make having to put up with all this noise a lot more worth it. I think it would relieve a lot of tension in these parts. I can see it in myself, all night long I have to listen to these assholes outside yelling like they're getting burned alive. Three in the morning and they're out there blasting that shitty music and yelling a bunch of shit. Tension, yes, the tension needs to be released. All I feel like doing is getting a gun and picking them off from the upstairs bedroom. That's what I call tense.

That's the problem though. All wind up, no release. No fire. No pow pow pow. Why can't these guys get into some heavy thing with the cops? All the time those choppers are hovering right over the block, they never do shit. What the fuck. Why can't there be one of those SWAT guys on the roof, someone like that guy Hondo from the TV show. I can see him now, his cap on backwards so he can see better, a cigarette dangling out of his mouth as he picks off those shitty little kids on their way home from school. Nothing like that ever happens here. All we get are these overweight social workers who come and hang out, score their drugs and leave. I'm not advocating death and destruction, well I guess I am but what the fuck? All bullshit and no death and mutilated assholes makes Jack a dull boy, dull and tense.

◄   ◄   ◄   ◄   ◄   ◄

Push them around. Don't you ever feel the need to kill them over and over? I do all the time. They make my teeth grind they make the bile rise in my throat. They force my eyes to hate. When I see them die, I feel good. I feel like I'm alive again. I feel like I've been re-born. I am part animal, part machine. Do you feel what I'm saying? Do you feel it? Yes you do, I know how you think. I know the whole thing inside out. I tell you, I think I'm going to explode. Have you ever felt like you wanted to rip your fucking face off? Burn it and feel the pain that comes when you live in this place. I want you to see this place in the middle of a fire storm because you know it would feel so good to know that they're burning like a fucking torch.

◄   ◄   ◄   ◄   ◄   ◄

Get lost in a vacuum and I'm an only man. Feeling mean and poor as I fall through your eyes. Getting lost all the time, you know how that makes it all seem too much. Getting cut loose, cut up, getting fucked up, and all the while thanking my lucky stars that I can still remember my name. I got home last night and it was there that it hit me. This is not home. Nowhere is home. That's it. That's the trip, that's the real above board on the level shit. And it stays with me and it stays with you and it runs like a river along my brain and it's turning on all the lights and I'm seeing all kinds of shit I never thought was there and it's blowing the circuitry until I find that mind frame where I can be sane amongst the bovines and the no minds and the killers and the fuckers and all the rest who failed the test and feel the need to send their F's my way like it's some kind of fucked up pay day or like a present when it's not your birthday and in the end it all gets so cleaned up that you would never know that someone died right here in this spot, someone who got lost and forgot and I tell you sometimes I want to forget my name.

◄   ◄   ◄   ◄   ◄   ◄

Sometimes I want to get a big gun and blow my skull apart. No more of those fucking black dreams to rip me apart during the incineration night. I want to put a black hole in my face. Big enough to put my hand through. I won't have to think about how I'll feel afterwards. By the time I find out there will be no more left to deal with. I'm not one of those to make a big production out of things. I would want to do it alone in my room. No note. No yelling out the window. Nothing to interfere. I've lied to myself for so long now I need the truth. I need to turn and see the black hole. I need the truth to come ripping through my skull. I need the truth to push my mind across the room. I need the truth to exterminate the lies I have been feeding myself. I can't stand it anymore. No more of those dreams. No more thoughts. No more wondering why. I'm sick of it. I'm sick of making shit up. I'm sick of lying, leaning my weight upon a hollow excuse. I'm sick of lies and I don't want to be sick anymore.

◂　◂　◂　◂　◂　◂

She was hiding something from me. I looked into her eyes. They were standing in front of something she didn't want me to see. I ripped her eyes out and looked into the holes. There wasn't much to see. Her secret was worthless. She was worthless to herself. She had thrown herself away weeks before. She couldn't bring herself to tell me. She had nothing inside so she hid her nothing. She tried to make it something to me. She knew when I found out I'd be gone. She'd be left all alone with her nothing.

◂　◂　◂　◂　◂　◂

It was cold and barren all around me. They were all buildings full of pigs as far as I was concerned. I had to come inside before I blended in with the wall paper suicide pig people. I'm not coming out. I don't want to be someone's paid hostage. I don't want to be a nail for some army of hammer-swinging monkey-suited thin-blooded neurotic paid to die by the hour lead brain slow boy flag waving television worshipping Jesus fearing fools, no, no, no, not me.

◄   ◄   ◄   ◄   ◄   ◄

I was riding in the subway going to Foggy Bottom. I heard a kid behind me say,
I want to kill!
And a man said
Sure, but in Europe?
I got off the subway with two beat up looking Oriental women. One had zit scars grinding deep into her face. I got on the escalator with a bunch of people and ascended into the light. I was standing behind this woman with tight pink pants on. The pants went way up the crack of her ass. I looked behind me. We were all looking at her ass. She was with a well built preppy guy, moccasins, tan khakis, gator shirt, Kennedy hair cut. He looked behind him and saw us looking. He put his arm around her as they stepped off the escalator and onto the sidewalk. We were walking on the same street but in opposite directions. The man and I both looked backwards, our eyes met. I waved, he didn't. Uptight.

◄   ◄   ◄   ◄   ◄   ◄

I was walking up the avenue. I saw a gold Mercedes parked with its hazard lights blinking. There was a man and a woman in the front. Two black guys come walking up the avenue towards the Mercedes. When they get to the car, one of them starts shouting and bouncing the car up and down with his foot on the bumper. The other one just stands there watching. The guy gets off the bumper and grabs the hood ornament and makes like he's going to pull it off, then he takes his hand off. He goes around to the passenger side and sticks his arm inside, he comes out with some kind of necklace. He goes around to the front of the car again and bounces it some more. Then he grabs the hood ornament again and pulls it off. He throws it across the street, it lands on a roof. He goes around to the passenger side again and yells into the car window. He turns away and he and his friend go walking on up the street.

◄   ◄   ◄   ◄   ◄   ◄

I'm exhausted but I can't sleep. Every time I close my eyes, these bright white dots go shooting through the space between my pupils and my eyelids. My body stiffens and jerks backwards to dodge the dots. My spine is an animal occupying my body. My jaws are clenched tight. When I notice I relax my jaw. A short time later my teeth are grinding again. My stomach is a hard knot. I'm sweating, my armpits and crotch itch. I feel like screaming but I'm afraid of scaring myself to death. My heart aches, I wait on each beat to be the one that jams my heart into my wind pipe. My head aches, it feels twice its normal weight, it feels like it's going to explode. I can almost see it ripping out of my skull, flying across the room and smashing against the wall.

◄   ◄   ◄   ◄   ◄   ◄

He took off his clothes and his watch and left them in a pile in the living room. He went to the bathroom and ran the water for the bath. He paced the hall waiting for the tub to fill. He didn't want to go into the bathroom until the tub was full. The last time he tried this, his face staring at him in the mirror made him chicken out. The tub filled with water. He walked in, avoiding the mirror. He picked up the razor and put it to his wrist. He took a deep breath and pressed down. The pressure on his skin made him stop. He wasn't afraid to die, that's what he wanted. He was afraid of the pain and the blood he knew he would see. He put the razor back to his wrist and closed his eyes. He pressed down firmly and evenly. He pulled the blade from his wrist to the crook of his arm. The pain wasn't sharp as he expected it would be. It was a deep and dull throbbing ache that he could feel in his chest and head. The razor dropped from his hand. His knees went a bit weak. He caught himself on the shower curtain which amazingly did not come down. He got in the tub and lay down. His breathing was heavy, the air felt tightly packed as he drew it in. He looked at the faucet and the soap holder. The air was getting heavier. The phone rang in the kitchen. He laughed and let out a long sigh, his eyes closed, his head tilted forward stopping when his chin hit his breast bone.

◀ ◀ ◀ ◀ ◀ ◀

I don't understand you. I don't think I ever did. For years I tried. I'm no closer now than I was then. It doesn't make me hurt but it makes me wonder. Back then I had ripped wounds and a head full of nothing. Thinking of you now makes me think that perhaps I haven't changed much at all.

◀ ◀ ◀ ◀ ◀ ◀

I have dirt under my nails from digging this hole I'm in. When they talk to me, they get my imitation. I treat the flesh on my hands like it's playtex. They shake my hand but they never touch me. When I extend myself to them, it's as if I have put a sign on my neck saying: destroy me. When I extend myself I always become the victim of some kind of cruel joke. Now I'm all for destruction, I think it's all right, but I would rather do it to myself.

◀ ◀ ◀ ◀ ◀ ◀

Downward spiraling man. Forehead pushed in, wall eyed. I rip his throat out. I push him. He falls away leaving a trail of exhaust fumes.

◀ ◀ ◀ ◀ ◀ ◀

She pointed her finger. His porcelain mask fell to the ground and broke into many jagged pieces. She looked at the face that she had never seen before. She walked away, leaving him alone with his undoing all around his feet.

◄ ◄ ◄ ◄ ◄ ◄

Florida Highway 1986. Lonely slum. I passed through on low wheels. It was hot outside. Shacks, gas stations that didn't work, dead corn in fields, children on the road, retarded and dulled by the heat. Two girls waved as I passed.

◄ ◄ ◄ ◄ ◄ ◄

The sun is setting on my street. I live on Sunset Ave. The drug dealers are having a meeting in the parking lot of the apartment across the street. They pull up in Cadillacs and BMW's. The little kids watch in silent reverence. To tell you the truth, it blows me away too. Seeing these guys with their gold and the nice cars, they look real smooth. Their hands wrap loosely around the steering wheels. Steering wheel one day, LA County prison bars the next.

◄ ◄ ◄ ◄ ◄ ◄

Clear blue sky, palm trees, offshore breeze, nice sunset. Well dressed black boys on my street selling drugs. Last night I was getting out of the car and one of the came up to me and asked, "Lookin?" I pointed the apartment where I lived and said, "No, living." He smiled and said, "I heard that."

◄ ◄ ◄ ◄ ◄ ◄

A fly was crawling across my window. I crushed him with one of the blinds. I watched him crawl with his guts trailing behind him in a snotty little trail. No I didn't stick my face in and clean it up with my tongue. You don't know me as well as you think you do.

I watched it crawl until it was too weak to haul its own guts. What a way to go. No complaining, no pleas for mercy. No cries for mamma. A while later I was looking out the window at the drug pushers across the street. I saw the fly again. It was still stuck the glass by its guts. Another fly was eating him. I wish I could be like that. My girlfriend blows her brains out in the bathroom and I take her body downstairs and live on it for weeks. I couldn't do that you know. I wouldn't have the guts. I thought of that fly again with its buddy standing on top chowing down. That fly has more guts than I do.

◄   ◄   ◄   ◄   ◄   ◄

Hello mom, do you read me? Over. Yes son go ahead. Over. Mom the sky is real red now and all you can smell is gasoline. You could look around at all the dead bodies and say that we're in some kind of hell. The choppers are so loud I can't even hear myself think which is ok in a way because it keeps out all the bad thoughts. Nothing to think about except death. It's not here yet but I know it's only a matter of time. Over. That's a big 10-4. Over and out.

◄   ◄   ◄   ◄   ◄   ◄

The Mexicans on their bikes
I see them around sundown
Riding slowly down the street
I'm still asleep when they go to work
They always ride fucked up ten speeds
Sometimes they pull into the store
A six of Bud
They weave one handed back into traffic
Sometimes I can look into their eyes
They always have that hard dull glaze
Hours of hard manual labor grinds the shine right off
Sometimes I think I see the same guy

I could be in Redondo, Hermosa, Torrance, Venice
It doesn't matter
I always see that same Mexican guy on the battered ten speed
When I look at him I think of overcrowded apartments
Too many days and nights of never enough
Too many mangled hands
Too many lies and broken promises
That keep you hungry and hanging on

◂ ◂ ◂ ◂ ◂ ◂

I sit at my table and listen to the noises outside. City sounds. I can imagine a new kind of jungle complete with its own animals, habitat and laws. The way one pusher whistles to another, each has a different sound and pattern. Like birds in trees. The police choppers, the motor scooters. The arguments, the fights, the gunshots. The eventual siren. The cacophonous blend makes me lock my door and keeps me up at night.

◂ ◂ ◂ ◂ ◂ ◂

When I was seventeen, I went to Spain. Nothing adventurous, just a school trip. I stayed in a hotel with a few hundred other bored, horny students from all over the USA. It was as if I never left home. It was a big party where everyone got drunk and nobody got laid. One of the cool things I did besides barely escaping getting raped by these drunk Spanish gay boys at a bar called the Don Quixote was to go to a bullfight. It was me, the students and all the locals. The locals didn't like us one bit. We always wanted the bull to win. We booed when they stuck the poor bastard with all the knives. There were three fights in all and they all ended the same way. They would make a big deal of killing the bull slowly and then the matador would put the sword through the bull's neck and kill him. They would drag the dead bull around the ring. Maybe to rub it in or ensure that the matador got laid. The last fight was the best. The moment came when the bull and the matador were looking into each other's eyes and the sword was about to plunge. The bull pulled to one side and swept his horn up and ripped out the matador's knee cap and chucked his ass up into the sucker seats. All of us Americanos were on our feet cheering like crazy. The locals were booing at the same velocity. They sent in another guy and he killed the shit out of that bull. They dragged his ass around the ring three times to let everybody know that you can't win when you're alone scared and crazy, pitted against a bunch of men with swords who aren't drunk and who need to get laid.

◄   ◄   ◄   ◄   ◄   ◄

So long alone. I wait for you. You see me standing there. I die inside. I watch you walk away. I sit in emptiness. Black hole, I'm falling in. Dead trip, I'm falling down. You took my onliness and turned it into loneliness. Needing nothing, wanting less. Filling up with emptiness. I torch my cell. I live in freezing hell. I wait and wait. I wait for you.

◄   ◄   ◄   ◄   ◄   ◄

The boy in the chip shop wasn't fucking with me. He was just standing there waiting for his order to come up. He was pale and lean. Nervous face. Acne, that gross facial hair that resembles fungus. I watched him lean against the counter tapping his coins. Like I said, he wasn't fucking with me. I had this overwhelming urge to kick his ribs and head in. I have no explanation for this. I just stood there and looked at his midsection and imagined myself kicking. I could feel the ribs against the toes of my shoes, just like that dude's head I kicked in Florida. That was the hardest I had ever kicked anyone in the head. I had no animosity towards this boy in the chip shop, no hate, nothing. That's why I was standing there wondering what my problem is.

The boy eventually got his order and left the shop. I can still imagine myself kicking his body across the floor of the shop. His body twitching and convulsing with each kick.

Driving home I imagined the car in a terrible accident where the driver's head was smashed into the dashboard. I thought of his brains and teeth mixed together with the food we had just bought. I could almost smell it. The smell would be like the one I caught while I was crawling around the site of where Katherine Arnold blew her brains out. There would be smashed bodies, steaming food and blue lights of the sirens bathing the wreck in rhythmic passes.

◄ ◄ ◄ ◄ ◄ ◄

I don't want a shoulder to lean on. I don't need it. The whole idea of "Someone, that special someone...!" is for me, a load of shit. I must be fully contained. No leakage, no spillover. Dependency is weakness. It's such a lie. Lying there in bed, in your lover's arms. *She's behind me, she believes in me!* No one is behind me. I am behind me. I believe in me. I don't need any support group to keep my head together. I know what I have to do, so I should just shut up and do it.

◄ ◄ ◄ ◄ ◄ ◄

I have children
They sit on basement steps
They lie curled in little balls amongst the shoes
My children have black eyes and broken fingers
Torn mouths and hopeless empty heads
I love my children
Their homes are big and small
Their needs are all the same
Their parents do not know me

◄ ◄ ◄ ◄ ◄ ◄

This is a cell I'm in. Fuck. Black head box and it's all corpses rotting in the hallway. Look at 'em rot. Dead youth in a school boy's uniform Iying in a hallway in my brain. The corpses can't move. I mean shit, man, they're dead and that's how I feel sometimes. Dead. Can't make anything move. I roll my eyes up in my head and think, all right, let's go! But all the dead school boys are just Iying there and I can see that were not going any place tonight.

◄   ◄   ◄   ◄   ◄   ◄

Walking down Main Street in Venice. I watch all the people go in and out of the stores like gerbils in a cage. There's always people eating in the window seats of those restaurants. I look at them. They look out at me and they look away with a troubled frown. I could never eat in a place like that. I would be afraid of someone driving by and shooting me. You know they always look at me when I walk down that street. I always look right into their eyes. They always look away. Like they got too close to something they don't like. I like that. I think that's the way it should be. As I walked by that bullshit factory on Rose Ave. I looked in the back where they take their coffee underneath the umbrellas. I thought how cool it would be to go through the place with a flame thrower. Like a real sanitation engineer. Hey fuck it man, it's a pig pile and if I don't like it I should move. Across the street from where I live there was a shooting the other night. Two girls got it on the front porch of 309 Sunset Ave. I was out of town the night it happened. Typical luck. I heard all about how the shots woke everybody up. And I heard about how this lady was wailing and screaming all night. Fuck I wish I was here for that. I would have been laughing and partying like a moth-erfucker. Blasting David Lee Roth out the window. Turning on the lights, dancing on the sidewalk. Laughing in their teary faces. High five-ing with the pigs. What a drag to have missed it. The other night I was walking by the place. There was all these white dudes hanging out in front. That's strange, I thought to myself. No matter. I pointed my finger at them and said, "Bang bang," then I laughed and went in my house. I'm glad that those two got shot the other night. Now things are real quiet around here. There's a lot of pigs around now but life is one big give and take, isn't it. Sure it is.

◄ ◄ ◄ ◄ ◄ ◄

I see why husbands beat their women. I see why moms and dads beat their kids. I see why they take oaths and break them. Make promises, forget and regret. I don't know why I didn't see it before. It's right there. In all their eyes. It's a lie. It's a lie and no one seems to mind. They find the most painless and elegant way they can to stand in line.

◄ ◄ ◄ ◄ ◄ ◄

The frail white people on the bus. They look so out of place. Mixed in like pieces of shit hanging from a Christmas tree. They're out of place and they know it too. Look at their faces. The slight discomfort, the nervousness, their thinly masked disgust. What a trip. They always look like they're being filmed by the police. I'm one of those white dudes. I ride the bus. I watch them and it makes me laugh inside. The Mexican girls with all that make-up. Big asses crowding over into the aisle. The homeys in the back smoking dope. The faceless workers and the whiteys.

◄ ◄ ◄ ◄ ◄ ◄

The ambulance came and took the bum's body away. The girl next to me looked out the window and said, "God, there's a lot of blood there." I wondered if the ambulance attendants curse under their breath when they have to haul away some stranger who stinks of his own wastes, who dies in a pool of puke, shit and urine. I wonder if they ever take one of those stiffs to a dumpster behind a 24-hour doughnut place and dump it. Or toss it over a bridge. Might be cool to dump the damn thing on your landlord's doorstep. Toss it into a swimming pool in Century City. The body is taken downtown and incinerated by a wetback who works for minimum wage.

◄ ◄ ◄ ◄ ◄ ◄

They get confused when their empty gestures cause no ripples in my pond. I'm a laughing man. Laughing like some kind of fucking dog in the hot sun. I laugh when their stomachs ulcerate. I laugh when they kiss their boss' ass as a career move. I laugh when they call me something because I know what I am. They can't make me feel bad when I don't play their lie game. Guilt is a word invented by some guy who owns a country club so he could have something to keep him up at night. Not my trip. I'm a laughing man. All the way to the gas chamber. All the way to the insane asylum. Laughing like a motherfucker.

◄ ◄ ◄ ◄ ◄ ◄

You can laugh your ass off at all this. All I can tell you is what I think. Take a look around at the lies flying so heavy. I can't think it's anything but the most crass set up there ever was. It's like getting sucked off so good that you don't hear the train that's coming to flatten you. I got some kind of bad trip vision. When I look around I see pigs everywhere. Pigs going in and of stores. Pigs going to work, to go lie and suck and kill. They suck so good when they sell you something. Motherfucking pigs are making me lose my mind. They got me crawling up a hot wall. They got me loading my gun. They got me laughing my ass off. I don't fear the violence that's coming. I don't fear the incineration. I'm swinging. I've been telling you that for years. Take a look around. See yourself for yourself.

◄ ◄ ◄ ◄ ◄ ◄

I was walking down Main Street today. These two women passed me and one of them said, "Nice hair-do." Then the other one laughed. They turned and went into a store. I was thinking to myself how great it would be to go up and smack her upside her head. It astounds me that some people think they can get away with such shit. I bet no one ever gave her a good one. Wouldn't that look on her face be worth a million bucks? To see her piss in those nice slacks she got on her husband's credit card, would almost be worth the arrest and beating by the pigs. Almost. I guess that's how they get away with it.

◂ ◂ ◂ ◂ ◂ ◂

That's my brain. Incineration is holy. Everything I do is holy. Every pig I incinerate, every lie I crush, every moment I don't take it up the ass is holy. When that incineration comes I'll be swinging from the rafters. I'll be feeling good because I'm holy. The holiest. That's why the pigs despise me. All pigs are jealous, that's why they get on their knees and suck. They see me swinging with no dirt on my knees. That's when they realize that they suck for me. You have to watch out for those pigs, they're vicious. It's all they know. Oh boy when it comes down is there going to be a lot of ball squeezing and backstabbing at the gates of heaven. Say there was a heaven. What if I came up to you swinging two sets of keys in your face? One set opened the pearly gates and the other to a new Porsche Turbo. Which one would you go for?

◂ ◂ ◂ ◂ ◂ ◂

I've got no romance left in me. I know I once had it. I have no need for love. You might have something to say about that, you might have a few names to call me. I'm not that desperate anymore. That's not to say that I've slacked off in the desperation depart-ment altogether, far from it. I have less time and less things in my mind to convince me of the need to support and perpetuate a lie.

Some will tell you that they need love to live. Well shit, people will tell you a lot of stuff, like how you owe a stranger your life to uphold the lie he's selling this week. Weakness is painless. Like sliding down a razor so sharp you wouldn't think to look down on the floor and see all the blood. The other night I looked down at her and almost forgot her name. It's just flesh. Put your tears in an envelope and send them to Hitler. They mean as much to his dead ass as they do to me.

◀ ◀ ◀ ◀ ◀ ◀

I used to revel in sullen amazement. All things around me made me spin. How someone could get in your face and lie, just rip you off like nothing. You thought you knew them so well. Nothing amazes me anymore. Not all the bullets in the world could make me wonder why. All these people talking about going to heaven or hell after they die. Hell is right here right now. War is at your doorstep all the time. There will always be a television set to turn up to drown out the poison. Lies are louder and stronger than the truth. Nothing amazes me anymore.

◀ ◀ ◀ ◀ ◀ ◀

I'm never wrong inside this room. Everything I think, everything I do is right and true. Even when it's a lie, it's my room. I know I'm lying, there's no one around to tell me any different. You could tell your friends that last night you were right about everything and there's nothing they could say to prove you wrong. That's why I don't like to leave this room. Outside it's all lies. You tell the truth and you get ripped off. You can get arrested or even killed. Inside my room I can tell the truth out loud. Sometimes it's the only time I get to be real. Because out there everyone is trying so hard to get away from what they are. Reality is the terminal machine. Death propelled. The truth is so plain that it reduces us to crummy bags of flesh. Weak and dependent. Shitting, pissing, eating, escapists. All of us, this is a drag for some. You can't rise above your asshole, you can only rise above those who think they can.

◄ ◄ ◄ ◄ ◄ ◄

I saw this dog run diagonally down the street one day. Right after it had gotten run over by a car. The dog was howling like its throat was going to come out of its mouth. Its guts were coming out of its stomach. They were tangled up in its hind legs. Made the dog run diagonally. I watched the dog go all the way down the block and around the corner. I could hear the howls for a while after that. I looked at the old black folks hanging out on their front porches. Their faces didn't even move. Now I'm sitting here wondering what kind of shit they must have seen to make that nothing at all.

◄ ◄ ◄ ◄ ◄ ◄

When I was young, I used to go to this park to play almost every day. One day I went there and I was heading towards this clump of bushes. There were all these policemen there. I knew from the TV that I had nothing to fear. I went over to where they were and asked if I could play in there. They told me to get back and then one of the park maintenance men pulled me away and said I should play over by the swings for awhile. The police didn't leave until it had gotten dark. I found out the next day that a little girl's body had been found right in the same spot where I had buried seven pennies. I dug up the pennies a few days later. I kept them because I thought they were important. Soon they were gone in the gumball machine.

◄ ◄ ◄ ◄ ◄ ◄

It was 360 degrees outside
The police had come dressed like friends

Acting like soldiers
They arrested everything
All the apartment renters
All the condo owners
The rich girls were trying to catch the pig's stare
In hopes of getting in a quick suck behind the bushes
To avoid prosecution
The rich boys could only offer credit cards and their assholes
The asshole offering had worked so many times before
It was no use, we were all going in
The last thing I saw before I passed out
All the rats and roaches cuffed and walking in a line

◄ ◄ ◄ ◄ ◄ ◄

Step back from the love hate game only to find that it's a game
played by a bunch of desperate liars like you and me. Do you ever
want to get past that chain gang mind? I got out, I stepped back
from the lie. I watched it smash, burn and hurl itself down the
street. I shook my head. I couldn't manage to feel sorry for any
of those fools.

◄ ◄ ◄ ◄ ◄ ◄

I was walking past the local cafe place today. There was a woman
in a phone booth out in front. She was talking away. She looked
at me as I passed and she started laughing. I spat on the glass that
was in front of her face. She recoiled and dropped the phone and
ran into the cafe. I kept walking thinking about what a pig she
was and how it was too bad that there was all that glass in the
way. About a block from the place, I heard someone coming up
behind me. I turned around to see a man with an apron coming
towards me. He asked me what the fuck I thought I was doing
spitting at that lady back there. I told him that he was a long way
from the restaurant and that he should go back before some-

thing really bad happened to him. He took his apron off and threw it on the ground. I took my gun out and I shot him. One less pig. To these people I should be a god.

◄ ◄ ◄ ◄ ◄ ◄

Stupid running man shut down machine
Breathing disease
The drunks piss in the bushes
Outside the cafe around the corner
Women in designer sweat pants
Step lightly over the rotting garbage
Like it's not even there
When they get out of their cars
I never even see them look down
They somehow avoid stepping in all that good shit on the ground
As if God wouldn't let it happen
Next time one of them falls on the ground in front of the sushi place
I'll step lightly over the body
Like it's not even there

◄ ◄ ◄ ◄ ◄ ◄

I need more than your shabby taste
You can't make it look good to me
I see it for what it is
You're looking real funny these days
One day you're going to be so high
That you'll float away
And miss all your appointments
You'll have nothing to say except
Roll another one

◄ ◄ ◄ ◄ ◄ ◄

I got filled up to the top
The noise and the colors pushing me around
One day I looked out the window and saw the whole thing was
a lie
It took me days, thinking on the whole thing
Seeing it from a new perspective
Everything started moving around
Exposing itself to me
I saw the dirt and the lies and the big one
The big lie
I went color blind
You might see it as a limitation
Living in black and white
I don't, I get tired of all the filthy colors
Trying to tell me that it's alright
Colors cover the truth
Colors tell me my shit doesn't stink
I don't need escape
I don't need confrontation
I know what I'm up against
At least I'm not fighting myself anymore

◄ ◄ ◄ ◄ ◄ ◄

You could lose your mind in this jungle. You could. It would be
easy. Or you could keep it. Hold on and ride. Like a soldier. Like
a mission soul. Like the Death Row man. Smiling and walking
down the hallway. Chomp down on the bit. Dig yourself in. Get
ready for the big storm. Oncoming. All around. 360 degree heat.
That's my ride. All the way alive. You could lose your mind in
this. Your soul could fall into the big abyss. Or you could
maintain. It's all you.

◄ ◄ ◄ ◄ ◄ ◄

Could you dig that all the way insane thing? Getting all the way into the thing. I'm not talking about casually. I'm talking about all the way insane in the house of war. No drug trip. No hotel room mamma's boy. The real thing. Swinging with it. I want to see the real thing. I laugh in your face. You blow smoke in mine. Let's see you do it. All the way. Why are you still here? I thought your art was going to kill you or some shit. Ah hell. I'll still buy the records.

◄　◄　◄　◄　◄　◄

Look over there in the kitchen. That's me swinging from an extension cord. I'm lying. That's just another dream. Another pass at the whetstone. The walls are so grey in here. And it's so cold except when it's so hot. Look in the kitchen now! Ten swinging bodies. All me all the time. Ten times dead. I feel like that right now. Ten times over and over. It's a meat house in here now. Of all the ways to go. Alone in an apartment dying over and over. Hanging like a dead cat. Look at my tongue. Black. Swollen. Look in the kitchen now!! Nothing. Dirty slob kitchen. Not even a corpse to show that I meant what I said. Just a liar. Here with me. Here with you.

◄　◄　◄　◄　◄　◄

Annihilation is all I can see. My teeth grind to powder as I accept, accept, accept. Swallow. Every day my vision draws into a tighter perimeter. I'm a one way brain. Soon I will be everything I see, everything I think, everything I hear. Everything I know tells me one thing. It all compacts into one. It all ends up in one place. Right into my head. Like a bullet smashing tissue. Mutilating existence. That's my incineration dream. That's my all the time. That's my all there is. Right here in the here and now. All mine.

◄　◄　◄　◄　◄　◄

Standing in the bathroom with my dick in my hand. Pathetic slobbering fuck looking into the mirror. Come like any other animal. Wash it down the drain. I feel mean now. I don't need the girl I was thinking about. That was a temporary weakness. I'll never do that again. I want to kill someone now. I want to see someone get destroyed, fuck that. I want to see a whole lot of people get wasted. I catch myself. Almost punched a hole in the wall. I killed romance. That shit was alright when I wasn't wise to the ways of the world. Now it's nothing to me. No girl can make me lose it. I must have been out of my mind. Stupid child. No more. It's just a place to put your dick as if you had no brains. Getting all bent out of shape. I tell you though, it's the lies that I couldn't deal with. Having to lie to not be alone at night. Lying my goddamn head off just to get laid. I can't do it. I'm glad that I don't feel the need to do that shit anymore.

◄　◄　◄　◄　◄　◄

You can tell yourself you're not alone
Lying in her arms, his arms, fighting so hard
Fighting until the tears come
And you're in the dirt again
Falling so hard when you didn't even move an inch
Rooms full of people say you're not on your own
How come I feel so bad when it's all over?
Maybe I was lying to myself
Telling myself the truth was bad
Telling myself a lie was my best friend
Killing myself ten ways
Making the alone the bad place to be
When it's the only place I've ever been
I think the lies I tell myself are the best
Airtight
I'm not going to bust myself
What the fuck, they cut me like a custom razor

No pain, no blood
Plenty of damage done
Invisible wounds up and down my arms
Lies are like that
They fill up an empty room at night
Your room, my room
That's the truth, the whole truth
And nothing but a liar's truth
Your room, my room

◄ ◄ ◄ ◄ ◄ ◄

I feel like a fool in front of her. I don't know what the hell I was
doing. My mouth was talking like it didn't belong to me. I lied a
lot, I had to. Sometimes they get let down when they find out how
frail you really are and you end up sitting in a cold corner all
alone. That's when I hate myself the most. Such a cold corner I
paint myself into. Now I don't talk to them. I don't lie. It feels
good. I'm alone a lot. That's good too. The other thing is a lie.
Temporary, confusing. Too fucked up. There I go painting
myself into a corner again. You know what I mean.

◄ ◄ ◄ ◄ ◄ ◄

I never felt like this before. Except for the last time I felt cold and
hollow. Like last night. It's just like beating off into the sink.
When you're staring at all that come in your hand and in the
basin, you swear you'll never do that again. You'll never go that
low. You'll never be that desperate. And then you find yourself
at the sink again, laughing at a mighty big joke. And you're just
another bluesman. And somewhere, someone is doing the same
thing wondering if you ever do. Well now you know.

◄ ◄ ◄ ◄ ◄ ◄

It's December 24th. I'm living in Venice. I went out for a walk tonight. The crack dealers were out on the corner doing their loud business as usual. I walked past Gold's Gym, the power line crackling. The smell of a drunk's urine in the bushes. Chicken bones and trash where the drunks sleep. I walk down Main. There are bums on the street trying to flag down cars to get money. They yell at me from across the street. I don't know what they are trying to tell me. I guess they are trying to sell me something. I walk past the laundromat, there's some bums sleeping on the benches inside. I stop and look at them. Their faces look the same color as their coats. I turn and walk back to my building. A bum passes me and wishes me a Merry Christmas. I pass the black guys selling the drugs. I don't want to go back inside. There's no place to walk around here without getting killed or depressed. This place really cuts me down. Someday I'm going to move very far away from here. The spray paint walls, the cheap smells, the screams coming from the apartments down the street. There's no place like this except for the hovel you might be living in right now. And you know as well as I do that we have to get out. Maybe I'll see you down at the train station. By the time we hit Arizona we'll be feeling real good. And when the sun comes up in Colorado and shines in through the window, it will feel really great. Better than this fake dirt lamp we got shining here in Venice.

◄ ◄ ◄ ◄ ◄ ◄

I used to work at this pet shop a long time ago, back when I was alive. I spent a lot of time taking out the trash. I was good at that, real good. I used to leave food out on the slab of cement behind the shop. After I took out the trash, I would sit on the stairs and wait. Soon the rats would come out and eat. They were pretty big, those rats. They would eat just about anything I put out there for them. One night I took out the trash and I put out a dead kitten for them. There, let's see you take that on, you bastards! They did. One came out and dragged it to a hole in the cement and pulled it down. The rat got it down about half way, and then it looked as if the little fucker was having trouble, the kitten was jerking around, its ass sticking out. Finally the kitten disappeared into the hole for good. If the hole was any bigger, I would have tried to stick the boss' kid down it. He was such a little pain in the ass.

I used to live in this apartment building with my mom. Right around 16th and Columbia in Washington, DC. The Park Plaza. I used to look into the alley from the balcony. I used to tell my mom to come out and look at the little cats playing in the alley way. She would look out and say nothing. One time my dad came over to the place to look around. I took him out on the balcony and showed him the little cats. He said, "Those are rats, kid."

My dad took me to the zoo once. We passed a large trash can. I went to throw something out and he told me to drop it on the ground, that I shouldn't use the trash can, there might be rats in there. I told him I could handle rats. I put the piece of trash in the can. As I was removing my hand, something grabbed it. This big fucking rat was trying to get out of the can by crawling up my arm. The rat jumped off my arm and ran into the polar bear cage. My dad was laughing real hard. All I can remember is him saying "Fuckin'-A!" a lot and his nose turning red.

◄ ◄ ◄ ◄ ◄ ◄

My dad used to drive me around on the weekends. When someone would cut him off, he would tell me to unroll the window and he would unleash all this shit at the poor fucker driving next to us. Whenever he would say, "Roll down your window, kid," I would get real scared, unroll it and sink as low as I could into the seat. The best one was when we were driving down Wisconsin Ave. In Bethesda. Some long haired guy cut my dad off. The window went down. My dad yells, "Are you a boy or a girl?" The guy got so mad that he ran into a parked car. My dad circled around and went past him again. The guy was shaking his fist. My Dad was laughing so hard I thought he was going to explode.

◄ ◄ ◄ ◄ ◄ ◄

Walking to the post office. December 26, 1986. Venice, California. Across the street from Gold's Gym. Budweiser, Haagen Daaz, Marlboro, the smell of garbage mixed with urine. A religious pamphlet, stained, stomped into the dirt. Ocean Ave. A Mexican man walks ahead of me. I pass him. A block later, he passes me running. A lit cigarette in one hand, a pack of cigarettes in the other. He runs across the street, down the block and into a liquor store. Walking back to the apartment. I see a black girl sleeping on a bus stop bench. Passing cars blow dirt all over her. I turn and go past Gold's again. You know that parking lot is always full of nice cars and bikes. I always trip out on that. The body builders are healthy and rich. I think it's funny to see some guy walk out into the light, sweating, crossing the lot, getting into his Porsche Turbo and tearing out of there. I walk past the gym and I pass the back lot. A man and a woman body builder sit against the wall and pass a joint between them. I keep walking down Sunset Ave. I see a man sitting on a low wall. Two white canes on the sidewalk in front of him. He has a sign on the sidewalk that says "Blind." I look at him. He's reading a book. I smile and pass him. He says, "Merry Christmas." I keep walking. All the kids are out for the holiday. They ride their new bikes, scooters and skateboards up and down the street, screaming at the top of their lungs. Bless their little hearts. Some older boys come out of the alley, they all wear those stupid warm-up suits, just like Run-D.M.C. They look at me and size me up. I wish they would fuck with me. I smile at them and walk into my building. I sit in my chair. In this room, no one fucks with me.

◄ ◄ ◄ ◄ ◄ ◄

There was a Rolling Stone magazine in my mail box today. It wasn't for me, it was for the guy next door. I took it in and read it through. I always read that piece of shit when it's free. The Talking Heads were on the cover. I read the thing. It was all about how the band is all bummed out that the singer is getting all the press and all they get to do is work on their little projects and live on their farms. Real hilarious. The last one I read had this thing on Run-D.M.C. and all they talked about was whether they should meet with Michael Jackson. Rolling Stone is some kind of magazine for the yups. The band can air out their little idiosyncrasies to a loving readership. That David Byrne guy is the yuppie messiah and his bandmates want some too! I read Rolling Stone to get me good and riled up. Makes me want to go out and walk over to Main Street and start kicking. I use it as a source to keep up on the yuppie pulse beat. I know, and you should know, that soon they'll be running this place and you've got to know as much about your enemy as you possibly can if you want to survive this earth trip intact. Like Sly Rambo once said, "In order to survive war, you must become war." Hey what the fuck, it sounds good and it makes sense. This one's free the next one will cost you.

◂　◂　◂　◂　◂　◂

To live alone. To live a life nobody knows. To cook soup in the kitchen and eat it without making a sound. To think of the things you'd like to do but knowing deep inside that you can't, because you're too damaged or shy or too totally fucked up. That must take a lot of guts. More guts than I have.

◂　◂　◂　◂　◂　◂

The difference between moderation and abstinence. The distance from close to almost there is invisible and unreachable to me.

◂　◂　◂　◂　◂　◂

I heard gunshots about ten minutes ago. Two of them and then nothing. I just heard sirens come to a stop a block over or so. I heard this one guy yelling over and over. Later. I went out and checked if I could see anything. I went all over the neighborhood. I couldn't find shit. I got back to my building, I saw these black dudes walking across the street. They were walking with some girl, and one of them says that she needs a man. They look over at me and one of them says, "How about that man?" I smiled to myself. Just my size. You take the first, buddy, the rest will take care of itself. Please.

◄ ◄ ◄ ◄ ◄ ◄

I was thinking about that girl that got wasted across the street. Wouldn't it have been great if they buried her in that strip of grass right in front of the apartment? Her friends could drop their cigarette butts and their empties on her face.

◄ ◄ ◄ ◄ ◄ ◄

The time spent alone will be hard at first. Each night will pass like a tooth getting pulled out of your skull by pliers. Without a doubt the first nights are the hardest. It's like when you get cold and you're shivering so hard trying to resist the cold and your body is shaking and your teeth are grinding and at some point you stop shivering and grinding and trying not to let it get to you because you become cold. More than just feeling it, you embody it. You're living it. That's how it is with the alone. After awhile the nights pass easily. You drip the alone from every pore of your body like a leaky radiator. The nights pass through you. They slash your wrists silently, bloodlessly. You start sitting in the dark, unable to move. Friends call and you don't want to go anywhere because you know that it would only be a temporary break from what will be waiting when you get home. That big, cold snake comes out and wraps itself around your soul and you go thoughtless, spinning into the night, imprisoned in your chair. In the dark you look at the light from the street, you listen to the sound of the traffic as it roars by. It always sounds like some kind of low grade war is going on outside. You don't wonder, you just sit still. Even when you're moving you're sitting still. Even when you're breathing, you're choking. Imagine that, choking on your own breath. Goddamn paralysis. Locked in, frozen. All confinement is solitary tonight. You snap into thought as a memory shoots into your head like a gunshot. Your head jerks. What was that, a shooting star? No just you and you. The nights are endless. They last all night and they come every night. They wait for you and you're never late. You're so damn punctual that you're sure that it's going to kill you and you're probably right. One of these nights. How will you know the one that will mow you down for good? They all look the same and they won't stop and you can't run and you can't hide and who are you going to tell about it. What are you going to do, get yourself a lover and that's going to be the end of your troubles? Even when you're lying in bed with this stranger and you're alone again and you're pretending that you're feeling real good and you use the word pretend when the real word is lie? You're lying to yourself, and it hurts and you know it. I tell you, I feel the lowest when I'm with some girl. I'm wrapped in her arms and I'm alone and I feel it so bad. I feel like I'm a rock and I think about this girl with this stranger in her arms and it repulses me and then I remember that the stranger is me and that makes me feel alone. I start feeling cold and I don't want to admit that I'm feeling cold and my body starts shivering and my teeth start grinding and finally I stop.

◄ ◄ ◄   ◄   ◄   ◄

I'm barely able to move. Shit has got me down. I can't look to anyone else. There's no answer in a lover's arms. Makes me think of a suicide man. Knocking on the door of an empty room. Losing it when there's no one home. There is only one place to find relief. There is only one answer. It's all a matter of barking up the right tree. I've got to bring it home. To me. That's where I have to go. I have to find all solutions in myself. Relief and resolution come from within. Tonight I killed all love songs. With a blood shot. One look in the mirror and I know that I have to know everything that I know.

◄   ◄   ◄   ◄   ◄   ◄

Alone in my room again. Writing to get out of it. Out of what? Out of it, you know, that prison mind. That gunshot wound feeling. I'm the diseased dog-eyed boy. Walking around my room. It gets so poisonous in here. I think I'm going to think myself to death.

◄   ◄   ◄   ◄   ◄   ◄

One of these nights. Merciful night. Sometimes I wish to be taken away. Into the black hole night trip. Deadened until I can't move, think or know any more. Sometimes that's the dead end dream I crave. The night seems to get to all of my wounds all at once. Tears holes miles wide, hours long, four walled in again. Sitting dreamless. Waiting for the next minute to crawl by, not missing a second of it.

◄   ◄   ◄   ◄   ◄   ◄

In the morning I sometimes sit at my table. I wonder how I got myself through the previous night. I sit there with my coffee thinking that I'm some kind of survivor of the Titanic or some shit. That's how I feel today. Last night was some kind of bastard. It's good to see the sun. I'm glad that I made it. Some kind of casualty.

◄   ◄   ◄   ◄   ◄   ◄

The whole place was cold tonight. I walked to the store through the shitty streets. This place has no soul. You could walk forever here and never get anywhere. As I was walking past the Minority

Work Force Center I looked around and all I could think of was Kerouac. His term "land sadness" or something like that. This place is a soul vacuum. I went by the laundromat. I saw the bums holding court on the benches inside, they were laughing like crazy. I was watching them so intently that I nearly collided with this big drunk guy. He looked like some kind of derelict water buffalo. I went into the ice cream store and as I left, I saw myself in the mirror. Shaved head, sunken face, too little sleep. Jesus I'm ugly, and those eyes. I can't control my eyes. I think they're not even part of me, the way they move in my head. Rolling. Came upon these three fat ladies. I had to go into the street to get around them. As I was passing I heard one of them say, "Oh, he's wonderful, he can get you excited about just about anything." Maybe she was talking about Adolph Hitler. I passed them and the lady stopped talking and then I heard one of them say something about the tattoos. I turned and looked at them as I walked backwards. I smiled my best. They looked like they were trying to swallow 1972 Buicks. Land sadness. The last woman on earth shakes her underwear. Dirt, empty beer cans and cigarette butts fall out.

◂ ◂ ◂ ◂ ◂ ◂

Hello war machine
My eternity
My long walk in the deep woods.
Ever lasting
Ever burning
You're all I have except my life and death
You are my reason for living
It's so hard to put into words
The explosions that I see
The trip that I'm on
Yeah and I ride

◂ ◂ ◂ ◂ ◂ ◂

I'm walking along the highway
I don't want to get picked up by a passer-by
I like it right where I am
Walking the depths of wherever it is I'm going
Highway
Walking alone at night
With those thoughts, those torn dreams
Small thorns in my feet
I push on
Dead silence, that's what's important
Death's vacuum, walking with it
Dealing with the all the time thing
And dealing on it

◂ ◂ ◂ ◂ ◂ ◂

Shot the dress off romance. She looks bad with no clothes on. You have to do it with your eyes closed. With a lie in between your teeth or you might throw up. I got tired. I'm weak. I can't carry all that weight. I had to drop the corpse and stop telling myself that it was good because it wasn't. I feel better now, but about what, I don't know.

◂ ◂ ◂ ◂ ◂ ◂

Hydra she wolf wraith-like bull whip divine witch ice-cold living-dead. Crosses boarders silently. Spider woman never forgets to kill for the sake of killing. But through the phone lines, a good friend of mine. I see the armies march. Unified, condemned. I'd rather crawl. Alone.

◂ ◂ ◂ ◂ ◂ ◂

We were in this room. Not a nice room, more like a room you wait to get the hell out of. There was a light screwed into the ceiling and it stared down and burned my eyes and made her skin look like fake leather. The room was hot, not hot like in summertime but fake hot. Hot from the heater that was in the corner. Heat that makes your nose feel like it's going to crack off. The windows were dirty. We were locked in a cell. We looked ugly to each other and we knew it. She said, "It's your birthday you know." I said I knew that it was, so what, she said that birthdays are special like and you get presents. I said I knew that too, big deal. She said, "I'll suck your dick for your birthday. I don't suck dick, I think it's sick. Just the thought of that fucking thing in my mouth makes me want to vomit. I don't like the way it looks, it's like putting a piece of intestine in your mouth. Christ, it makes me sick but it's your birthday so I'll suck your goddamn dick. Pull it out and I'll do it." She pulled up a trash can next to my leg. I asked her what the hell that was for and she said that it was for if she threw up in the middle and also when the stuff came out she was going to spit it into the can, there was no way she was going to swallow that. She said that she might even spit it in my face if I tried to stick it down her throat. I didn't want to do it. She said, "Why the hell not, don't you want your goddamn dick sucked? I said I'd do it." I said that she made me feel more ugly and worthless than I had ever felt in my whole life and I just wanted to get the hell out of there and why was she so damn mean? She asked, "Since when is sucking dick a mean thing? Christ, I offer to put that monstrosity, that ugly, dirty fucked up thing in my mouth and you're telling me that I'm mean? Come on, let's go! She slapped my leg and yelled, "Come on birthday boy, pull that thing out, come on, let's see that goddamn thing!" I just sat there looking down at the floor with my hands between my legs. I felt like shit. I felt real bad and there was no place I could go. She ran around the room yelling a bunch of shit at me, telling me that I fucked bad and that I had a small dick. She called me toothpick. She said, "Come on, let's see that little toothpick. Where is it, where is it? It's so small I bet you can't even find it!"

◂ ◂ ◂ ◂ ◂ ◂

The wives of all the guys in my graduating class. Are you kidding? You must be kidding. You want me to put that thing in my mouth? I never. .. You must be kidding. What planet do you come from? I'm calling the police. You're sick. Get out of here right now. Put your clothes on and get out!

◄ ◄ ◄ ◄ ◄ ◄

I come to see her again and she acts like she doesn't know me. I ask her what her deal is. Why is she acting like this?" She asks what I'm doing here. I tell her that I've come to see her. She says that I'm wasting my time. I tell her that I wasn't wasting her time the last time I was here. She says that was last time. She says, "I just wanted to fuck you because you were in a band. That doesn't mean I have to like you. I don't owe you shit." I tell her I know that but she doesn't have to be that way about it. She says, "Who cares? You were something I used to show my girlfriends that I wasn't afraid of assholes like you. Now why don't you just be cool and get out of here?"

◄ ◄ ◄ ◄ ◄ ◄

"You know you're stupid looking. You look ugly. No girl is ever going to fuck you. Boy I'm glad I don't look like you. Holy shit am I glad that I'm not you. I was in a bad mood until you came. Now I have something to be thankful for. My god, that face! You're so fat. Look at those zits. I bet you beat off a lot don't ya? Do you even have a dick at all? You're a fucking reject man. You're cursed! That's a great name for you. From now on you're 'The Curse.'"

The Curse got his face flushed down the toilet almost every time he went to the school men's room. The Curse got his food tray pushed into his lap a few times a week. The Curse couldn't tell his folks because his dad would try to fight the other kid's dads. The Curse learned to hold his bladder all day long. The bus ride home was excruciating, each bump made his jaws clench.

The Curse never went to the school football games. He did once and about two hundred of them started chanting, "Curse, Curse, Curse." There was a penalty given out by the school's disciplinary board for not coming to the Friday game when it was played at home. Three hours on Saturday, in full uniform. It was worth it to miss the game and serve the hours. To get to school by public bus took him almost two hours each way. It would be late afternoon by the time he got home. Still it was worth it, not to see them, not to hear them. Well worth it.

◄ ◄ ◄ ◄ ◄ ◄

January 1987. So much shit comes along and kicks holes in me. Sometimes I feel like a rusty old can. A friendly face can be like a funeral. It dents me and it hurts. Like when he came by today. He was sitting on the floor and we were talking about how this guy's fallen down and that guy's all fucked up and I look at him and he's looking at me and I know we are feeling so goddamn ancient. No glory. Just like old men talking about how they were alive once, and how good it felt. And when we talk about what's happening now, there's this deathly ring to the words as they go back and forth and it makes me feel like I want to die right now. I suffocate while taking deep breaths of air. The room gets smaller. All the wall hangings fade a little. Everything I've ever done comes back to me with a cheap taste. Goddamn that hurts, to feel like you've never lived. Especially when you look in the mirror, and see that you have.

◄ ◄ ◄ ◄ ◄ ◄

Sometimes I feel like going down to the recycling plant. Turning myself in, jumping into the inferno, getting melted down, coming out again as someone else. Scrap metal man.

◄ ◄ ◄ ◄ ◄ ◄

I dodge the holidays like bullets. New Years in Venice. All these dudes were shooting off guns. Sounded great outside. Like a war. But it's a tease because I know that no one got shot, but the homeboys were airing out their weapons all the same. There were shotguns. There were handguns and fireworks. Too bad it can't be like that all the time. Maybe I would love my woman more if I knew I might not see her again after I had gone out to do the laundry. Everything would be more important and real if there were bullets flying every night here in Venice.

◄   ◄   ◄   ◄   ◄   ◄

Little old man, age thirty. Your head lifts slightly to sympathetic applause. They love you and they think you're kind of cute. A cute little junkie. They laugh a little while they applaud. You sing and fall down. Kids and junkies are a lot alike. They get lost a lot, they have to be led to the places where they eat and sleep. Their behavior is accepted. Come to think of it, they're exactly alike, except no one considers a five year old who falls down and vomits a lot a genius.

◄   ◄   ◄   ◄   ◄   ◄

They get disillusioned because they had illusions. The postcard that was glued to their eyes got filthified by reality. Their dreams rotted and fell away. They broke down and caved in. I saw them crawling. And with my boots, I marched over them.

◄   ◄   ◄   ◄   ◄   ◄

Those dead dream cities, shit. You have to march through them. They're killing themselves to live and they'll kill you too. I take a look around the place I live and I can see that reality swept through this place like a search and destroy mission.

◄   ◄   ◄   ◄   ◄   ◄

I was talking to Tom the other day and he was reminding me of all that shit we were talking about then. Like in that Burger King where I was telling him about tattooing babies and making my book covers out of the flesh of kids. And I asked him, "I said all that shit?" And he said, "Yeah." And I said, "Man, I must have been on a roll because I can't remember the last time I came up with something that good."

◄ ◄ ◄ ◄ ◄ ◄

Sometimes when I think about all this stuff I did, I get real depressed. It was as depressing then when it was going on as it is thinking about it now. So I write about it and all the other shit I seem to have a lot of when I'm miles past the last disaster. But there's those times when I look back and try as I might, I can't make anything funny or anything else out of it, except for the piece-of-shit drag that it was. It's like trying to get juice from an orange made of granite.

◄ ◄ ◄ ◄ ◄ ◄

I want a woman who will remind me of every lie. A woman who will laugh every time I tell her that I want her. A woman who will tell me over and over that everything I have ever done is nothing much. A woman who will make me want her in spite of all the things she says. A woman I can come to who will turn me away and tell me that I'm on my own. A woman who will smile at me every two months. A woman who will kick me out of bed the next day and tell me not to be late the next time. Otherwise it's too easy to get dull and lifeless. To fall into the death trip: mindless, rotting, ego annihilating, love. I want ferocity. Savagery. Claw marks. Venomed fangs. Sweat. Hot rooms. Broken furniture. Insanity.

◄ ◄ ◄ ◄ ◄ ◄

You make me feel so fucking old. You make my knee hurt. I sit on the bed and watch you cry. Are you ever happy? You make this place into a prison. There's no place I can go to get away from your misery. Now you got me going. Head hurts. Knee hurts. I'm miserable just like you. I told myself that I wouldn't let you bring me down. But I let you because I ran out of breath. I fall back winded, wounded, weak. Like trying to swim through mud. If I had a penny for every tear of yours, I would buy this apartment and give it to you. So you could have your own place to be so damn sad.

◄ ◄ ◄ ◄ ◄ ◄

I limp to the post office. Cars pass me and beep. Jangles my nerves like a tambourine of razors. I'm in pain and scared all the time. I see that guy looking at me and if he comes over and tries to fuck with me I'll try to rip his goddamn head off just so I know for sure he'll leave me alone. That's how bad I want to be left alone. Because I'm feeling brittle and tense. Walking around in this cheap city with all these tender monkeys in my face. Pushing me with their fear as they drive by in their getaway car realities. Safe in their ignorant police dreams.

◄ ◄ ◄ ◄ ◄ ◄

Every time I breathe in I suffocate. I wake up and all I can think about is the lie. The lie stinks. Every time I go outside, all I can see is the lie. Every time I go outside and don't kill a pig, I lose a little. I sell out to their fucked up dream. It's no dream, the lie is killing me. The lie does not kill them because they eat shit for a living. They can't taste it. On this planet, I'm what you call a saint. But I'm a loser because I'm caught up in the lie. On the streets I lose my mind when I see them. I want to push their picture over and watch the colors come spilling out onto the ground, into the gutter. Pigs drove by me yesterday, gave me some kind of look. Made me want to kill them right there. The lie. All of them are the lie. A big rotten balloon with stretched out skin, waiting to explode. Every day I stay here I lose a little. Every day they get me and I know it and it hurts. What am I? I'm all things that are in the space between everything and nothing. I am all of that. I will probably end up being all things. I can handle that. Every time they look at me, they know what I know and they don't like to look into my eyes. I used to feel bad when I would look at someone and see them bum out that I was looking at them. I felt bad because I was insulting their lie. In feeling bad, in feeling that shame and blame, I was fueling the lie! Me! I was doing that. I saw the light. I see right through them. It's all in the way of the truth, their lives. They look at me while they're eating at the restaurant, their eyes drop quickly to their plates. They don't like what they see. I put ripples in their pond. That's a good thing. The only truth they see all day, of course they don't like it. I used to feel on the outside of everything but now I feel like I'm on the inside of all things, looking outward, looking inward, always looking. Like he says, "I am the eye in the bird's eye of your mind. To live all things." To run free in the burning fields of their insane. I must swallow my mind and soul every day to make sure they don't get a drop. I must be all me for me. All one. The big one. The mighty number. The only number that doesn't lie to me.

◂ ◂ ◂ ◂ ◂ ◂

I had a knife in my hand. I wanted a gun in my mouth. I was standing there with a knife in my hand. But what I wanted was a gun in my mouth. Standing there like a stupid fuck waiting for a death trip so bad. But not bad enough. Far from bad enough. Not close to anything. Smell my fear. Breathing animal. I want a gun in my mouth. Take care of me bullet. Deliver me from my small time life. My small time fear. So easy to wish for the thing that will kill me. Especially when it's nowhere in sight.

◂ ◂ ◂ ◂ ◂ ◂

No love runs through my insane field
Hate and death make me twitch
Otherwise I'm dead
I don't understand what keeps me alive
It makes me feel no way in particular
Always
All ways
All one
In my mind
Right here
Now

◄ ◄ ◄ ◄ ◄ ◄

The drug dealers are back again. The police chased them out but they came back. The shitty music blares all day long now. The cracked out arguments go all night again. I guess if I want to get any sleep around here, I'm going to have to go to the gun store and buy a "party pack" of shotgun shells.

◄ ◄ ◄ ◄ ◄ ◄

Love is flawed. Hate is pure. Real to me. I burn pop song lies in my room at night. Laughing at the doormat boys. Their cry eye faces. Hard dick blueball realities. Painful little mind. Writing love songs to the fucking moon.

◄ ◄ ◄ ◄ ◄ ◄

I see that little girl everyday. She always runs to wherever she's going. Christmas came and left her with a bike. Now she rides up and down the street. It seems she never gets tired. She always plays by herself. I saw her the other day standing with her bike next to all these other kids who were much older than she. She wasn't even paying attention to them. She was standing there because they were. The older ones were smoking and talking a bunch of loud mouthed shit. All at once she got on her bike and sped away like she had some important place she had to be. Today she's playing alone with a ball. She runs up and down the street chasing it as it bounces past the crack dealers hanging out in front of the apartment building. I wonder if she'll ever get out of this neighborhood without turning into to some poverty case criminal fuck up. She probably won't. That's too bad. She's got more on the ball than all those crack dealing idiots ever will.

◂ ◂ ◂ ◂ ◂ ◂

Pigs came to the crack house last night. All the crack dealers scattered like roaches throwing their stash over the cement wall as they went. The cops shined their little lights and tried to find the stash bags. But to no avail. The pigs rolled out and chased two dudes down the alley. They nearly ran over two other guys who were crossing the street. That would have been so cool. Total carnage. The bad guys killing the bad guys for a change.

◂ ◂ ◂ ◂ ◂ ◂

I went to the airport to pick up my mother. I went through the security check and the beeper went off. The man told me to go back through and empty my pockets I went through after I emptied my pockets and the beeper went off again. I told the guy that it was the steel toes in my shoes. I took the shoes off and went through again and I passed. The security types were all making these remarks about my appearance and I stood there instead of going down the hall. They said a few more things and then they kind of shut up. I said, "I can't understand what you're saying, maybe you should speak more clearly." They just kind of stood there and looked around and then one of them said that I looked like I just came out of prison. I said that I have been in prison all my life in their world. I went on to meet my mom. They called the police on me and this pig stood behind me until my mom came.

Every couple of minutes I would turn around to see if the pig was still there. I smiled at him. Eventually my mother came and we left. These people are so fucked up. They start this shit, they take no responsibility when it comes back to them. All they do is shift their shit to someone who is paid to enforce some trip they aren't even that clear about. No one takes the responsibility for their actions it seems. They find ways to get themselves out of it. They lie to everyone they deal with. They lie to themselves, and they wonder why they hate themselves.

People earn their living by hating themselves. Their jobs destroy them, every minute they are being humiliated and degraded and it gets to the point where they have been neutralized into anonymous conformity. They get programmed to think that other people are better than they are. They are taught to shirk their responsibility and sell their souls for a poisonous dream that's the cause of their torment and self hatred. Self hatred makes jobs for head shrinkers who enforce the conformity and self hate vibes. Weakness breeds weakness. Fear keeps the fear in the minds of the weak. The strong are hated. The weak are hated. People who hate themselves are weak. People who love themselves enough not to play fear games on others are strong. Weak people are dangerous. They are not responsible for themselves. They take their weakness out on others.

◄ ◄ ◄ ◄ ◄ ◄

You fucked her!
No I didn't (Oh shit)
Yes you did you bastard how could you?
You fucked her even if you didn't.
She looks over my shoulder as I write.
I ask, "Oh are you mad about something?" I see the look on her face get all mean. She looks at me again and goes upstairs. This was going to be a funny thing, this conversation I was going to write, but now I lost the thread of what I was going to say. The

timing was perfect though. Every time she walks by she sneaks a look at what I'm writing and I stick my head in the way and she gets all mad and says that she wasn't trying to look. Come on, just mind your own business and you wouldn't get yourself all bent out of shape. Life is hard enough without all this torment. Oh well. What the fuck, there goes another idea. It's hard to stay in a good mood around here sometimes. I do my best just to stay afloat.

◄ ◄ ◄ ◄ ◄ ◄

It's impossible to get away
The phone rings and I'm trapped with the voice
What an insult
What an invasion
How dare they
I should take it off the hook!
Oh no, but I couldn't do that
Imagine no one being able to get in touch with me
A fate worse than death!

◄ ◄ ◄ ◄ ◄ ◄

Sullen sunken eyed mamma. Tonight I send a prayer out to you. I can't see you and I don't know your name but I know you're out there. You're sitting in the kitchen looking at the roaches. The apartment smells like insecticide and baby shit I know. The child is crying, always crying, no matter what you do. He's long gone. I know what you're thinking. It would be easy to dump it down the incinerator chute. No more crying. No more insane nights kneeling on the ground tipping over the ashtray as you change it. That child has no name. You would be free to starve it out alone. That's why I'm sending my thoughts out to you tonight. Please, give it one more day. I can see it. The fat detective standing out on the sidewalk, looking down at the tiny corpse and then looking at his watch. He takes the metro section of the

LA Times and covers the still, shriveled, shape. You're upstairs with your door locked. You hear the detectives walking down the hall knocking on all the doors asking if any one knows anything about the child they found in the dumpster. They forget so fast so completely so good. It's as if they were never kept up nights. Some are thanking you as they lie in the pig's face. There's nothing I can tell you to make you change your mind, I know that. One more day. Dead-eyed mamma. I see you burning its arm with your cigarettes. One more day. You could snap its little neck with your thumb and index finger. Give it one more day.

◄ ◄ ◄ ◄ ◄ ◄

They see no corners and no straight lines. I see the corners and the angles. They don't question. They eat poison and call it caviar. They kill themselves at their jobs and tell others to be like them. They hate themselves. They preach self hatred self destruction and conformity and call them virtues. They talk about love but there's always money on their breath. They lie to themselves constantly. White lies are okay. Lies are okay. The truth is okay after it's been twisted and distorted into something more acceptable, like a lie. Lies are polite. The truth is rude and they don't use it unless they want to hurt one of their kind. All those who live outside their shallow lying reality are hunted down and destroyed. Victims of the lie are criminal. There's a place for them. The liars built it. They built a bigger one for themselves to live in. They call it the free world. And it's like everything else they say. They don't take responsibility for their lives. They pay analysts, priests and police to do it for them. They pray to God to deliver them from the hell they created. If there was a God, she would kill them all.

◄ ◄ ◄ ◄ ◄ ◄

It hurt when I found out she dug her lies more than my truth
It hurt when she finally broke down and saw the real thing

She was so let down
She felt like she had been ripped off
My truth incinerated her lies
I asked her if she loved me
She said that I wasn't the person she thought she knew
I told her I was right here
I was a lie to her lie
I let her down
I couldn't feel bad for being myself
It hurts to think that when we were looking into each other's eyes
We were looking at strangers we thought we knew so well

◄ ◄ ◄ ◄ ◄ ◄

Look at those streets running wild. Cars bullets killer sex ma-
chine drug boys twisting to death grip monkey rhythm. Can you
get a grip or is it running too fast too wild too much right now
all the time? The streets are boiling underneath your feet and all
the lies in the world can't stop that mother with the screwdriver
who wants to come into your face. Can you touch that madness,
can you put your hand in that fire? Can you do that or is it moving
too fast, too clean, too all the time snapping and twisting and
showing its teeth? It's melting all around you all the time. The
rhythm is real and random and it's so goddamn scary that it's got
to be the truth. Oh yeah, that truth bullet ripping your face off
again. Truth making your brain all naked and confused. Makes
you want to go up to a stranger and grab him and beg him to lie
to you so you won't lose your mind to the madness that too much
truth brings. All the eyes are on you now, did you know that?
Sure you did, oh yeah, those eyes are putting a burn on your skin
and you want to get out of that skin so bad. Look at that war, look
at that all the time reality. It walks with you, it talks to you, it's
all around. It's hot! It's cold! It's 360 degrees outside!

◄ ◄ ◄ ◄ ◄ ◄

The fuckers are killing me. The weak fuckers. There I am, the fool again. Putting myself in a place where they can get me. The weak bastards are all over the place. They suck my blood with their suckass shit talk. They will destroy me if I'm not careful. There's nowhere I can go without one of them getting in my way and fucking with my trip. Their word is nothing. Their word is worth as much as they are. It's their trip, their ball of confusion. The roots of their weakness snares my feet and brings me down to their level. It's like: "Here's a paddle, let's move through my shit together." That's the trip. They're worth as much as their word. They aren't worth shit. They always seem to get me. Their checks bounce. Their promises send me on children's games goose chases. They are weak and they make me weak. They are disease. They should be destroyed. Any disease that should be destroyed must be destroyed.

◂ ◂ ◂ ◂ ◂ ◂

If you're not strong inside yourself I don't even want to be near you. Don't even look at me. I don't want to know your name. Life is too short. The closest thing I can come to love, is respect. To me, respect is miles beyond. That's the problem. Love can exist in spite of a total lack of respect. To me, that's a fucking fat lie. I can only carry myself. I can't respect anyone who can't stand on their own two feet. If you want me, then you must want yourself ten times more. You must be strong. Otherwise go fall in love and lie to yourself as you beat yourself into happiness.

◂ ◂ ◂ ◂ ◂ ◂

They left you like you knew they would. They went away and you fell like a stone. All the way to the bottom of your room. I see you, yes I see you. Sitting in your chair, hating every minute of it. Falling like a stone without even moving. It hurt you to know that you were right about all the shit you wanted to be wrong about. They always leave you. You put yourself in the right place to get left.

◄ ◄ ◄ ◄ ◄ ◄

I'm burning out. I did a show last night out in Phoenix, AZ. This girl came up to me and told me that she really liked what I was saying. I said thanks and I tried to get away as fast as I could. She said that it's important for me to keep doing this. She was worried that I might burn out if I kept going as hard as I have been. She told me that it would be so terrible if I burned out. At that moment I felt more scorched than I had for a long time. Having someone telling me this made me want to do it kind of. Now I'm sitting here feeling very burned out. Promoters burned me. Airplanes burned me. Liars and death machines. I don't want to leave this room. I want to stay here and maybe if I'm lucky I'll evaporate or something. The phone rings and I hate the person on the line before I pick it up. I don't want to talk. I don't want to see anyone. I don't want to move.

I don't want to think. My eyes are heavy but I can't sleep. I start thinking about the weak fuckers that I find myself involved with, makes me think I'm as stupid as they are. Or at least as weak. Ah, those fuckers, those neutralized fuckers. Numb dead men jerking me around again. There's no such thing as keeping your promise. There's making it halfway and talking it the rest of the way. A lot of people are real good at it. They're weak and they're all over the place. The drag is you can't do it all. You have to leave some of the details to strangers, and you get what you get. You get sold out by someone that won't even remember your name.

◄ ◄ ◄ ◄ ◄ ◄

Me and Ian. Shit man, we used to walk down the street, we were perfect. No lie. Walking down to the laundromat to get some cokes. We were flawless. We had our sweat, the scabs on our knees and a whole bunch of stories. We would hang out in the parking lot as if our lives depended on it. We lived on the Avenue. Even when there was nothing happening there was always something happening. Everything was happening on the Avenue. Someone tried to hold up the lady who worked behind the counter of the deli! No way! Fuck yea! What happened? He went across the street to the rug store and tried the same thing after the deli lady wouldn't give it up. What happened at the rug store? Fuck I don't know, it's still there. Yea.

It was so simple that even we couldn't possibly screw it up. Going down the street to get some cokes. Better get some extra ones because it's hot as shit out tonight. Perfect. Hanging out in another parking lot just to watch the sun go down. Wanting to watch it go down because the day had been so great that you wanted to say goodbye to it personally. I was so fucking stupid. I was perfect with my sweat and my days and nights out on the Avenue like it was never going to end. No shit man, you should have seen us walking down the street! We just did it like it was the most natural thing in the world because at that time it was. I know I couldn't walk down the street that perfectly again. I got too smart. I got so smart that I got stupid to the point to where now I need bigger and more dangerous things to get me off.

I got Tylenol and coffee to help me cope with my current imperfection and intelligence. Goddamn. You should have seen us walk down the street. We were perfect.

◄ ◄ ◄ ◄ ◄ ◄

Tonight me and my girlfriend were walking down the street going to the store. We were right about to cross the path of an alley and I heard the sound of a car engine even though I couldn't see its lights. I grabbed her hand and we came to a stop. Right then this plain clothes cop car comes tearing out of the alley with its head lights off. The car came to a stop and then I saw the reverse lights come on right as we were crossing behind it. The pigs backed up and nearly wiped out my girlfriend. She looked at the car and called them assholes. The pigs heard her and gave her this dirty look. She and I stood and stared at the guy in the driver's seat. He zoomed off into the parking lot of the apartment where the drug dealers hang out. The druggies saw the car coming from way off. I heard them yelling commands to the guys inside to lock the doors and be cool. The pigs circled the block and were roaring down the street back towards the apartment and I heard one of the drug boys say, "Look out, he's coming hard." I thought that sounded cool.

This kind of shit happens all the time and I always come to the same conclusion. You call in the air strike and incinerate the fucking place. The pigs the poor, all of them should be destroyed. Melt the whole fucking coast from Santa Barbara all the way down to Long Beach. To clean this place up by conventional means at this stage of the game would be impossible. There's no social reform that I can think of. There's only one way to solve my problems here. To cleanse with fire. Any disease that should be destroyed must be destroyed. Hail hail annihilation.

◄ ◄ ◄ ◄ ◄ ◄

We were always pushing for war. No I'm not talking about some sweeping history essay here. I'm talking about me and my bro hanging out talking about the real things needed to get this country rolling again. I'm not talking about a war in some South American country or some shit. I'm talking about right here. These kids with their bullshit music and stylized decadence. The grown-ups with their bullshit excuses for getting away with murder. Let's give everybody guns and let this place get really wild for a change. It would be great. It would be war time all the time. Life would be more precious. Love would be a real thing and not just a way to get laid. War would put things in their proper perspective. The fat have gotten too fat and the thin too thin. It's time to kill some pigs and party down.

One From None

My mind is behind a locked door
I can't get out
I feel like punching my head in
I get mad at myself
All the stupid shit I get myself into
All the shit I have to take
I never get tired of it
I never get finished with being frustrated
I can't let go
No compromise?
Bullshit
I get compromised all the time
I do it to myself
I am weak
Everything that happens to me
I let happen
It's all in my head
I have killed myself a million times
I never get tired of killing myself
What a way to live
What a fool

❖   ❖   ❖   ❖

You can't hold me
Your tears don't imprison me
Your love no longer leeches my soul
Your love makes me hate love
In your eyes everything becomes a move
A sleight of hand
I don't have shit up my sleeve
I don't play games
I have a headache
My skull feels like it's going to come out of my mouth
And you ask,

"What does that face mean, what have I done now?"
I feel like educating your face
I don't want to lose anymore of myself in you

❖　❖　❖　❖

At some point they show their true colors
After the break up
After the trial
After the contract is signed and broken
Their true colors stink
These days
I find it hard to get along with them
I want to push them until the colors come out
And sometimes I hate them so much, I push and see
I do the same to the ones I like
The ones I don't care about
I smile at real nice

❖　❖　❖　❖

I closed my door
I saw the world frowning at me
I sat shut away from their downward spiraling universe
I stared at the walls
My universe frowned at me too
Shut away
Turn away
I want an eject button I can push
So I can get out of myself
When my universe frowns at me

❖　❖　❖　❖

I don't believe in opposites
Black the opposite of white?

Right the opposite of wrong?
No opposites in my mind
Free to think
Opposites divide
Opposites make the mind trip
No opposites in my mind
I see no opposition

◆　◆　◆　◆

I want to take a screwdriver
Mutilate my face
Find a beautiful woman
Make her love me for what I am
Then say I don't need it and walk away

◆　◆　◆　◆

This train ride
That's all we got tonight
What a mean game to be left with
The lonely drunk man in the dining car
Cowboy hat and boots
Holding a Budweiser
Swaying with the train
Trying to start conversations with all that pass
Lonely cowboy
From nowhere
Heading to Chicago

◆　◆　◆　◆

The first day back is the hardest
When I get off the boat and see all this
I freak out
It's not paranoia

It's pig reality
When I get back here I think
I will never get back out there
I look out the window
I listen to all the talk
All I think about is getting out again
I wait
Simmering in the coat of a lie
I do my best to maintain

◆ ◆ ◆ ◆

Memories don't hurt like they used to
Last year they cut and burned
It was my fault
I would go back and check on my memories
Like they were some kind of investment
When I would return to these places
To these people
I became lost inside
I think that people fear the fact that all things pass
All of a sudden you find
That you should have left the party a long time ago
All the great things that happened
Come back to make you feel crummy
You have to let go otherwise you get dragged
So many ways to burn out

◆ ◆ ◆ ◆

I'm going to sit in this room until summer
It will be a great long wait
I am in cold storage
I sit looking at the walls
Thinking about women, music and the heat

I want it all
I look out the window at the gas station
I try to imagine that I am somewhere else
Can't wait for the summer
A good chance to die

◆   ◆   ◆   ◆

Celine rocked.
Goddamn!...they're dead!...walking corpses...and so
young!...from now on I push them all away...call me any damn
thing you want...I don't care!...they're dead....the pretty ones
too!...so hard to talk to them...a waste of time...so empty!...I can't
figure out what makes them go...too bad...life is over so
quickly...oh well...I used to care...things have changed and I see
that I must have been out of my mind to think that I could have
woken them up!...they're dead...can you imagine that...trying to
wake the dead...what a joke!...more powerless power to them!

◆   ◆   ◆   ◆

Think of all those people in their rooms
Lights off lights on
Sitting pacing screaming at the walls
Staring at them in clenched silence
Like a prison term
That's where I go
I get unhinged trying to deal with people
I feel like an idiot for opening my mouth at all
I sit in my room and play Black Sabbath records
I pretend that I am Bill Ward
I pound the air to Iron Man
And try not to break the typewriter
All the war vets in their rooms
All those who have been brushed aside
Thrown away, shut down

They know that the world is full of lies
Mean, fragile and up to its teeth in death and bullshit

✦　✦　✦　✦

Obscure search for truth
Cutting through a jungle full of lies and liars
I trip over vines
Cut my face looking around
I can see you though real clear
I'm always looking at you
Every move you make
All the ways you kill yourself
All the ways you run around
There's nothing here
Empty time spent passing empty time is making me insane
The truth is one person in a room
Looking out the window
Waiting on the storm

✦　✦　✦　✦

All my war stories are old
They hang like old clothes in the closet
No one wants to hear old war stories
It's all I have right now
My mouth flaps dry in the air
I am in this room pacing the floors
Sun up sun down grinding my teeth
Jumping at shadows waiting
I don't want to think about that old war any more
It's driving me up the wall with bad insanity
I need new war
High on war

✦　✦　✦　✦

All the beaten down men got on the bus long before I did
I look at their cheap clothes and run down shoes
Their bags of junk
Their faces look like they're going to drop off their heads
Most of them are holding transfers
It's late
Look at these guys riding into the night
Like a sad song played out of a cheap radio

◆   ◆   ◆   ◆

I hate to feel need
I look at her and I need
I feel it burn
I have a black gift
I heal myself into a mass of scar tissue
Unparalleled in insensitivity
I numb myself to myself
Instead of listening to my need
I don't feel the cuts and I can't taste the blood
Like having a headache
Blowing your brains out to stop the pain
Stupid and gutless
But it's easy and it hurts so much
That it doesn't hurt at all

◆   ◆   ◆   ◆

Stop the headache
Cut off the head
Stop the bleeding
Drain the body of blood
Stop the war
Kill both sides
Stop hunger

Starve them to death
Stop crime
Put everybody in jail

◆　◆　◆　◆

He sits in his room night after night
No one comes over or calls
He makes no sound
He looks at his hands
He looks at the floor
He listens to his breath
He doesn't look at the clock
Time doesn't matter
His hands don't matter
He doesn't matter
He pays no attention to his thoughts

◆　◆　◆　◆

There were things I wanted to tell you
I couldn't get it together
I couldn't get past your eyes
After you were gone it hurt to have kept quiet
So easy to not say what you think
To not do what you want
Hard to take rejection
Easy to hurt someone else and not know it
Easy to make it hard

◆　◆　◆　◆

They will try to destroy you
At all times on all levels
All the things that go bump in the night twist your balls
Listen to how they talk

Sounds like trash falling out of their mouths
Every sound, every motion wants a piece of you
You must:
Disown
Disavow
Discard
You must break it over your knee
Dislocate
Take a look around
Look at all the animals looking at you

◆   ◆   ◆   ◆

They're all strangers to me
Sometimes I want to be known
I feel like I am at the bottom of a hole
I want to kick all the strangers
Inside
I fall into her eyes
Please know me
I am lost
I can't talk
I don't know
Please know me and understand

◆   ◆   ◆   ◆

They will try to destroy you
That's all I know right now
I go out and that's all I can see
Walking killer diseases
Fucking knife heads
Fear running wild
Seeing the real thing and calling it something else
Walking away with ground staring eyes

Pretending all the way to the grave
Like they got five hundred years to live
You will try to destroy me
If I'm not careful I'll help you
Like waltzing with a lie
Instead of walking with fire
Fuck it
I will crush you with my life
You are disease

◆　◆　◆　◆

I am the man in the frozen night cell
I am the man behind the shrieking red hot walls
Unhinged from the earth
My eyes are endless windows
All things compact and fall in
All the time I try to sweep my mind clean
The garbage piles up faster than I can burn it
In my room I am the bullet
I am the axis
I am the reason to pull the trigger
I am snapped off from the earth
I don't miss a thing
In my room nothing is missing
One of these days I will come to my senses
I know they're in here somewhere

◆　◆　◆　◆

In my hot room I am rising
I am a dead man right now
Come into my room and kick me
I need to feel you
I don't care how you do it

I need to feel
Touch me hard
Grab me
Shake my bones
I need to feel it
Shaking hot insane driven in
Pull me out
Pull me apart
I need it
Can't you hear the war sounds
The fire at our backs
Come into my room
In this lonely heat I am freezing
Burn me up
You know how to do it
Burn me beyond recognition
I don't want to know who I am
Turn me to ash
Burn me white hot
I don't want to see myself
You know me
Burn my flesh
Make me hear the animal sound
Destroy me

◆ ◆ ◆ ◆

I am close to no one
That's the way it is
I have no need to bleed for you
It doesn't feel good
Makes no sense
I am not cold blooded
I am a stranger
I go so far and that's all you know

No one gets close to me
Walk away
Don't say a word
It's no use
Lies take up too much time
Too much pain already

◆   ◆   ◆   ◆

I chew holes in the fabric of creation
I am the survivor of the all night room
I don't look for ways out
I know where I am

◆   ◆   ◆   ◆

Soon I will be gone again
Another tour in the van
Today I wrote a list of the things I need to do
Before I get to get the fuck out of here
At the top I put:
Rollins-bailing man
Like Pere Ubu
Done it so many times now it's like breathing
The last few days are like countdown
Take a look around the small room
Enjoy the last few moments of clean and quiet
I am twenty-six
I wonder how long I will be doing this for
I wonder what will stop me
Waiting to go is harder than the tour
Maintaining everyday
Listening to these people talk
Dealing with people who have no idea
I will be in shitty clubs the rest of my life

I feel at home in those dark shit holes
I will bury all these fuckers

✦   ✦   ✦   ✦

I keep my madness to myself
It's all I've got
Your eyes don't do anything for me
When we go, we're gone
I keep waiting for one of you to touch me
All you do is touch my flesh
I talk to you and I get so cold
Better than it used to be
Used to get all hung up on you
I won't play these fragile human games
You used to frustrate me with your shallow embrace
Now you don't make me feel anything

✦   ✦   ✦   ✦

I am death's custodian
I clean up after myself
And wait for death to blow out the flame
Death is inside me all the time
Like a friend but better
No lies
No judgment
The tap on the shoulder at the end of the trail
Death calls out in even tones
Everyday louder and sharper
The later days will be thunderstorms
With my life I serve death
The path is direct and I am on my way
The shortest distance between two points
Is the truth

✦   ✦   ✦   ✦

I could drown in her shallow eyes
I could feel like crust
But

✦   ✦   ✦   ✦

Big Larry the black fag
We used to hang out at the Old Europe parking lot
I would watch him park cars
We would hang out on the avenue and talk
So much bullshit
Sometimes all we could do was laugh
He would sometimes reach over and grab my dick
I would say get off me you big black fag
We would laugh like shit
He would look at me with these watery eyes
He would say:
White boy, you got no box, you got no ass
What are you going to do?
I didn't know
I asked him why the hell didn't he like women
He laughed so hard he nearly fell of his crate
He said that there was something about that big old piece
Just hanging there that really did it for him
I told him that women were what was happening
He laughed hard as shit
Asked me how I knew that
I didn't know shit about women
Much less anything else
All I had was a milk crate under my ass
And this big black motherfucker grabbing my dick
I told him that I was with women all the time
He laughed so hard
I thought his eyes were going to fall out

✦   ✦   ✦   ✦

I am trying to solve this problem inside myself
I am too nice for my own good
Seeing the people that I have to work with
I should be a real fucker
So I can keep my head above water
I am working hard
Makes me mean as shit
Nice guys have a lot of friends
Then they fall and have none
They cry and wonder why
The friends you have when you're down
Are the only ones that matter
We have one thing in common
We have a lot less friends than we think

◆ ◆ ◆ ◆

I met a guy once
He had been locked away in solitary for a stretch
When they came to let him out, he didn't want to go
He liked it better in there
Said it was a world that he could understand and control
Sometimes I think it would be better to stay in a cage
It gets hard to take the shit that these fakes put across
They should be careful
Someone might take them out of the picture
Just for a laugh
Or because they have the blues
The world is big
You see how people react to the terror
The size and the noise
Freaks them right out
They wish for the cage like I wish for the cage
Sometimes I want to kill you
Make you wish you gave me the cage

Before one of your pigs takes me out
I am going to take a few of you down
I have the blues from the size and the noise
Where's that cage?

*   *   *   *

I am the axis tonight
All things
Can't shut off my mind
Can't stop the eyes from seeing
The overload never comes
I become selfless
I do all things for no reason
No reason is the reason
All things tonight

*   *   *   *

The lies that come out feel good to say
Sound good to hear
Truth is sometimes painful
Sometimes people like to get out
There's always someone else who wants to get out
We find each other
We dig the lies

*   *   *   *

Walking on a dark street looking for a friend
Looking at the faces that pass me by
Wondering if anyone knows me
Someone without a hollow, ringing smile
Someone who won't pass me by and ease the pain
I like the faceless faces
Perfect strangers in all the right places

Something to ease the pain
I have a long face
It falls to the ground
Looking for something to ease the pain

◆ ◆ ◆ ◆

We can get together
Talk, sing the old songs
We can keep each other's spirits up
After awhile it sounds real
We will believe it
With lies we can ease the pain
To kill the pain would be good
Looking for a way out of it
At the end of the night we separate
We becomes I
And then it gets real
That can be hard
The night gets cold
The emptiness so huge
The everything so all the time
That's why we cling
Like leaves to a shivering tree
Trying to hide from death
By running headlong into its mouth

◆ ◆ ◆ ◆

Gun in mouth blues
I am breathing in night air
I am going to take the big breath
This is important
The stars are in the sky
They shine like diamonds

Cold and far away like me
Like this whole fucking place
The walls are singing tonight
It's all coming to me
All things are compacting into one
Life is a joke
A tease
Now :
Shot in the dark
Knee jerk
Oily smoke
Brainless
Hot man
Filling the room
With the rising sun

◆　◆　◆　◆

I have come back to you swinging man
I left you in that room years ago
I went out into the light and looked around
I have come back into the darkness
To bask in your rancid creaking rhythm
I can hear you swing back and forth
I can see liquid dripping from your mouth
Sticking your tongue out, making fun of the world
I see why now
They make me feel like they made you feel
Hollow and alone
Emptied and gutted
I must tell you right now
Silence is the most powerful sound I have ever heard
The things they said feel good
Don't
You could never fit in

So you made your own place
That's what I need to do
I feel pushed out of everything
I wish I could have seen you kick out the chair
It would have been great to see your eyes
But then again
That wouldn't have been too good for you
The best things are done alone

◆　◆　◆　◆

Take my hand
Come into this dark room
Get down on the floor with me
Let's get slain
Lick the sweat
Taste the blood
Hear the sound
For once
For real
I need something real from you
I want you so bad
I want to taste you
I need to feel your teeth in my flesh

◆　◆　◆　◆

I took you to you
That's what you wanted
I think I did a good job
You got mad when I left you there
You cursed me
For the stench of your trash
Well, it's all you now
Sooner or later you'll see

The sun shines outside the sewer
It's easy to come away empty handed when you don't reach out
It's hard to believe you when you say you're choking
When you have your hands around someone else's throat
It's all you and you now
If you lean too far to one side you will fall
You'll have to pick yourself up off the floor of your soul
Scar tissue is stronger than normal flesh
It's all you for you now
All things inside
The poison
The medicine
All in you for you

✦ ✦ ✦ ✦

When I look at you
I want to destroy your smile
It sits on your face like a lie
You look good
I want to know the truth about you
I want to get close to you
When I do, you see that I see through you
Your heart beats like a small bird
You know me well
That's why you can't handle me
It hurts me to act a fool
Pretend I don't see you for what you are
All of you keep me on the outside
I want to believe your lies
Turn myself off and feel you
But I can't stop seeing through
All of you

✦ ✦ ✦ ✦

He sat in the dark room and waited for her
She was not his friend
He tried friendship for years and knew the truth
He wanted someone to be nice to him for an hour
He was lonely
It made no sense that someone would find him attractive
That someone would want to be with him for what he was
In his business everybody wanted something
There was always an ulterior motive, a game being played
There was something wrong when someone was nice to him
And they weren't getting paid
Every time someone wanted to shake his hand
He wanted to say:
What are you after?
How much do you want?
He was not a bad person
He just couldn't identify
He sat and waited for her to come
She was a whore
Not off the streets, she was high class
His manager got her for him
There was a knock on the door
He opened the door and she came in
She looked at him and smiled
She looked down at a card in her hand
Asked if his name was Frank
He nodded
She went into a speech about the things she wasn't into
Rough stuff, anal sex, S&M
He nodded
He spoke:
It's hard for me. I'm not used to this. I need you to be nice to me
for awhile. I want you to pretend that you know me and like me.
You don't have to take off your clothes unless you want to.
Maybe you could just put your arms around me for awhile.

Could you do that for me?
She put her arms around him
He closed his eyes
He felt good
She looked over his shoulder at the television
She almost started to laugh out loud
She wanted to ask if she could light a smoke
What a crack up, this rock star
Her little brother had all of his records
If he knew what he was really like, he would throw them out
After a short time he pushed her away
Gave her a wad of money
Said: It's all there, thanks
Get out

✦　✦　✦　✦

Don't talk to me about your training
What the fuck are you training for?
There is a difference between making someone happy
And inflicting your happiness on them
Don't drag me through your happiness
Your unhappiness was bad enough

✦　✦　✦　✦

They don't lie a lot
They just don't tell the truth very often
Truth does not mean much to them
You can lie to them, or tell the truth
Makes no difference to them
Walk on them if you want
Eat with their forks
Destroy them for the hell of it

✦　✦　✦　✦

Animals in pain
Sweating and screaming
Bullets blowing brains across apartments all over town
The janitor hangs himself in the basement
Had a falling out with God
Leaves a note saying he was sorry for his life
Hot night breaks jaws
All is fair in love and hell
If you don't like it, crawl on your hands and knees
And stick your head in the oven
Breathe deep
Dying in rooms
Crying out from plaster tombs
Heroin worship
Nightmare in the womb
Sliding down the icy spike
No way but out

✦　✦　✦　✦

Another gun in mouth blues
Another day, no answer
Fist through the mirror
Fist through the wall
Pull back
The pain
Over and over
Gun in hand
Itchy finger
Perfection
Pull back
Shut down
So far down
So far out
All the way

✦　✦　✦　✦

Ok on my own
Around people, I come apart
Waste energy
Could have put it into the work
They will never understand you
Best to move silent and unseen
Like the wind
Like a disease
Like dreams

✦ ✦ ✦ ✦

Look at me
Look closer
You see the distance grow
It cools and widens
You see that we are ugly
There is nothing left but the truth
It locks you with cold lips
You feel the lump in your throat grow
You can't get farther away than too close

✦ ✦ ✦ ✦

Fevered brain
Bad water in the river
Foul taste in my mouth
Bile spit taste of blood
My eyes feel warm in their sockets
Ugly mind
It's real
She said that she didn't think I was like this
You are everything you say I am

✦ ✦ ✦ ✦

There are a few good times left
I drink from their streams
Like a parched soldier
I take their damp rags and wring drops into my mouth

✦ ✦ ✦ ✦

This wonder
The uncompromising will to destroy
I turn to the wall
They all fall away
The feather people
Inhale
Exhale them right out of the room
They don't even know
What a joke

✦ ✦ ✦ ✦

I will endure
I will turn to stone
I will maintain
I freeze like ice
A bullet of thought
Ice cold reality
Straight and clear
Everyday I see it clearer and clearer
It compresses itself into diamonds in my brain
Elimination
This is beauty like I never knew

✦ ✦ ✦ ✦

I kneel down on the floor of my room
I pull back a section of the curtain and look outside

Half an eyeful is all I can take
Every pig eye in every house tries to catch me
They're like an army of diseases
I pull away from the window, I've seen enough
I crawl on the floor to different parts of the room
Can't stand up
Snipers, fuckers, pigs, you never know
Steely sounds from outside
Traffic talk
Metal dumb animal suicide pain gibberish
Soon the night will come
I will be able to breathe again
I will pull into my head
The place where I fuck and kill them all
Where I destroy myself
Where I smash myself into a million pieces
Grow scar tissue
Stronger than ever
Doomed to endure and prevail

◆　◆　◆　◆

I reach deep inside myself
I rip out a handful of bleeding crackling wires
I squeeze the juice out
I burn them out
I want to see where the truth lies
I want to see where it all breaks down
I walk down the mouth of every beast I can find
So I can see what's at the end
That's the only part that interests me
The end
The rest is all getting there

◆　◆　◆　◆

Sometimes while playing
Too much heat, too little air
The end of each song forces me to my knees
I reach for the water and try to breathe
When the last song has finished with me
I go staggering outside for real air
As I walk I think about how funny it is
One minute I am in the middle of hot lights and strangers
The next I am on some street with all the air I want
Feeling like I could do it over again
I get one sliver of relief
I wrap it around me like it's some kind of badge
Happens every night the music tries to kill me

❖ ❖ ❖ ❖

Together
Two strangers
Clawing each other's flesh
No words
Waiting room eyes
Dry mouth
Dry everything

❖ ❖ ❖ ❖

I touch her
Doesn't matter who she is
Feels the same
Tastes the same
Makes me empty

❖ ❖ ❖ ❖

Crawl to me
Get in line

Bend over
Swallow
Take it day in day out
Breathe in breathe out
Breathe no fire
Dead dreams but no fire
Kill yourself
Get up do it
Turn it on turn it off
Bend yourself into a shape
Dead room death row
Empty headed hollow man
Spinning hanging choking
Get up and do it
Become it
Live it
Believe

✦   ✦   ✦   ✦

Curling up and dying inside
Crawling into a corner because I know no one will be there
All the bad trips in your mind
All the asylum sweat
No mirrors in my room
I don't want to see myself
Endless time spent trying to destroy time
Crawling on the floor waiting for something to end
All the dying time in my room

✦   ✦   ✦   ✦

In the morning I felt stupid and cold
I didn't want to ask her what her name was again
We both laughed after she said

Will I see you again?
She said she was only joking anyway

✦   ✦   ✦   ✦

Some people don't need much to live on
Hell some folks live on pennies a day
I was right about to wrap my arms around that girl
But at the last minute
I jumped back and wrapped them around myself

✦   ✦   ✦   ✦

What's the matter, are you burning out? Are words failing you?
Things not like they used to be? Funny taste in your mouth, eyes
hurt. Does life feels like a square wheel that's crushing you under
its tread? Feel like your brain is dripping out of your ears? Feel
like your face is going to slide right off your face? Do you think
about death and when it's going to come to you? Do you think
that your life is coming to a grinding halt while it's moving too
fast to even understand it before it's all gone rushing past? It's a
wonder the sidewalk doesn't swallow us whole.

✦   ✦   ✦   ✦

Downward into silence
Downward into darkness
I am falling into myself
I can see my skull shattering
Falling inward
I am caving into myself
The pieces fall to the bottom
I sit here and stare at the ground
I can feel it
I don't want to stop it
It's what had to happen

It is the ending place for me
Here in me

♦   ♦   ♦   ♦

I am the only one who can fix me when I break down
If I can't fix me then all is lost
I wish this weren't true
So many times I wished for the mercies of a woman
To heal
To take the pain away
I read about it somewhere
Tried it a few times
Too much pain
My instinct is to reach out
I see now that instinct is not always right
It hurts

♦   ♦   ♦   ♦

It's funny
These people try to bum me out
Calling me shit
They're not telling me anything I don't already know
When they talk shit
It's lightweight compared to what I say about myself
They will never be as hard on me as I am on myself
So fuck them
Love me, hate me, it's all the same

♦   ♦   ♦   ♦

Back in LA sitting on the front porch
Taking in all the smog
I must have forgotten how fucked up this place is
Those helicopters, they're like the state bird

Every time they go by I flip them off
Maybe one day those little pigs will see me
Dive bomb the house and kill me
I always think of heat seeking missiles
Wouldn't that be great
Have a pickup truck
With a rocket propelled grenade launcher in the back
And a five CD changer in the front
Loaded with Black Sabbath
Cruising the blvd.
Hot woman in tow
Smoking those lawmen

◆ ◆ ◆ ◆

6.29.87 Silverlake California
Been home four days now
Feeling useless
What did I expect when I got back here?
I always forget how empty and small this still life can be
Been here four days and I can't remember any of it
It's like I've been dead
Hard to sleep
Nothing makes sense except to leave again
The phone is ringing
Let it ring
I don't want to talk to them

◆ ◆ ◆ ◆

There was nothing in here tonight
I sat in this room and waited
Death did not come
A couple of weeks ago I was in Florida
Riding down a road, looking at the Everglades

Smelling the rotting swamp
Everything was alive and moving
Including me
I am a dead battery now
A shell for past experiences
An almanac
A reference book on what was and how much it hurt
I am an old war story
If I could have the big wish come true right now
I would want an enemy to embrace
Anything but this unchanging stillness

✦   ✦   ✦   ✦

In New Jersey she said:
 "It's always been a dream of mine to have you inside me."

In Rhode Island six people came and no one clapped.

In Pittsburgh she said:
 "You're the most gorgeous man I have ever seen."

In Minneapolis the pigs arrested Joe.

In Des Moines she said:
 "Its so exciting when you come inside me."

In New Brunswick he said I was a hippie.

In Birmingham he said I was:
 "A no-talent jerk that stole freely from bad sources."

In Madison she said I was a typical asshole.

In Washington I quoted Hitler and made her cry.

In Athens I tried to fuck behind the police station.

In St. Louis she said that she hates all men.

In New Orleans he said that someone was coming to kick my ass.

In Pensacola she walked away from me, wordless.

In Daytona beach she said I was a pig.

In Miami bugs crawled on my face and I couldn't sleep.

In Jackson she said:
    "It's hot and things move slow around here. That's why we fuck a lot fight a lot eat a lot and drink a lot."

In Philadelphia I fucked in a men's room stall.

In Columbia he said:
"White power alright." I said: "Heil Budweiser."

In Vermont I saw him get hit by a car.

In Albany I saw him get taken to the loony bin.

In Boston she said that her friend hadn't washed her shirt since I sweated on it.

In Lincoln twenty people came and they all sat in back or left early.

In Memphis he pounded the stage with his brass knuckles.

In Hoboken I spat puke for the last three songs.

In Chicago I spat puke for the last four.

In Cincinnati I spat blood.

Here in LA I wait to go.

✦   ✦   ✦   ✦

People get lost
The alarm clock goes off and someone loses their way
All of a sudden five years have passed
Same job
They look at themselves in the mirror
Can't understand where it all went
A dirty underhanded trick
Someone gets lost and destroyed
People walking the streets like dumb animals
Smart enough to be cruel
Handcuffed to the television set
Another beer can opens
The sun goes down on another day
Self destruction slow and complete
What nasty things we do to ourselves

✦   ✦   ✦   ✦

Do you ever get the feeling that when you show someone your affection for them, you are assaulting them? Like you should probably leave them alone? Your affection, no matter how sincere, does not necessarily mean a damn thing to the person you are giving it to. Love can corner you. When you intrude on someone with your affection, you might find yourself trying to knock a strong door down with your shoulder. Either you break the door or you break yourself. Something almost always gets broken. In my mind it runs like this:

I'm going to like you, whether you like it or not. I'll wear you
down until you relent and swallow this big lie I have for you.
Don't move. Don't live. I love you.

♦   ♦   ♦   ♦

Tell me when to stop
Tell me when enough is enough
I don't understand
Don't let me hurt you
Sometimes I go too far

♦   ♦   ♦   ♦

This cold box sterile room
The very thought makes me weak
The disease crushes me in its fist
The naked girl next to me
A lie
She makes me feel weak
No, worse
I find an excuse for my weakness in her eyes
I do all the bad things to myself
I try to blame them all on someone else
I am too smart for that now
In here I waste away
My soul atrophies
I need to be in front of something that's trying to destroy me
I want to destroy it, whatever it is
In here I destroy myself
That's what weakness and disease is all about
I should know

♦   ♦   ♦   ♦

I get calls from crazy girls
Late at night
They sound like they're calling from another planet
The other night one calls from some bin in OC
She tells me that her parents put her there
They no longer want to see her
Her older brother told her that she is ugly
She believes him
She starts to cry
She says that he goes out with a girl that got named
Ms. Huntington Beach
She asks me if she is ugly
I tell her she's not ugly at all
She says that her brother is a big fan of mine
And he wouldn't believe that we are talking right now
She tells me that she lives in a ward
A lot of other kids around her all the time
A tough weird reality
Almost thirteen years old
She asks if she can call again some time
I say sure
She says goodbye and hangs up
I stare at the ceiling and try to fall asleep
I feel so lonely right now

✦   ✦   ✦   ✦

1:22 a.m.
Phone rings
Long distance
She is off medication
Nervous about starting up with the new shrink
Trying to get her friends off drugs.
"She works her ass off all week. Gets her pay on Friday and it all
goes up her nose. She's trying to quit but it's hard."

She says that all of last year she was on medication
She sat in her room and stared at the wall
Her family pretended that she wasn't there
She goes to bars to be around people
She can't be alone for too long or she starts to slip
She says she is coming out to LA
She sounds like she's talking in her sleep
I tell her that I have to get up in a few hours
She gets mad
She tells me that I'm trying to avoid her
She calls me a few names and hangs up
Another night warped

✦   ✦   ✦   ✦

She calls me from a bin out in the sticks
Tells me all about getting strapped down
Tells me that she's getting better
She can't feel it now
But they tell her that she's getting better all the time
I think of her as she speaks
Shitting her pants
Men in smocks putting electrodes into her head
I think about lab rats
The smell of shit
All these people getting better
Bright lights
White sheets
This stranger

✦   ✦   ✦   ✦

A girl called me once
Told me about her times in the home
One morning she woke up and saw a girl hanging

Her urine in a puddle
She said that she better hang up
If she didn't she wouldn't be able to stop talking
And it gets her upset

✦ ✦ ✦ ✦

Three pigs had me in the shadows
Rainy night in Santa Cruz
They wanted to work me over
I saw one of the pigs getting his gloves ready
He didn't ask any questions
I tried to steer the pigs to the street light
I wanted there to be some witnesses
Someone would get to see a guy in gym shorts
Standing in the middle of pouring rain
Get his ass kicked by a pig
Did you hit her?
No
Are you sure you didn't hit her?
I looked over at the pig with the gloves
He was on his toes
He wanted me to say yes so bad
No
He looked so let down
Like a child with a broken toy
I kept him in the corner of my eye
You never know when a pig is going to cheap shot you
They let me go
That's another reason stockpiled on a mountain of reasons
Why I laugh when I read about a pig getting killed
Imagine one of those pigs dying while a Crip laughs
I think it's wonderful
Like flowers and puppies and peace and love
And Hallmark greeting cards, frisbees, picnics

Music and a pile of dead pigs burning
Whoa yea baby, rock and roll all night long

◆   ◆   ◆   ◆

Be careful of people
People on their way up
People on their way down or out
These punk rockers turned stoner record executives
So funny that they survive
Watch out for people who want to help you for no reason
Everyone is out for something
Watch your ass
People are everywhere

◆   ◆   ◆   ◆

She makes me feel invisible
When I touch her and she looks at the wall
I feel like I am not there
Her face holds no expression
Every once in awhile she smiles
I hang onto the sparks
The light in her eyes makes me forget the blank moments
When she makes me feel like a piece of furniture
I am leaving her
There is one place for me
The road is always there for me
My endless friend
I will die on your shoulder
No woman will ever understand me
I won't waste my time with it
The road waits to destroy me

◆   ◆   ◆   ◆

After this is over I will return to a small dark room
I will sit and stare into the darkness
No one will come
No one will touch me
There will be no calls
My life is a hollow scream
My memories no longer haunt me
They have been exterminated
My present reality is wreckage
That will take me the rest of my life to pull out of

◆　◆　◆　◆

I am in myself
All the way in down and through
I sleep with myself
I feed myself
I fuck myself
I hear what they say
Strangers have touched my flesh
Made me want to destroy it
Sometimes it all seems so alien
I turn on myself
I try to hurt me
I should know myself better by now
I don't
I hear the things I say
Makes me want to turn around and ask who said that
Sometimes I want to end myself
I get trapped and scared
Cornered in my corner
I get revenge on myself
I can smell myself
I want to turn myself off right now
Lose myself

Hide from myself
A tragic summer holiday

✦   ✦   ✦   ✦

I will make black music all night long
I will scream in the dark
I will go deep into the night
As if the rising sun would incinerate me
Which it has before and will again
Destroying my black music
Incinerating my black night dreams
Making all my words unspeakable

✦   ✦   ✦   ✦

For some there is no music
No lights
No fire
No untamed madness that breathes life
There is work
Anguish
Frustration
Rage
Despair
A dullness that rings like wooden thunder

✦   ✦   ✦   ✦

It is violent summer in my brain
Napalm summer rain inside
The sound is getting so loud
Exterminating parts
The signal so clear
The light so bright
In the distance

The sound of animals dying
Important famous deadly sounds
An evil siren singing to me
It's all unraveling
One more night of this prison and then it's freedom time

◆ ◆ ◆ ◆

Alone is best
Better than women
Why bother
At the end I am alone anyway
That tells me everything
There is no strength in numbers
Listening to them talk is depressing
Better off alone in the soldier brain
In my man hole
All these tours push further into myself
They're all strangers
It's cold everywhere
You look for warmth in their eyes
You get stung hard and dropped
I am better off alone
The other pain is a lot worse

◆ ◆ ◆ ◆

Some nights I look into their eyes
I see rows of empty houses
The trail is endless friendless and full of lies
Ice cold places, vacant faces
I had to get away from their leeching complacency
Or explode completely
Self expression, they can't touch it
Their dead hands can't pull it down

It's a mute lesson that screams
A vision that blinds
A heat the freezes
A fulfillment that empties and leaves me with myself
Again and again
I can't get enough

♦ ♦ ♦ ♦

There are dark and cold times you have to stumble through alone
There are days when there's not a cloud in the sky
But when you look out the window you see rain falling
There are times when the leaves are sitting still on the trees
And you would swear you were in the middle of a storm
You look in the mirror
Wrap your arms around yourself
And you don't know if you're there at all
The most simple things cause torment and confusion
All the lines run together
You look for the closest hole to fall into
This is when you must remember what you are
You must get back to the real number
You are a number
The number is one

♦ ♦ ♦ ♦

I am the reason
I am the bullet
I am the number one
Tearing a scar in the sky
You should have seen them screaming and hitting me
My eyes were ripping holes in the rafters
They can't touch me

They don't know me
They can't ride with me
They can't destroy me
I've got a limp and an inside mind
Attitude armor with all my teeth jammed together
After the show I was in the shower trying to beat off
Nothing happened
I had to laugh
I'm dying piece by piece
Dancing like a dirty shadow in the chicken lights
The roar in my ears
War is all
It defines me
I have my good times
Crawling through the wreckage
I have my bad times the rest of the time

◆　◆　◆　◆

It's over
The jewels in your eyes have turned to coal and died
When I touch you I lie to myself
When we are together we are dead
We are rag dolls
Nothing to say
We walk hand in hand with a lie
Trying to be as deaf dumb and blind as we can
Kissing each other with razor lips
Sticking knives into desperate flesh
Making the pain mean something else
Ignoring the blood
It's over
It's dead

◆　◆　◆　◆

Drove into Milan Italy today
Looked out the window at another filthy city limit
Wondered how many had passed before my eyes
The dirt and the poverty doesn't faze me
They have quite the opposite effect
The garbage and the stench are the welcoming committee
I enter these places life a knife
I exit like a bullet leaving a skull
In between I walk trails through their guts

◆ ◆ ◆ ◆

I've been stuck with bad nights where all I could do
Was keep my brain from running down my neck
I've been held down in dirty cities
The air burned my lungs
The food made me swear off food
Reduced me to a figure of fun
I've been through eyes and ears
Assholes, keyholes, broken noses
Vomit, sweat, blood and alienation
On and on, over and over
I am stuck with my understanding of all this
At least I'm not stuck with you

◆ ◆ ◆ ◆

Every night I spend in these stinking shit holes
I get stronger
Hot nights, no air, tasting my own puke
Listening to strangers telling me what to do
Hitting me, grabbing my dick
Spitting on me, throwing cups of urine
You think that makes me want to curl up and die?

I get stronger
No weak ass piece of shit with a mouth and an attitude
Can fuck with me

✦　✦　✦　✦

Past midnight
Walking down a street in Vienna Austria
I saw a whore standing against a wall
Hips out, shoulders back, headphones on
Staring straight across the street
I walked by and gave her a wave
Her eyes bored right through my pointy head
I kept walking, thinking how tough and awesome she was
Three short Asian men passed me and went over to her
I hid in a doorway to watch
They looked her over
It looked like Snow White and the Three Dwarfs
But more fucked up
She stood there looking over their balding heads
Like they weren't there at all
They took a few steps back and held a short conference
They came back and one of them spoke to her
I saw her laugh
They walked away fast
What the fuck you shits
What do you got
Nine inches between the three of you?
Yea, I'll do all three of you
No sweat
What's the matter?
You scared of a little pussy?
You fucking runts
Get the fuck out of my face

I watched for another minute
She adjusted her headphones
And returned her gaze to the street

✦   ✦   ✦   ✦

Not human right now
I want to break things
If you were here, I would want you to touch me
Show me something, take me out of this thought
I am lost in my eyes
Touch me
Teach me a lesson that I forgot
I am high on war

✦   ✦   ✦   ✦

In times like these I have to remember who I am
What I am
Where I come from
I come from war
My parents are war
I will survive
I will destroy
In times like these I think of three things
War
The number One
The forward roll
Deal with it

✦   ✦   ✦   ✦

You make me feel cold
When I talk to you I feel stupid and small
I tell you I miss you

You tell me where it's at with your silence
I hang up the phone and look at the floor
The room is cold
One on none
That's the way it is
I get harder, I learn things
Things become clearer all the time
The idea of reaching out to someone else
Lodges in my throat and burns
I think about you tonight as I sit in this nowhere
Why are you like that to me?
Why do I sit here and torture myself thinking about you?
Long distance never felt longer

✦   ✦   ✦   ✦

I'm looking for something to scare me out of my skin
I'm following myself
Playing jokes on myself
Injecting myself with nightmares
I wait in dark corners to jump out and scare myself
I've got to get away from myself

✦   ✦   ✦   ✦

I am inside pulling in tight
Inner core getting harder
The number One growing in my brain
My eyes see clearly
My ears hear perfectly well
I've been through the flesh mill
Carousel funeral march, a parade of lies
Tears and fake inspiration
They don't move me
I know what they say

Little words from little planets
Their lies don't cut me
Their touch doesn't make me feel
I am all the time
And just because they can't see it
Doesn't stop the truth bullet from ripping through my brain
Work
Strength
Solitude

◆　◆　◆　◆

I am the keeper of the inner war
All these people trying to shove their peace down my throat
Telling me to get in love's line
Sometimes it's hard to find war
I look around and all I see is peace
They would like me to trade my fangs for dentures
If they could they would make me crawl for peace

◆　◆　◆　◆

Yes I am negative to you
Yes I am all those things you called me
All the things your mamma called me too
I am all the things you can't get to
I am huge
I am invisible

◆　◆　◆　◆

Be careful
I am not given to emotion
Self possession is my thing
The feeding fist will be mine

I am the bullet
The casing
The charge
Like the bullet, I will go through you
Or your fucking mom
If I become flattened
Destroyed
So what

✦　✦　✦　✦

One of many truths
In all my life
I have never had an experience that came anywhere near
The level of awareness I have achieved
Through an action of violence or aggression towards a human being
Breaking someone's nose is more memorable than the best sex
So many nights I crave a body to destroy
Sometimes I get it

✦　✦　✦　✦

I am the only man street walker
I am the footstep sound moving past your window
I pass through your dreams at night
When the cars pass me they send echoes through my head
Street lamps glow
Reflections come up from the rain drenched sidewalk
I air out my brain at night
Lose an entire day of useless commotion
Do my best to get back to myself
Try to remember whatever it is

✦　✦　✦　✦

12.6.87
Got off the plane eleven hours ago
Already it's getting to me
I re-live this over and over
The first evening back in the room
Everything is covered with dust and grime
Takes me all night to find half the stuff I'm looking for
I don't remember what's in this place anymore
Been gone four and a half months
Been cleaning the room for hours now
Servicing it
The new old cell
I'm back

◆　◆　◆　◆

I got a letter from a girl
Ten pages long
She's been off heroin two weeks now
She says she was on for eighteen months
She says she loves me
She wants to die while fucking me
She hates life
She hates her parents
She tells me that we have met before
She is a model
I put the letter back in the envelope
A piece of paper falls out
Her portfolio
Pictures of her in bikinis
I remember her
There's a number on the paper
I call it
A woman at the other end says she's gone
Before she left, she forged a check for two hundred and fifty dollars

I tell the woman about the letter
She says that the girl is messed up
Now I'm sitting in my room
Wagner pounding the walls
Sometimes people invade me
I read the letters they send me
It's as if they have moved into my brain
I hate the feeling of being crowded
When I'm alone in my room

✦ ✦ ✦ ✦

I was on the bus going east on Sunset
This guy gets on
He goes all the way to the back
His head goes from side to side
He looks at everyone coming like they're going to attack him
He looks frantic, like a caged animal
He keeps looking at me
I see a name tattooed on his neck
He has tattoos on his face
He comes over to me and asks me where I get my stuff done
I tell him about Rick
He tells me that he is covered
But has never gotten "a real one"
He says that his homeboys do his work for him
And now that he is "out"
He wants to get a lot of it covered up
He just finished three years straight time
Northern California
He was only supposed to be there for eighteen months
But had to stay because of fighting
"The north and the south don't like each other.
There was a lot of rioting. I had to stay."
His nose is running and he keeps scratching his face

He says he can't get off heroin and coke
Today he is drinking beer to try to keep his mind off it
Yesterday he could barely stop himself from stealing a car
"I'm a dope fiend, man."
The cigarette behind his ear falls behind the seat
Takes him two stops but he gets it back
He looks at me closely
"You're that guy. I seen you in magazines that
my homeboys send me. You're that Rollins dude."
He went to his last two parole hearings fucked up
They found the dope in his urine
They will probably send him back for another year
He says it's ok
That's where all his friends are
He has been out four weeks now
He has a night job
He spends all the money on dope
He gets up to leave
He is off to meet his friend
They are going to try and score
"Hey homey. Don't get no tattoos on your face. No one understands."

◆　◆　◆　◆

I tell you
He's in love with her and it's tearing him apart
The oldest and coldest story going since death
He loves her
She loves junk
She gets high
He gets lies
She drags him through her methadone treatments
She always goes back to smack
To hold onto her
He started shooting too

That's what I call true love
He isn't hooked
He's just been checking it out for three months
She left him

❖   ❖   ❖   ❖

That last phone call was a good one
Hearing that girl lie her ass off
I like it when people lie so earnestly
Makes me know more about how you all work
She is all cleaned up
She sounds like a witch
Almost as funny as the call that came right before hers
The ex-boyfriend not knowing how much of an ex he is
Telling me how he is going to get back with her
He told me that she said
That she and I shoot up together
And it's alright by him
He has a few of my records
But don't share needles ok?
That's rich
You all are better than MTV
I ask her about the guy that she wasted and used back there
She starts laughing like she and I are in this together
She says that he got in over his head
And his mother is lucky she didn't make the check out for more
I guess mom is lucky
You make me hate

❖   ❖   ❖   ❖

They are a disease
Something I never wanted
To stay strong I must stay away from them

I fuck myself up when I am around them
Every day I go without being touched
I get stronger
I see clearer
I can feel the precision
To want makes me feel alive
To feel so alone that I might disappear
Makes me want to live
Better than company
I want to build walls where there are none
So I can have something to break through
The night passes so slow
The silence slices into me

◆ ◆ ◆ ◆

It's the road I'm on
It takes me the long way
Around everything and everyone
I keep going, getting farther out
Sometimes I can't find things
Can't find words
Can't find a way
There's often a feeling of great loss
It's just the road I am on
Sometimes I get locked out of myself
It keeps me away from you
Even when I don't want to be
It hurts
If I knew what to say to you
I would scream it until you noticed
But when I look at you
No words come out
It's just the road I'm on

I never asked you to come along
I will never ask you
I like where I am
I wish I could like where you are

✦   ✦   ✦   ✦

I have been off the road for three days now
The sinking feeling is strong within me now
Some people called me today
I had nothing to say
I pulled the plug
It's better now
I have not touched a woman in five months
I think about what I would say to one if she was here right now
I can't think of anything

✦   ✦   ✦   ✦

This fever that I feel
Here alone in this room
I am untranslatable
Solitary refinement is keeping me together right now
A current runs through me
Sometimes I expect to fly apart
Their existence drains me
This fever that I feel has no language outside myself
Trying to talk makes me feel so cold

✦   ✦   ✦   ✦

Back in LA for awhile
At night I sit on the porch and look to the west
I can see the lights of Hollywood
Sunset Blvd. roaring like a diseased beast

This is the perfect place for the air strike
I was on Hollywood Blvd. tonight
Looking at the whores and punks and tourists
This place is dead already
Lying on its side, exhaling bad breath
I could clean it up
Call in the air strike
Do this place a favor, it should be incinerated
It's what happens when a city falls apart
The scum come out to hunt the scum
Leeches leeching leeches
The same tired black blood being passed
Mouth to mouth, needle to needle
Cleanse with fire
End this petty glittering palace of emptiness

◆   ◆   ◆   ◆

Riding on the bus west on Santa Monica Blvd.
Nonstop ugly people
Some guy's dick in my face
The bus makes a turn, he leans into me
At Western Ave. more people get in than got out
The bus driver says to give your seat to a senior citizen
There's all these old folks hanging on for dear life
They look around to see if anyone is giving up a seat
No one moves
The bus driver repeats the request
All the seated look at the ground
We hit Beverly hills and everyone starts looking better
Except the sleeping drunk, breathing in my face
This fat guy in a security guard outfit is trying to talk to all the
people in the back. He's sitting next to me and he keeps trying to
catch my eye. I look straight ahead. He talks to the Mexican

ladies in their maid uniforms. They don't know much English and they try to be polite. They smile and nod. The pig doesn't get it. The bus driver keeps slamming on the brakes and I keep falling into him. We pitch and toss.

A real ship of fools
I do my business and get on the bus and head east
Back to beautiful, pulsating, vibrant, now
Fabulous, cosmopolitan, metropolitan
Silverlake
Home of the stores that close at eight
And who cares anyway, the food on the shelves is stale
Why go outside at all
There's more aggravated assault than last year
Not one girl on the bus to look at
The side windows have been kicked out
Who cares, we're on a lark!
Pulling away from a stop a fist slams the glass where my head is
The bus pulls over and a man gets on
He's pissed off for almost getting left behind
Two old ladies get on
The driver pulls away fast
One of them falls and hits the floor hard
I guess the driver didn't see her white cane
Bad luck
A few stops later a group of homeboys get on
I can smell the wine and pot as they pass
I know I am getting close to my home
All the whites are getting off the bus
Two stops to go
I laugh out loud thinking about the guy
That walked out the back door right into a light pole
I did that when I was in 6th grade
I get out
Sixty-three minutes after Santa Monica

The stores are closed
The leather boys are out
Good night

◆　◆　◆　◆

Night time
Walking to the liquor store
Only thing that's open at this hour
I can see the lights of Hollywood
I can hear the sound of the freeway
Sounds like a war drawing to a close
Like an animal spitting out its last mouthful
Everything looks cool under the crime lights
The cars that pass me all sound like they are dying
Nothing runs well in this neighborhood
I do my business at the store
The Asian man never says a word to me
I walk out and pass the gay diner
All the faggots in the window check me out
So nice to be wanted
Two gay boys pass me
One says good evening and gives me the up and down
The other one laughs and they keep going
Under the crime lights nothing grows
Everything stays so it can die over and over
I get back to the room
I have found a new way to punish myself
All I have to do is go outside

◆　◆　◆　◆

I live in this room
I had to make it a good place to go
It's cold in this room

I had to make it warm in my brain
The bathroom stinks
It crawls into my nose
I smell it when I stand over the sink jerking off
I am alone in here
Some need others to make their place a good place to be
I think that would ruin it
Out there is fucked up and filthy
Full of cheap weak nothings and nowheres
Not in here
What makes this place so good is the fact that in here
I don't have to explain shit to anyone
Too much time is taken up explaining
Trying to make yourself look good to someone else
That shit doesn't matter
It wastes your time
You don't owe anyone an explanation
When you get into that shit you end up lying at least once
That's a taste of cancer right there
I got so tired of it
I had to get off that bus
No one will ever understand you
They just won't
That's why my phone is unplugged tonight
That's why my door is locked tonight
That's why my gun is loaded tonight

◆　◆　◆　◆

It's winter time
I'm in the same place I was last year
The winter brain
I crawl the walls
I wait for the hot nights
I've been here a week

My head is getting smashed on bullshit
I walk the perimeter of the room
I avoid human contact
They make me want to kill
I can't take the talk
After what I have been through, I just can't take it
In my head it's summer
Incineration
Loud, violent and real
I want to put my fist through
I want to destroy
I have to maintain
The room gets so small at times like these
I don't talk to women
I don't like the way they make me feel
I want to wreck myself on something
War in the summer
I will fucking kill you
It all happens in the summer
I got it good last summer
I know what I am made of
Every night I shoved myself down my own throat
Some nights it hurt so bad I don't know how I got through
I can't find anything that good anywhere else
This room is sucking life out of me

❖   ❖   ❖   ❖

Last night I was in the kitchen
This roach runs by me heading for the stove
I nailed it with my index finger, knocked part of its guts out
The roach kept crawling, dragging its guts behind
I pushed it back so it couldn't get away
The rear legs gave out, it kept crawling
The guts started to pick up dirt and bits of food

It still kept going with all the new weight
I wondered if I would be able to keep on crawling
With my guts hanging out of me like that
I would have done something lame
like gone into shock and died
Finally I killed it
Tonight I was at the market
I got my food and was walking towards the door
There was a small line to get out
A woman with a walker was having trouble getting out
People were bumping into her, getting around her
They couldn't wait that long
She nearly got knocked over a few times
Still she kept on crawling
She had a hunched back
She edged up to a trash can
I saw her bend over it
I wondered if she was looking for food
I got closer and saw that she was crying
Her tears were falling into the trashcan
Tears out with the garbage
I could hear her crying
Crying into a trash can as people pushed by her
At some point, every living thing is made to crawl
They'll always make you crawl if they can
She looked so lost there under the Christmas lights

✦   ✦   ✦   ✦

They invade me with their calls
Months ago she called me
Told me that the medication was making her overweight
Now no longer on the medication
Nor depressed or overweight
The last time she called was in the middle of the night

She wouldn't stop talking, said she was falling apart
This time she is in love
She asks me what I'm doing
I tell her that I am working
I don't want to talk about it, I just want to do it
They spend so much time talking about it
They talk themselves in and out of insane asylums
Talk talk talk
Like they have all the time in the world
Like they have all of my time as well
I felt like throwing the phone across the room
Finally she released me
I had my room to myself again

◆   ◆   ◆   ◆

We could get away from here
Give them all the slip
It wouldn't last long
You would be surprised how fast they find you
I was just thinking of you
You who I've never seen
I don't know if you exist
Perhaps we will find each other in this mess
Do you ever feel closed in?
Like you could walk for miles and go nowhere?
Do you feel the distance when you're close to someone?
When you see the truth and wish you didn't
I can't get away from the truth
The sands of the hourglass are the scars that I bear
Is there somewhere we could go?
A house that's burning?
A place that's like you and me
Temporary

◆   ◆   ◆   ◆

Sitting in the room, I should be gone
There's nothing left but the road
I laugh at the lines in my face
Tell me about your broken dreams
About your broken television set
About your fear
We take up all of our time
We waste a life thinking that we have to live correctly
It makes us shrink back from the sun, retire to the shadows
There are some that walk away from the world
They are the ones that get written about
We make a few into heroes so we can live through them
Some of them are stupid enough to wait around for the praise
They lose the sound that roars in their ears
They forget the feeling of the pain
It's sad to see them go out like they do
Best not to talk about it
Best to go on and head for the jungle
When you go, if you ever do
Do it right
Head out for the darkest part

◆   ◆   ◆   ◆

A few weeks ago, I was in Germany
Did this show in Munich
I could feel my guts falling through my shoes as I spoke
After it was over
People were coming up to me, shaking my hand, hugging me
The nicer they were, the deeper I sank
These girls were waiting to meet me
I didn't want to mess with it
I got out of there
I remember the rest of the night in the hotel room
I carry it like a hunch back
Night by night, I freeze out parts of myself

What is there after it's all gone
Truth, I'm coming

✦   ✦   ✦   ✦

I am the human unraveling thing
I peel layers and cast them off like some kind of animal act
It's ugly
The human navel orange
I like things that are ugly
They tell me everything
An addiction to truth will leave you in a pile on the floor
Make you sick of yourself
Rip yourself apart
Walk until it falls away
Seek darkness until you see blinding light
Know that there are too many cowards in the world
They speak the loudest

✦   ✦   ✦   ✦

I pulled myself away from them
I needed to find myself
It's easy to get lost, too easy, too painless
I want to know when I am bleeding to death
Walked out of the room of sporadic sexual encounters
Didn't feel good
Life burns and freezes me
A lot of times it leaves me alone
Taunts me
Makes me think that I will break
So let it break, I want to see the pieces
At least I'll know something
I need to know something
Even if it kills me

✦   ✦   ✦   ✦

Post Lhasa Club Blues
Did a show about two hours ago
Was up there spilling my guts for a long time
All these people were there, and all the lights were on
It felt good
Now I'm in my room alone
3:30 in the morning
It's the emptiness that makes it hard to sleep
When you can't take your mind off your mind
Maybe it's not good to feel that good
The other side of it is too much sometimes
Like right now

◆ ◆ ◆ ◆

Don't let them look at you for too long
They will make you the axis for their woes
If you're not careful their problems will become yours
And if you can't take the weight
They'll call you every name in the book
They have a way of calling revenge self-affirmation
And they will affirm themselves on your flesh all night long
Watch out for the weak

◆ ◆ ◆ ◆

I'm ok but my heart is stupid
It goes places that I would never go
I have a leash that I keep it on
Doesn't always work
Never learns from pain
Stupid

◆ ◆ ◆ ◆

No friends in this city
I like you so I'll tell you straight
Don't try to get close to me
No one does
When they think they are
They hurt themselves and they don't feel it
I don't want you to hurt yourself
If you try to get close to me you turn yourself into shit
The best thing for you to do is to walk out of this place
If it's a game you're playing, you will lose
You don't want to be a loser in a place like this
Just because we fuck, it doesn't mean anything more
Than that we fuck
I'm not someone who cares about you
You haven't ripped me off yet, so I like you alright
I'm telling you, the best thing to do is to get out of here
I will make everything turn on you
It's all I know how to do
I will laugh in your face and you will cry
You have no friends in this city
No one does
I am the glittering saint of hollowness
You see how I shine
You see the other fools lined up behind you
Just because you're at the front of the line
Doesn't mean that you're not in line
Do you see what I mean?
Walk away before you crawl

✦   ✦   ✦   ✦

I am weak
Looking to get stronger
When I open my eyes all the way
It's all there is for me

Kindness is strength
It's easier to close a door than to keep it open
Hatred is easy
Frustration is life on pause
These are truths that are hard for me to deal with
I learned a lot this year
I think I am stronger than last year
Self creation is painful
Trying to take my parent's blood out of mine
Trying to stand on my own two feet
Without leaning on someone else
Looking to myself for total strength
To be
One
From
None